THE GEOPOLITICS OF GAS

Common Problems, Disparate Strategies

THE GEOPOLITICS OF GAS

Common Problems, Disparate Strategies

Shebonti Ray Dadwal

INSTITUTE FOR DEFENCE STUDIES & ANALYSES
NEW DELHI

PENTAGON PRESS

The Geopolitics of Gas: Common Problems, Disparate Strategies
Shebonti Ray Dadwal

First Published in 2017

ISBN 978-81-8274-900-9

Published by
PENTAGON PRESS
206, Peacock Lane, Shahpur Jat
New Delhi-110049
Phones: 011-64706243, 26491568
Telefax: 011-26490600
email: rajan@pentagonpress.in
website: www.pentagonpress.in

In association with
Institute for Defence Studies and Analyses
No. 1, Development Enclave,
New Delhi-110010
Phone: +91-11-26717983
Website: www.idsa.in

Printed at Aegean Offset Printer, Greater Noida, UP.

CONTENTS

1

The Problem of Plenty

In 2000, in an interview with *The Telegraph*, the iconic former Saudi oil minister Sheikh Ahmed-Zaki Yamani had predicted, "Thirty years from now there will be a huge amount of oil and no buyers. Oil will be left in the ground. The Stone Age came to an end, not because we had a lack of stones, and the oil age will come to an end not because we have a lack of oil."[1] At the time, there were not too many takers for Sheikh Yamani's prognosis. But less than two decades later, his predictions appear almost prescient. As climate change concerns have seen a new determination by several nations to replace "dirty" hydrocarbons with cleaner fuels, dire predictions of renewable energy resources (solar and wind in particular) and nuclear energy replacing oil, gas and coal are making the rounds. Adding to the debate is the fact that over the last decade, the prices of renewables have plunged, signalling that the time lag between the transition from fossil fuels to renewable energy may be shorter than earlier expected.

This raises the question whether the end of the hydrocarbon era is nearer than anticipated. Not yet, if the International Energy Agency's (IEA) *World Energy Outlook 2016* bears out. According to its November 2016 publication, the era of fossil fuels is far from over, although it

1. "Sheikh Yamani predicts price crash as age of oil ends", *The Telegraph*, June 25, 2000 at http://www.telegraph.co.uk/news/uknews/1344832/Sheikh-Yamani-predicts-price-crash-as-age-of-oil-ends.html

does state that renewables have and will continue to see the largest growth in demand across the globe. But the IEA also says that natural gas, which also belongs to the hydrocarbon family, is projected to be a "big winner(s)" till 2040, and that it is expanding its role at the cost of coal and oil.[2] In the US, for instance, natural gas is also replacing nuclear- powered plants that are being phased out.[3]

Given that natural gas *is* a fossil fuel, why is its share of the global energy basket increasing, when most countries are attempting to move towards non-carbon emitting energy resources?

While oil dominated, and continues to be the fuel of choice for the transport sector, coal was the predominant fuel for the power sector. Natural gas, a latecomer in the hydrocarbon family, can be a substitute for both oil and coal, due to its lower carbon-emitting properties. Hence, in a world that is increasingly becoming more concerned with the impact of climate change, natural gas is seen as a less polluting option.

Second, countries usually take decisions about energy choices based on resource availability, and in this respect, natural gas is far ahead of both oil and coal, thereby contributing to the energy security of nations. Speaking about the future of natural gas, the executive director of the IEA, Dr Fatih Birol says that there are good reasons to be upbeat about the future for natural gas due to "its relative abundance, its environmental advantages compared with other fossil fuels, and the flexibility and adaptability that make it a valuable component of a gradually decarbonising electricity and energy system."[4]

Third, apart from availability, the price of fuels are, more often than not, a major determinant in opting for a particular energy resource. In fact, that was one of the reasons why coal and oil were preferred by many countries over natural gas. Hence from the second half of 2014,

---

2. "*World Energy Outlook 2016* sees broad transformations in the global energy landscape", *World Energy Outlook 2016,* International Energy Agency November 2016 at http://www.iea.org/newsroom/news/2016/november/world-energy-outlook-2016.html
3. James Conca, "Natural Gas — Not Renewables — Is Replacing Nuclear Power", *Forbes*, May 16, 2016 at http://www.forbes.com/sites/jamesconca/2016/05/16/natural-gas-is-replacing-nuclear-power-not-renewables/#399022764abb
4. See Note 2, *World Energy Outlook 2016*

when the price of natural gas dropped drastically for reasons that will be explained later, it appeared logical that the time for gas to outshine its hydrocarbon cousins had come. In fact, prior to that, in its 2011 *World Energy Outlook*, the IEA had brought out a special report titled *Are we entering the Golden Age of Gas?* wherein a rather optimistic picture of the gas market was painted.

However, since 2014, that optimism has abated considerably. Despite the abundance of supplies that have flooded the gas market following the shale gas revolution in the US, there are few takers for a variety of reasons. First, the price fall makes it difficult for producers to recover the huge capital costs required for gas infrastructure, both for liquefied natural gas (LNG) as well as pipelines, particularly those involving cross-border projects. Third, the recovery in global economic activity in many parts of the developed world, which are the largest consumers of gas, has been more modest and uneven than anticipated. Fourth, in some countries (notably China), which were seen to be major drivers for it – the demand for gas has not gathered pace due to the economic slowdown in that country. And lastly, the pace of increase in growth for renewable energy, both for climate change factors as well as more technological initiatives, have made them more competitive vis-à-vis other fuels)

Nevertheless, there is hope that the demand for natural gas will pick up, albeit later than was forecast, as it is the most suitable as a transition fuel between the age of fossil fuels and clean energy.

Natural Gas Trajectory

The Chinese are believed to have been the first to discover how to use natural gas in 500 BC, when they used gas seeping to the surface to form crude pipelines out of bamboo shoots to transport the gas, which was used to boil sea water to separate salt. However, it was Great Britain that was the first country to commercialise the use of natural gas in 1785, when natural gas produced from coal was used to light houses, as well as streetlights.[5]

5. *Natural Gas: History*, Natural Gas.Org at http://naturalgas.org/overview/history/

Until the 1990s, natural gas was by and large perceived as a by-product of oil fields, with no market and used for re-injection into oil fields to increase production, flared or neglected. As a result, since the end of the First World War and for most of the 20th century, oil was the prevailing energy resource that dominated the energy security discourse, over which many a battle has been fought. But over the last decade-and-a half, with concerns of global warming and climate change increasing, and the linkages between the use of hydrocarbons, particularly oil and coal, and carbon emissions, the search for cleaner fuels has gained ground. Given that renewable energy resources are not commercially competitive vis-à-vis hydrocarbons and are not likely to provide the volumes required to satisfy demand, natural gas, despite being a fossil fuel, was seen as the best choice to bridge the gap between dirty fossil fuels and renewable energy, making it an ideal "bridge" fuel. Furthermore, with opposition to nuclear energy growing following the Fukushima Daiichi disaster, much of the demand for power from nuclear energy was expected to be replaced with natural gas.

Other factors that favour natural gas over other fossil fuels include facts such as natural gas is more widely dispersed geographically than oil or coal. With reserves that are more geographically dispersed than oil, gas is more abundantly available, much of which can be developed and produced at relatively low cost, the total recoverable reserves of gas are projected to sustain current production for over 250 years, with all regions having recoverable resources equal to at least 75 years of current consumption.[6] According to the IEA, the estimated remaining technically recoverable natural gas resources is around 752 trillion cubic metres (tcm), while the BP states that global gas supply is expected to grow by 1.9 percent per annum or 172 billion cu feet a day (bcf/d) or 4.8 bcm/day, to reach a total of 497 bcf/d (14.07 bcm/d) by 2035, that is from 21 percent in 2010 to 25 percent by 2035.[7] (see graph) At the

6. "Are we entering a golden age of gas?", *World Energy Outlook 2011* Special Report Factsheet, International Energy Agency, 2011 at http://www.worldenergyoutlook.org/media/weowebsite/2011/WEO2011_GAG_FactSheet.pdf
7. *BP Energy Outlook 2035*, January 2014 at http://www.bp.com/content/dam/bp/pdf/Energy-economics/Energy-Outlook/Energy_Outlook_2035_booklet.pdf

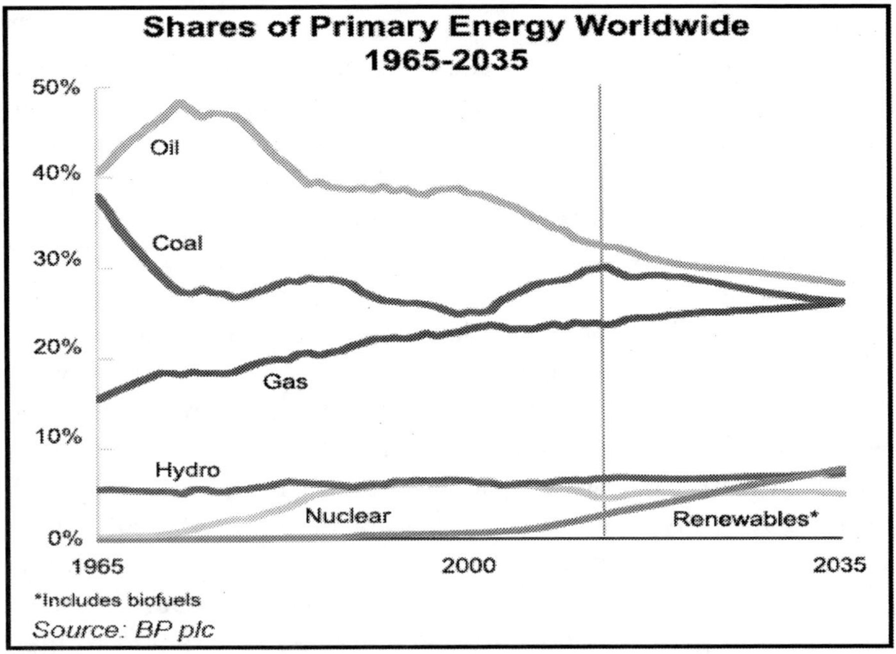

same time, "unconventional" supplies of natural gas, including shale gas, tight gas and coalbed methane (CBM) have been growing steadily for decades, roughly tripling the resource base that can be economically recovered.[8] Since natural gas resources can be produced from all the volumes of rocks that contain oil as well from tight sandstones, shales and coals that contain no oil. Hence, the global volumes of sediments capable of producing natural gas commercially are at least twice and probably closer to several times the volumes of rocks capable of oil production.

Second, despite being a fossil fuel, gas is a cleaner burning fuel than either coal or oil, and emits around 40 percent lower than coal plants, while new gas power plants emit 66 percent lower carbon than existing coal-based plants because of their higher efficiency levels. Similarly, in the transport sector, many countries are opting for gas- (compressed natural gas or CNG) powered vehicles, driven by rising

8. "Global LNG: Will new demand and new supply mean new pricing?", Ernst & Young, 2013 at http://www.ey.com/Publication/vwLUAssets/Global_LNG_New_pricing_ahead/$FILE/Global_LNG_New_ pricing_ahead_DW0240.pdf

air pollution. Interestingly, in March 2014, Royal Dutch Shell also announced that it had started selling a premium motor oil that is derived from natural gas, instead of the traditional crude oil. Around 40 percent less carbon than coal as a fuel is used in the power sector. Hence, for countries that are looking to reduce their emissions, gas is the preferred choice of fuel. Moreover, gas is a far more versatile fuel than oil or coal. Apart from being used in the power, residential and industrial sectors, it is now being seen as a cleaner alternative in the transport sector. Hence in a situation where 27 percent of energy was being consumed in the transport sector, which was dominated by oil at 93 percent, a switch to natural gas, in the form of compressed natural gas (CNG) or LNG would involve a massive jump in demand. This is being seen in several cases with the growth in natural gas-fuelled vehicles witnessing a jump of 23 percent between 2001 and 2011.[9] Although nuclear and renewable energy are cleaner than hydrocarbons, they are not cost- competitive when compared to fossil fuels; moreover, they cannot provide the volumes required to meet galloping demand in the emerging economies. Natural gas being a relatively cleaner fuel than coal and oil, is therefore attractive as a "bridge" fuel before renewable energy can compete with fossil fuels.

Finally, unlike oil, which is a fungible commodity with a global benchmark price, and hence vulnerable to price volatility due to disruptions in production or supplies,[10] the gas market is structured differently and therefore less prone to disruptions.

Changing Trends in the Gas Market

Unlike the oil market, which is global in nature, the gas market is fragmented and largely regional, with inter-regional gas trade comprising only 30 percent of global gas consumption. The three main markets are the North American market, the European (EU) market and the Asian market, which is dominated by LNG.

9. Chris Le Fevre, "The Prospects for Natural Gas as a Transport fuel in Europe", The Oxford Institute for Energy Studies, OIES Paper: NG 84, March 2014 at http://www.oxfordenergy.org/wpcms/wp-content/uploads/2014/03/NG-84.pdf

10. Geoffrey Kemp, "The Challenge of Iran for US and European Policy", in Richard Haas (ed.), *Transatlantic Tensions: The United States, Europe, and Problem Countries*, Brookings Institution Press, December 2010, p.62.

Being regional in nature, the pricing of the gas varies from region-to-region. For example, the North American pricing mechanism is tied to the price of natural gas quoted at Henry Hub (HH), whereas European gas pricing is largely based on oil product prices. However, gas in Europe is also traded in other exchanges, albeit virtual in nature as against the physical trading hub in the US (HH), such as the UK's National Balancing Point (NBP), the Netherlands' Title Transfer Facility (TTF), and Belgium's Zeebrugge Hub. Nevertheless, only 34.8-37.7 percent of Europe's gas supplies are priced off spot markets, as Russia, a major and largest supplier of gas to European markets, insists on trading gas based on oil-indexed contracts, on the ground that stable oil-indexed gas prices were necessary to fund capital-intensive exploration and production projects. Moreover, according to Gazprom, Russia's largest gas company, hubs are not sufficiently liquid to generate any meaningful price signals and that producers should not be burdened with both the pricing and the reservoir risk, given that although the production costs of gas and oil are similar, gas costs about 30 times more to store and transport than oil. Hence, gas importers cannot avail of the benefits of supply security and flexibility (in contract pricing) while paying a lower hub price that reflects the value of only the commodity.[11]

In the Asia-Pacific region too, gas prices are linked to crude oil, known as the Japanese crude cocktail (JCC) which stands for Japanese customs-cleared crude and is an average price of a basket of crude oils that enter the Japanese market, which is the largest gas importer in the region.[12]

The majority of gas trade is conducted between 10 to 30-year contracts, with prices being generally adjusted on a quarterly basis, and linked to the price of oil. These long contracts gave rise to rigidities, as the buyer was required to pay for a specified minimum quantity of gas at the contract price, irrespective of whether the gas was actually utilised.

11. Nigel Harris, "Should Natural Gas Prices in Europe and Asia Be De-Linked From Oil?", The Oxford Princeton Programme, 2015 at https://www.oxfordprinceton.com/news/latest-news/338-should-natural-gas-prices-in-europe-and-asia-be-de-linked-from-oil.html

12. Roberto Aguilera, *et al*, "The Asia-Pacific Natural Gas Market: Large Enough for All?, *Energy Policy*, Vol.65, 2014, pp. 1-6.

Although the gas market has been evolving and changing over the last decade or so, the factor that has hastened the process and brought about immense changes in the outlook for gas was the introduction of fracking technology in the US which led to a revolution in the gas – and oil – sector. Due to the surge in gas production in North America, the leading oil and gas consumer in the world, namely, the US, has not only cut its oil and gas imports substantially, it is now poised to become an exporter.

This surge in supplies has not only brought surplus gas in the global market, it has also resulted in downward pressure on prices in the US, which in turn is impacting on prices in non-American markets.

This rigid, regionally structured price regime is now gradually changing, with both Europe and the Asian countries moving away from oil-indexation towards more competitive gas-on-gas pricing. For example, some companies are changing contracts which involve a hybrid formula linking pricing to gas *and* oil, as opposed to linking prices exclusively to oil. In 2012, the BG group reportedly concluded a deal with China's CNOOC, wherein 70 percent of the price was linked to oil and the remainder linked to Henry Hub. Again, in 2012, KOGAS and GAIL India signed 20 year contracts linked to HH prices from Cheniere's US-based Sabine Pass facility.[13]

Some of these changes were brought about due to various factors including the rising price of oil, and forecasts that prices would remain high in the foreseeable future for various reasons. Subsequently, however, oil prices have decreased substantially, setting off a debate whether gas prices should be de-linked from oil; the emergence of new LNG markets in China, India, South East Asia, Latin America and West Asia; the growth in Japanese gas demand following the Fukushima nuclear accident and the government's decision to cut back on nuclear power, and replacing it with gas-based power; political turmoil in West Asia, popularly called the "Arab Spring", which curtailed exports from some countries like Libya; the growth in LNG supplies and most importantly, the shale revolution in North America, which freed up

13. Jane Nakano, Michelle Melton, "Coming Changes in the Asian LNG Market?", CSIS, March 28, 2014 at http://csis.org/publication/coming-change-asian-lng-market

large contracts of LNG that were originally bound for the US market. This, in turn, led to a fall in hub (Henry Hub) prices due to the oversupply in the US market. Apart from the US, several new gas producers have also entered the market. As a result, large quantities of conventional gas is also emerging from a number of regions – namely, Africa, the Mediterranean, Australia and the Arctic, added to the global supply base. And finally, following the agreement between Iran and P5+1 over the Iranian nuclear issue, the decades-old sanctions that were imposed on Iran were lifted. Although the re-entry of Iranian gas into the market will take a while given the state of the country's gas sector, it is expected that large supplies of Iranian gas will add to the increasing gas pool in a few years.

LNG as a Harbinger for Change

Although pipelines dominate global gas trade at around 20 percent of the total, LNG trade grew quickly in the late 1990s and 2000s. However, from 2010 its share of the global gas trade has stabilised around 10 percent, although it has the highest growth rate of the gas supply sources (which includes domestically produced and consumed supplies), expanding at an average of 6.6 percent since 2000,[14] with some analysts stating that it now rivals iron ore as the world's second-biggest traded commodity, after oil. While the IEA forecasts that natural gas demand globally would grow at about 1.6 percent per year through 2035, the growth in LNG demand is expected to be even stronger. Although the first commercial liquefaction plant was built in 1964 in Algeria, and growth was slow till 2000, since then, LNG's growth trajectory has been swift, with average annual growth of around 5-6 percent per year, albeit till 2020, when growth is expected to dip slightly.[15] This growth is based on the fact that more than 30 countries

14. "The World depends on Natural Gas", *IGU World Gas LNG Report*, 2016 Edition at www.igu.org/sites/default/.../IGU-World%20LNG%20Report-2015%20 Edition.pdf

15. International Energy Agency, *World Energy Outlook 2012*, October 2012 at https: //www.iea.org/media/workshops/2012/energyefficiencyfinance/1aBirol.pdf, and "Global LNG: Will new demand and new supply mean new pricing?", Ernst & Young, 2013 at http://www.ey.com/Publication/vwLUAssets/ Global_LNG_New_pricing_ahead/$FILE/Global_LNG_New_pricing_ ahead_DW0240.pdf

have proposed plans to build or add LNG liquefaction capacity, many of them being newcomers to the LNG market.

At present, the largest consumers of LNG are Asian countries, namely, Japan, South Korea and Taiwan, respectively. An exception is China, as it imports gas via pipelines from Central Asia and Myanmar, and is poised to import large quantities from Russia. Due to the lack of overland contiguity, there was a high level of dependency of most Asian countries on LNG imports. Traditionally, LNG in Asia is priced based on a price mechanism tied to the Japan Customs Cleared Crude price (JCC), also called the "Japan Crude Cocktail." The contracts, which are skewed in favour of the suppliers to ensure they get a return on their large infrastructure investment, are long-term, and once finalised, remain in place for the duration of the contract which is usually 20-30 years, and are rarely up for renegotiation, although some limited volume flexibility exists in some cases, such as allowing the buyer to reduce the volume slightly by a fixed amount. They are also subject to a destination clause, which prohibits a buyer from re-selling LNG in the market.

As a result, by mid-2011 prices rose in excess of $15/mmBtu from a low of $7.18/mmBtu in 2009, and further touched $18/mmBtu by the end of 2014, compared to $8 to $10.70/mmBtu in the European hubs and the Henry Hub (North American prices within a bandwidth of $2/mmBtu to $6/mmBtu between 2009 to 2015. At the same time, the Asian spot LNG prices from mid-2009 to early 2011 remained significantly below the JCC price during this period. Hence, when the Fukushima Daiichi accident occurred in 2011, and Japan began importing more LNG to replace its closed nuclear power stations, which resulted in a tight Asian LNG market, prices went up further.[16]

However, since then, several new LNG supplies have entered the market, chiefly from Africa and Australia, as well as from the US due to the shale gas revolution, leading to a surplus in supplies. The fall in oil prices too had an immediate effect on oil-indexed pricing with spot prices in Asia being set at around $6/mmBtu compared to $15/mmBtu

16. Howard V. Rogers, "The Impact of Lower Gas and Oil Prices on Global Gas and LNG Markets", OIES Paper NG 99, Oxford Institute for Energy Studies, July 2015.

for terms sales, as it takes four-five months before oil prices are fully reflected in contract prices.[17] As a result, several LNG importers switched from long-term contracts to the spot market or shorter term contracts as well as employing a hybrid form of contract, which involved a mix of European and US hub-based pricing formulae.[18] In the first quarter of 2017 however, LNG prices have recovered somewhat, with Asian spot LNG prices ruling around $7.50 per mmBtu, almost at par with NBP benchmarks.[19]

As the spot market for LNG grew, there were some calls for moving away from oil-indexed pricing to a hub-based one. In Asia, there were some suggestions that an Asian hub be created which would be indicative of regional trade. To retain their markets, long-term suppliers began offering concessionary prices in order to remain competitive, although given the high costs in developing new capacity, LNG prices are unlikely to collapse much further, particularly in Asia.

With oil prices looking to remain depressed for a while, as OPEC members inclined to maintain production quotas to retain market share by driving out high-cost production, hub-based cargoes may not remain cheaper, as low gas prices have seen several planned LNG plants being cancelled or put on hold. As in the case of the oil market, if the gas market becomes globalised, a cyclical trend in prices may take place in the gas market, leading to increased price volatility, as low prices will eventually lead to a tapering off in supplies, while high prices will lead to a supply glut.

At present, the gas market – particularly the Asian LNG market – is in a state of flux, with no sure indication about which way it will head. At the end of the day, contracts and pricing mechanisms will have to suit both producers and consumers, which in turn will require

17. Anne Kat Brevik, "The Tide Has Turned for the Global LNG Market: A Look Ahead to 2015 and Beyond", Thomson Reuters, February 10, 2015 at http://blog.financial.thomsonreuters.com/the-global-lng-market-a-look-ahead-to-2015-and-beyond/
18. Tetsuo Morikawa, "Outlook and Challenges for Gas Markets in 2015", The Institute of Energy Economics, January 2015 at http://eneken.ieej.or.jp/data/5914.pdf
19. Oleg Vukmanovic and Mark Tay, "Global LNG-Asia prices hit parity with British gas benchmark", *Reuters*, February 3, 2017 at http://www.reuters.com/article/global-lng-idUSL5N1FO5T3

a market-based mechanism to be in place. However, as in the case of the oil market, with security objectives taking precedence over economic ones in several countries, prospects for a competitive, market-based and deregulated gas market may be limited.

Growing Geopolitics

Despite new supplies coming into the market, natural gas resources, like oil are not evenly distributed. Around 70 percent of the world's known conventional gas resources are found in a region which stretches from Russia, Central Asia and West Asia. Moreover, natural gas reserves have been found in the Eastern Mediterranean Sea, which the United States Geological Survey in March 2010 assessed of having a potential of around 112 tcf (3.17 tcm).[20] Since the revenue accrued from energy sales/exports are often the economic backbone of exporting countries leads to political and economic interests of States taking precedence over commercial competition. In order to defend their national interests, States engage in strategic behaviour, which is reflected in policies that are geopolitical rather than commercial. This factor is expected to increase, as along with demand, the supply source of gas also expands with the discovery of new sources of gas emerging. With competition in gas-exporting countries poised to increase, States often strategically manoeuvre in order to affect gas flows.

This proclivity of some countries to use their gas exports as a foreign policy tool and influence gas flows raises concerns in gas importing countries over dependence on gas imports. On the other hand, gas-exporting countries, particularly those which are dependent on transit countries or a small number of markets are also concerned over losing market share to competitors and are weaving their energy policies into their foreign policy strategies. Similarly, some of the large energy consuming countries are leveraging their market as a diplomatic tool, and ensuring that the promise of long-term demand is being tied into their relations with energy producing countries. While energy –

20. "Assessment of Undiscovered Oil and Gas Resources of the Levant Basin Province, Eastern Mediterranean", U.S. Department of the Interior, U.S. Geological Survey, Fact Sheet 2010–3014, March 2010 at http://pubs.usgs.gov/fs/2010/3014/pdf/FS10-3014.pdf

more specifically oil – has always played a major role in traditional geopolitics, the growing debate on carbon emissions and its fallout on global warming has turned the spotlight on gas as a 'bridge' fuel in the transition from fossil fuel-dominated global economy to cleaner, greener energy resources.

Although gas is used worldwide, some countries are more important for the gas market as their policies and strategies are expected to either influence the way in which the gas market evolves, or conversely, whose polices will be impacted by unfolding events in the gas market. Although the following countries are the main movers and shakers of the gas market, several newcomers have emerged more recently. However, as their activities and policies are more commercially oriented, they have not been dealt with separately.

The United States of America

The US has perhaps been the largest contributor to the changes that have taken place in the energy markets, and more particularly in the gas market. The American energy revolution brought about by fracking technology, with the commercial exploitation of shale assets having had wide-ranging geopolitical consequences. Apart from being closer to realising its goal of being 'energy independent', the US is now poised to become an energy superpower, rivalling Saudi Arabia and Russia in the oil and gas markets. For the first time since 1971, energy will no longer be perceived as a strategic liability for the country, and it can now take policy decisions without having to factor in complex obligations based on energy security considerations. Instead, the US' new-found energy bounty is set to boost its leverage around the world.[21]

As US production continues to increase, it is putting downward pressure on global gas – and oil – prices, thereby reducing the geopolitical leverage that traditional energy suppliers have wielded for decades. For example, in 2012, while US gas prices stood at $3 per million BtU (mmBtU), Germans paid $11/mmBtU and the Japanese

21. Robert D. Blackwill and Meghan L. O'Sullivan, "America's Energy Edge: The Geopolitical Consequences of the Shale Revolution", *Foreign Affairs*, March-April 2014 at

paid $17/mmBtU. Gas customers in various parts of the world will now have the advantage of negotiating better terms with traditional suppliers, and loosen the geopolitical grip of these producers from Russia to West Asia.[22]

These changes may also see the emergence of new partnerships, which will have considerations for the energy markets at its base, but more importantly, will have far-reaching geopolitical implications, the contours of which can be seen in the China-Russia gas deal of 2014.

Finally, the US fracking and shale gas revolution may well have the greatest impact on the current pricing mechanism, as cheaper US hub-based resources may instigate changes in the current regional status of the gas market and nudge it closer towards a more globalised orientation, akin to the oil market.

Russia

Its natural gas reserves are perceived to be the backbone of the Russian energy sector, and more importantly, a powerful tool of the country's domestic and foreign policy. Not only does it play a key role in establishing Russia's credibility in the global energy economy, it is an important tool in a number of significant foreign policy initiatives as it allows Russia's integration into global trade. Through joint ventures and foreign investments, both within and outside Russia, Russian business has been able to be integrated into global economic relations, gradually making Russia a full-fledged participant in the global economic system.[23]

With around 1,688 trillion cubic feet (tcf) (47.7 trillion cubic metres) of natural gas reserves as of January 1, 2013, Russia accounts for about a quarter of the world's total proven reserves. At present, 76 percent of its natural gas is exported to Western Europe through a vast network of pipelines controlled by state-owned Gazpromand transiting through Ukraine and Belarus.[24]

---

22. Ibid.
23. Tatiana Mitrova, "The Geopolitics of Russian Natural Gas", Center for Energy Studies, James A. Baker III Institute for Public Policy, Rice University, February 21, 2014.
24. Russia, US Energy Information Administration, March 12, 2014 at http://www.eia.gov/countries/analysisbriefs/Russia/russia.pdf

When Vladimir Putin took over Russia's presidency, in line with his policy outlined in an article he wrote in 1999, he moved to take control of the natural resource sector, as he felt it was too important to be left entirely to market forces. Putin understood that energy resources and exports could be used to leverage Russia's economic and geostrategic revival, and after nationalising several independent oil companies, the government systematically set about to monopolise the European market, ruthlessly preventing any alternative suppliers from emerging, either by buying gas from regional rivals at above-market rates, or preventing any alternative transit routes from coming up by engineering conflicts and even terminating supplies. Being Eurasia's largest gas supplier, Russia has a huge influence on the prices as well as geopolitical leverage. However, Russia's most effective weapon is its gas network, and it has assiduously prevented any rival network or route to come up. Whenever any former Soviet state has shown an interest in integrating more closely with the West or NATO, Russia has used pricing disputes to terminate gas exports. Some cases in point are Belarus and Ukraine, both of which are important transit states through which Russian oil and gas exports are sent to Europe.

However, these strategies have left client states, sometimes with the support of the US, to explore alternative supply sources as well as to seek reorganisation and reform of their energy sectors, which, if successful, could see Russia losing its market monopoly.[25] The recent sanctions imposed by the West following Russia's annexation of Crimea has added to Russia's economic troubles, at a time when Russia needs foreign investments to develop new gas reserves in Siberia and the Arctic to replace falling production from more mature fields. At the same time, the emergence of new gas producers is cause for concern for Russia. With new entrants in the gas production market growing, Russia will be facing tough competition for markets.

As a result, Russia is now seeking to diversify its market to the east and has been negotiating with potential Asian clients for markets. In May 2014, in what is being seen as the biggest deal in the energy

---

25. Jonas Grätz, "Deflating Russia's Gas Pressure", *Policy Perspectives*, Vol. 1, Issue 1, Center for Security Studies, September 2013 at http://www.css.ethz.ch/publications/pdfs/PP_01_08_2013.pdf

market, Beijing and Moscow ended months of fractious negotiations and signed a $400 billion agreement wherein Russia would supply China with up to 38 bcm of gas annually between 2018 and 2048. The deal is being seen as a reiteration of the role geopolitics plays and will continue to play in energy issues. Nevertheless, Russia will have to overcome several challenges and introduce reforms in its gas sector if it has to continue to retain its grip as a gas superpower.

West Asia (Iran, Qatar)

Although Iran has the second largest gas reserves after Russia, the sanctions imposed on the country have not allowed it to gain access to the technology or the financial resources it desperately requires to become a global natural gas and LNG player. The sanctions also deprived it of agreements on major pipeline deals to transport gas to Europe or Asia. But following a deal between Iran and the P5+1 nations on capping its uranium enrichment programme in July 2015, many of the sanctions have been lifted, making it possible for Iran to come out of decades of international isolation. However, while Iran has embarked on a large-scale plan to rejuvenate its ailing gas – and oil – sector, it will have to overcome several hurdles, many of them emanating from its own domestic politics, before it can position itself as a leader in the gas market over the next decade. As in the oil market, where its regional rival Saudi Arabia stands in its way, Qatar, the US, Russia and more recently Australia, stand in its way.

As the current reigning LNG superpower, Qatar's natural security policy is driven by increasing its international profile in order to protect itself from the perils of its vulnerability as a small State sandwiched between the two regional giants, Saudi Arabia and Iran. Using its vast gas resources – the third largest in the world – it has gained an international presence far beyond it size. However, it is now facing competition from new producers, particularly in the Asian LNG market, which is its traditional domain. Australia is constructing liquefaction plants that will more than triple its annual LNG-manufacturing capacity to 85 million tons by 2018, surpassing Qatar, and even American producers have signed contracts to supply Asian LNG buyers at competitive prices. As a result, Qatar stands to lose some market share and may cut prices to retain markets. To hedge itself against increasing competition, Qatar has bought stakes in oil and gas fields in diverse countries as well as in international oil companies such as Royal Dutch Shell and Total, both of which operate LNG plants around the world.[26] Whether Qatar succeeds in manoeuvring itself in an over-supplied and increasingly competitive market will be a testimony of its survival skills and business acumen.

Turkmenistan

Turkmenistan, which is estimated to hold around 17 tcm of natural gas reserves– currently the fourth largest in the world – adopted a foreign policy that was premised on "positive neutrality" following its independence in 1991. While "neutrality" allowed it to build strategic relations with all countries without joining any blocs, it also allowed it a way out of its dilemma of maintaining relations with Russia on the one hand, and forging relations with other countries on the other. Iran is already a market, albeit limited, although pricing disputes with Tehran have seen flows decreasing. Moreover, with Iran now poised to become a major gas exporter following the lifting of sanctions, the need to find other markets has become all the more critical for Ashgabat.

At the time of independence, Turkmenistan, a landlocked country, was completely dependent on the Soviet-era pipeline network to transport its most valuable asset, natural gas, to other markets. Hence, while in the initial years of independence, it continued to use the Russian network, pricing problems with Gazprom saw Ashgabat cutting off, or threatening to terminate gas supplies from 1997. Subsequently, frequent disagreements over pricing, and Ashgabat's attempt at finding alternative markets have exacerbated frictions with Russia, and recently, the latter terminated supplies from Turkmenistan completely.[27]

---

26. Robert Tuttle, "Qatar's LNG dominance challenged", *Washington Post*, April 18, 2014 at http://www.washingtonpost.com/business/qatars-lng-dominance-challenged/2014/04/18/90b06cda-c66c-11e3-9f37-7ce307c56815_story.html
27. Martha Brill Olcott, " Turkmenistan: Real Energy Giant or Eternal Potential?", Belfer Center, Harvard University and James A. Baker III Institute for Public Policy, Rice University, December 2013 at http://belfercenter.hks.harvard.edu/files/CES-Pub-GeogasTurkmenistan-121013-1.pdf

However, by 2009, Turkmenistan had found a ready client in China's CNPC, to which it supplies 35 bcm currently, with plans to double supplies by 2020. Nevertheless, unwilling to become dependent on a single market, Ashgabat has also been negotiating to further diversify its market. Negotiations for two more projects are being carried out – the first, which envisages transporting 33 bcm per year of gas from the Galkynysh field to South Asia through the Turkmenistan-Afghanistan-Pakistan-India (TAPI) pipeline, and the second, the 30 bcm per year trans-Caspian pipeline (East-West Pipeline) to Europe through Azerbaijan, with supplies from its Caspian Sea reserves. Both projects are uncertain, however, the first due to security issues given the conflict-ridden route of the project, as well as disputes over giving stakes to the companies involved in exploration, production and transporting the gas, and the second due to legal disputes with other Caspian littorals over sovereign rights as well as Azerbaijan.[28] Hence, although Turkmenistan has the potential to become a major gas supplier to European and Asian markets, it has to overcome several obstacles, including its own land law policy, and manoeuvre through regional geopolitical tensions before it can take its place among the world's gas giants.

Australia

Currently the second largest LNG exporter after Qatar, and poised to become the leader by 2020, Australian gas producers are not in an enviable position as continuing low prices from 2014 has seen it under pressure from Asian buyers to renegotiate prices, particularly after its massive $54 billion Gorgon project – the most expensive in the world – comes on line. In addition, three unconventional coal seam gas (CSG) projects are under construction in Queensland, one of which has commenced production. Most of Australia's current LNG production is exported to Asia; more than 80 percent is exported to Japan, while

28. Andrew C. Kuchins, Jeffrey Mankoff and Oliver Backes, "Central Asia in a reconnecting Eurasia: Turkmenistan's Evolving Foreign, Economic and Security Interests", Center for Strategic and International Studies, CSIS, June 2015 at http://csis.org/files/publication/150513_Kunchins_CentralAsiaTurkmenistan_Web.pdf

China and Korea account for much of the remaining share.[29] However, following the slump in prices, concerns regarding the viability of the Gorgon project have risen as supplies from new suppliers are undercutting the project's potential, rendering pricing below production costs. Nevertheless, the project's partners are optimistic, banking on the hope that prices will not remain low forever and that growing demand from the Asia-Pacific countries which are the main buyers of Australian LNG, would see demand – and prices – go up again, albeit over a period of time.

While Australia will certainly be a dominant actor in the gas market over the next decade, particularly in the Asia-Pacific region due to its geographical location, currently, the decisions taken on natural gas development and marketing are based on market considerations and not driven by geopolitical considerations.[30] Hence, a separate chapter on Australia has not been included in this book.

Arctic

Prior to the drop in the price of oil and gas, the Arctic was seen as the last frontier for the world's hydrocarbon resources, setting off fierce competition among the Arctic littorals. Following a US Geological Survey report published in 2008, which estimated that the region held 22 percent of the world's technically recoverable oil and gas resources, as well as the opening of sea routes following the melting of sea ice, fierce competition broke out among these nations, with each vying to expand their sovereignty and territorial space. The issue became more complicated as non-Arctic observer States too tried to expand their reach in the region. Over the last few years, some militarisation has also taken place, with some States making overlapping claims over large swathes of territory, and moving troops and equipment into the region.

---

29. Natasha Cassidy and Mitch Kosev, "Australia and the Global LNG Market", Reserve Bank of Australia, March 2016, *Bulletin,* at http://www.rba.gov.au/publications/bulletin/2015/mar/pdf/bu-0315-4.pdf
30. Ronald D. Ripple, "The Geopolitics of Natural Gas: The Geopolitics of Australian Natural Gas Development", Belfer Center, Harvard University, and James Baker III Institute, Rice University, Center for Energy Studies, January 2014 at http://belfercenter.ksg.harvard.edu/files/CES-pub-GeoGasAustralia-011414.pdf

Since the drop in oil and gas prices, some of the lure of the region has dissipated, as it is unlikely that the Arctic's energy and mineral resources will contribute to the global energy market till after 2025.[31] As long as energy prices remain low, exploring for hydrocarbons in the Arctic makes little economic sense. However, given that the region may be the last fully unexploited space with abundant energy resources, it is likely that the geopolitical competition that was seen a few years ago will return.

While the countries and regions mentioned above are producers and exporters of gas, countries that rely on importing their vital energy supplies and are therefore seen as a being vulnerable. However, given that energy security is as much about the security of markets as the security of supplies, the need for retaining and protecting market share make producers just as dependent on sustainable demand from key economies. The shift in economic dynamism towards the East over the past two decades is often seen as a rebalancing of geo-economic leverage, with some major Asian economies using their markets for geopolitical gains. Hence, these countries are seen as an important anchor for the global supply-demand balance and an influential force in global energy markets.

China

For China, the changes taking place in the natural gas and the overall energy markets have given rise to concerns as well as opportunities that could be exploited to its advantage. On the one hand, for China, whose rapid economic growth allowed its international profile to grow, energy security is critical in order to maintain its growth trajectory as well as ensuring that its domestic climate remains peaceful. However, its huge economic growth has meant a commensurate rise in demand for energy and despite large investments in domestic production, its demand has outstripped domestic supply, rendering the country dependent on increasing imports. Moreover, its energy security concerns have usually centred around its access to energy resources

31. "Opportunities and Challenges for Arctic Oil and Gas Development", Eurasia Group Report for The Wilson Center, Washington, D.C. January 2014 at http://www.wilsoncenter.org/sites/default/files/Artic%20Report_F2.pdf, accessed on May 22, 2014.

often from unstable regions, and transported through sea lanes that are dominated by the US navy. The US' pivot Asia policy along with the shifts that have taken place in the energy market due to the shale revolution have also created concerns of encirclement, pushing China to adopt an aggressive posture over territorial claims in the East and South China Seas, both to control the energy reserves in the region as well as to counterbalance Washington's network of alliances in the Pacific. Beijing is also trying to lessen its dependence on sea-based transport, and the timing of the recent deal with Moscow is a sign that it is hedging its vulnerabilities to ensure its energy supplies.

At the same time, the US shale gas revolution has benefited China as it has driven oil and gas prices down. The freeing up of US-bound gas supplies are now available for other consumers and can be negotiated for better terms.

Nevertheless, in its pursuit of enhancing its energy self-sufficiency, China is also trying to develop its own vast shale resources, given that it has the world's largest reserves of shale gas. The US EIA estimates that China has total reserves of 1,211 tcf (34.3 tcm) of shale gas, almost 50 percent more than the 862 tcf (24.4 tcm) in the US. Although issues about the economics and environmental consequences of developing shale gas have to be taken into account, it also has the potential to transform China's energy landscape, provided China gains access to the technology.[32]

Finally, China is well poised to replace the US as the largest energy market, and while it has leveraged its growing demand to form loose energy alliances and partnerships with several oil and gas producing countries in Eurasia and West Asia, as well as Africa and Latin America, it remains wary of its vulnerability to supply disruptions, particularly in its maritime periphery. Moreover, faced with a slow-down of its domestic economy, the China's leadership began looking for new avenues to sustain growth at a time when other developing countries are experiencing rapidly rising demand. In 2013, Chinese President

32. Gal Luft, "What does America's shale gas revolution mean for China?", *Journal of Energy Security*, July 25, 2013 at http://www.ensec.org/index.php?option=com_content&id=452:what-does-americas-shale-gas-revolution-mean-for-china&catid=137:issue-content&Itemid=422

Xi Jinping first mentioned the plan, known as the One-Belt-One-Road (OBOR) project. At the heart of the plan, which involves more than 60 countries, representing a third of the world's total economy and more than half the global population, lies the creation of an economic land belt that includes countries in Central Asia, West Asia and Europe, as well as a maritime route that links China's port facilities with the African coast, through the Suez Canal into the Mediterranean and eventually into Latin America. The project aims to redirect the country's domestic over-capacity and capital into infrastructure development to improve trade and relations with ASEAN, Central Asian and European countries, as well as gain improved access to the Persian Gulf and the Mediterranean Sea, as well as to the Indian Ocean and South China Sea through Southeast Asia and South Asia.[33]

India

Where the Chinese gas market had earlier held out the promise for gas exporters, India is being seen as a market with huge prospects. According to the IEA, India is, or will be, the surprise factor in the coming decades as its high economic growth has seen its demand for energy, growing at a pace that is faster than any other country. Although coal and oil will continue to form the backbone of India's energy sector, the government has declared that it plans to shift to a gas-based economy, both by boosting domestic production as well buying LNG, to meet its commitments to curb growing carbon emissions. According to the IEA, India's natural gas demand will grow by 4.2 percent per annum to 2035, with demand growing from 5.3 billion cubic feet per day (bcf/d) or 0.15 bcm per day in 2012 to nearly 18 bcf/d (0.5 bcm/d) by 2035. Despite the optimism regarding increased domestic production, its gas output has been falling due to lack of investment and the low domestic prices which act as a disincentive for the producers. Hence, India is expected to become

33. Xuming Qian, "The Belt and Road Initiatives and China's Middle East Energy Policy", *International Relations and Diplomacy*, October 2016, Vol. 4, No. 10, pp. 611-616 at https://www.davidpublisher.org/Public/uploads/Contribute/586b5db7853d6.pdf; Francis Cheung, "A brilliant plan: One Belt, One Road", Credit Lyonnais Securities Asia (CLSA) 2015 at https://www.clsa.com/special/onebeltoneroad/

more dependent on imports, which currently stands at 40 percent of demand. As of now, the bulk of India's LNG imports come from Qatar through long-term contracts, while the remainder is purchased on short-term and spot deals. India had also tied up a 20-year agreement with ExxonMobil's Gorgon facility in Australia, with supplies beginning from 2016-17, and another 20-year contract with Cheniere Energy from the US, with deliveries expected from 2017.[34] However, given the crash in prices, India is now negotiating with these suppliers for better terms, preferring to pick up cheaper gas from the spot market. It is also looking at importing piped natural gas from Turkmenistan, under the TAPI project, as well as from Russia and Iran following the lifting of sanctions from the latter. Nevertheless, given that plans are afoot for constructing at least five more terminals, it would appear that India intends to import LNG as opposed to piped gas.

What Lies Ahead?

The era of gas has been brought about by the fracking revolution and the unlocking of vast amounts of shale gas that was previously considered uneconomical to extract. The resultant pace and scale of US shale gas production, has changed its status as the world's largest oil and gas importer to that of a potential exporter. The implications of this go far beyond economic factors. Not only have natural gas prices in the US plummeted – from $13 per million British thermal units (mmBtu) in 2008 to around $3.80/mmBtu – leading to a scramble among US producers to find overseas markets. This has not only raised the potential of increased gas supplies globally, as supplies intended for the US market are now freed up for other customers, but it has also created the potential for other countries to explore their own shale resource base for domestic use as well as commercial production, which may lead to dramatic geopolitical changes.

As more supplies enter the market, leading to greater liquidity, it could lead to a change in the structure of the current gas market, from a predominantly oil-indexed and regional one to a competitive gas-

34. Charles Ebinger and Govinda Avasarala, "Natural Gas in India: Difficult Decisions", Belfer Center, Harvard University and James Baker III Institute, Center for Energy Studies, Rice University, October 2013.

on-gas priced market, that is more global in nature. Given the wider-than-oil but still uneven distribution of gas resources in the world, geopolitical factors will gain ground in the gas market, as countries may increasingly use their resources or markets as an instrument to further their broader geopolitical and economic interests.

However, given the nature of the gas market as well as the infrastructure required for gas, there are numerous challenges that will have to be overcome before gas can replace oil, or for that matter, other competing fuels. Gas infrastructure – both for piped gas as well as LNG – takes years to build and involves huge costs. Moreover, given the high reliance on fixed infrastructure, finding alternative supplies in the event of disruptions can be difficult, as the gas spot market is relatively small, despite growing liquidity, and requires more liberalisation, along with more contractual flexibility with regard to re-directing cargoes.

Finally, the future of shale gas is still uncertain, and the current production surge can be reversed in a few decades, causing a rise in prices, which will affect consumers all over the world, similar to that in the oil market. Already, with a rise in oil prices, a concurrent rise in gas prices has also taken place, reiterating the need for a de-linking oil and gas prices.

Therefore, while significant changes are taking place in the gas market, which over the years will have far-reaching consequences and implications for the global energy market as well as geopolitics, it may take a while before the golden age of gas can become a reality.

2

THE UNITED STATES OF AMERICA – THE GAME CHANGER

"Energy independence" has been a mantra that has been stated as a goal by successive American presidents and leaders. But not only did the US become a net energy importer by the 1950s, by the early 1970s, it had become the largest importer of oil. Since then, the one of the cornerstones of the country's foreign policy was dictated by the need to not only secure an uninterrupted flow of oil, but to ensure that it was priced affordably. With the West Asian region holding the largest oil reserves, it was only natural that the region was a major focus of its foreign policy. Hence, during the Cold War, US strategy was primarily aimed at ensuring that the vast oil reserves of the Persian Gulf states did not fall into Soviet hands. When Washington lost influence over one of its key allies in West Asia, following the Iranian revolution in 1979, and subsequently the invasion of Kuwait by Saddam Hussein, its policy was geared towards preventing these countries from threatening the US' oil-rich Arab allies. When a sanctioned Iraq tried to sell its oil in Euros, threatening the dollar's hold over the oil market, Saddam Hussein was removed.

Interestingly, although the US was till recently the largest importer of oil and gas, the West Asian region per se was not a major source of oil or gas for the US. But oil being a fungible commodity meant that irrespective of where production disruptions occurred, the stability of the entire oil market is affected, mostly due to the impact on prices as well as being a major source of supply for its European and Asian allies. Hence, although the US' primary sources of oil – or for that matter gas – imports was not the West Asian producers, the instability of the region had an impact on the US economy as it not only meant higher oil import bills for itself and its allies,[1] but also because oil and gas revenues sustained the reign of its West Asian allies. Moreover, with oil being traded only in dollars as per the 1945 agreement between the US and Saudi Arabia, it was essential that Washington exercise control over this vital commodity. And in so doing, it was also vulnerable to the impact of oil-related politics of the producing countries.

Now, for the first time since the 1970s, the US has an option to distance itself from the geopolitics of the oil market, and particularly that of the West Asian oil producing countries. With production of oil and gas averaging around 8.6 mbd in 2016 and natural gas production at 769 billion cubic metres (bcm),[2] the US is not only in a position to cut its oil and gas imports, but also to become a major global supplier.

This change in its energy scenario was made possible through the breakthrough in horizontal drilling technology combined with developments in hydraulic fracturing (fracking) technology, due to which the economic feasibility of production of oil and gas from shale formations has increased. As the US has substantial shale formations, and has seen a rapid increase in the production of shale oil and gas, there are reports from the Department of Energy (DoE) that with a combination of energy efficiency measures, lower consumption and huge production of shale gas as well as oil, it would not be long before a shale resource-driven US would not only be in a position to reduce – perhaps even end its energy imports – but would enable it to call the shots in the global energy market, thereby gaining a tremendous geopolitical advantage. Only, now the US' energy geopolitics will be driven not only by its oil production, but also by gas.

1. Stephen P.A. Brown, Hillard G. Huntington, "Assessing the US oil security premium", *Energy Economics*, Vol. 38, 2013, pp. 118-127.
2. "U.S. Petroleum and Other Liquids, Short-Term Energy Outlook", US Energy Information Administration, DoE, June 7, 2016 at https://www.eia.gov/forecasts/steo/report/us_oil.cfm, and "Natural Gas Production", *Global Energy Statistical Yearbook 2016*, at https://yearbook.enerdata.net/world-natural-gas-production.html

According to the recent *BP World Energy Outlook 2017* projections, while fossil fuels will continue to provide the majority of the world's energy needs, meeting two-thirds of the increase in energy demand out to 2035, there will be a shift in the energy mix. Driven by climate change concerns, natural gas, including shale gas, along with renewable energy resources, nuclear and hydro energy, will now dominate the global energy basket. Moreover, gas – which is projected to be the fastest growing fossil fuel, as well as the cleanest – will meet much of the increase in demand as coal and oil combined.[3]

A Gas-Based Resurgence

When Barack Obama took over the presidency in 2009, the US was already reeling under the impact of the economic recession that had taken over the Western countries. It was not surprising therefore that Obama's campaign rhetoric focused on economic recovery as well as the re-emergence of America as a global energy leader.

The energy policy adopted by him during his first term underscored the point that a global race was underway in taking over the leadership over the development and manufacture of clean energy technologies, with countries like China and even India playing to win. He exhorted the American people to take back the mantle of energy leader. In his State of the Union Address, the President proposed an ambitious but achievable standard that by 2035, the US would generate 80 percent of electricity from a diverse set of clean energy sources – including renewable energy sources like wind, solar, biomass, and hydropower; nuclear power; efficient natural gas; and clean coal, and called for investors to move billions of dollars into the clean energy economy, creating jobs across the country and reducing air pollution and greenhouse gas emissions. In his *2011 Blueprint for a Secure Energy Future*, the Administration outlined the government's priority as maintaining America's leadership in Research and Development (R&D), which was critical to winning the future and deploying innovative technologies that will create quality jobs and move towards clean energy economy that would further reduce the country's reliance on oil.[4]

3. *BP Energy Outlook 2017* at https://www.bp.com/content/dam/bp/pdf/energy-economics/energy-outlook-2017/bp-energy-outlook-2017.pdf
4. *Blueprint for a Secure Energy Future*, The White House, March 30, 2011.

Despite the focus on renewable and alternative energy resources, hydrocarbons and the need for imports would continue to be an important area for the country's energy policy. Like his predecessors, Obama too talked about the need to free America from energy import dependency, and specifically from the Persian Gulf region, and advocated increasing domestic production of hydrocarbon resources by opening up environmentally fragile areas in Alaska and the Gulf of Mexico.[5] But, as he stated in his first address to the nation after winning his second term, his strategy towards achieving "energy independence" was based on the natural gas boom in North America and not on the need to reduce energy imports from other regions.[6]

As a result, despite the fact that almost all US presidents since Richard Nixon have been talking about the need for energy independence, or rather, the need to reduce dependence on Persian Gulf for its oil imports, it is for the first time that the goal seems to be realisable. Based on a policy that combines a number of factors such as a resurgence of domestic oil and gas production including from areas that were hitherto closed due to environmental concerns, greater efficiency standards in energy consumption across the board, and wider spread of renewable energy and the commercial viability of US shale gas production, never since the 1970s has the US been closer to becoming an energy provider as against a net energy user.

Now, in 2017, the election of Donald Trump has seen the balance tilt even further towards fossil fuels. His vow to "unleash an energy revolution" by reversing regulations on oil and gas drilling on federal land and offshore exploration, including shale resources, and speeding up approval of new oil pipelines, including the Keystone XL and the Dakota Access[7], under his "America First" energy plan, has seen

5. "Obama Announces Plans to Achieve Energy Independence", *The Washington Post*, January 26, 2009 at www.washingtonpost.com/wp-dyn/content/article/2009/01/26/AR2009012601147.html?sid=ST2009012601175

6. "Obama's 2013 State of the Union Address", *The New York Times*, February 12, 2013 at http://www.nytimes.com/2013/02/13/us/politics/obamas-2013-state-of-the-union-address.html?pagewanted=all

7. Jeff Brady, "'America First' Energy Plan Challenges Free Market Realities" National Public Radio (NPR), February 7, 2017 at http://www.npr.org/2017/02/07/513905161/trumps-energy-shift-could-bring-higher-gas-prices-analysts-say

natural gas production rise to 73.7 bcf per day (2 bcm/d) in 2017, up by 1.3 bcf per day from 2016 levels. In 2018, the forecast for natural gas production is another 4.1 bcf per day increase from 2017. Moreover, this American bonanza of natural gas – and oil – exports are also poised to increase. While LNG exports are expected to rise to 12 bcf per day (0.339802 bcm per day) by the end of 2017 and if cross-border pipeline trade with Canada and Mexico are factored in, it may become a net exporter of natural gas by a margin of as much as 15 bcf per day (0.424753 bcm per day).[8] If these forecasts bear out, it will have huge implications for the energy – particularly the global – gas market. Traditional LNG exporters like Russia and Qatar have already sounded their concern over losing key markets in Europe and Asia respectively. Already there are reports that Cheniere's Sabine Pass LNG terminal in Louisiana exported 11 cargos in December 2016 to China, Japan and South Korea, Asia's largest gas markets.

The 'Revolution'

Although the first recorded extractions of shale gas took place in 1825 in Fredonia, New York, the fracturing or 'fracking' technology has only recently matured to a level where commercial-scale production has become viable. However, it was only after 1976 when the US government began investing in gas research as part of the Eastern Gas Shales Project that the potential of shale began to emerge. From 1980 to 2000, tax incentives were given, to promote shale drilling, providing the stimulus required for technology innovations. But it was only in 2006, that the 'revolution' was formally launched in the Parshall field in Bakken-Three Forks, North Dakota – originally discovered in 1951 – that has turned global energy production upside down,[9] putting the US back in control of the energy markets.

While the shale gas revolution has ensured that the US' concerns over dependence on energy imports have been allayed for now, it is

8. "Natural gas prices in 2017 and 2018 are expected to be higher than last year", Energy Information Administration, US Department of Energy, January 23, 2017 at http://www.eia.gov/todayinenergy/detail.php?id=29632
9. "The Shale Gas Revolution: What You Need to Know", *Allegro Development*, 2013 at http://www.allegrodev.com/whitepapers/Allegro—The-Shale-Gas-Revolution.pdf

in the strategic domain that the US stands to gain the most. At home, increased production of shale resources has not only bolstered the US economy by bringing down the price of oil and gas at the pump as well as its energy import bill, but has also contributed to the economy by creating thousands of jobs across the energy sector. According to data contained in the 2015 Annual Economic Report of the President transmitted to the Congress, the total employment in the oil and natural gas industries, including extraction and support activities, increased by 133,000 jobs between 2010 and 2013, and continued to grow through 2014.[10]

The rise in energy production has also led to the recent improvement in the trade deficit. Hence, while in 2006, the total trade deficit was 5.4 percent of the GDP, by the end of 2013, the trade deficit had fallen to 2.8 percent of the GDP, the lowest since 1999, barring the crisis-affected year of 2009.[11]

Moreover, the greater availability of gas, and the concurrent fall in retail prices, led to a shift from coal-based generation of power to more gas-based generation, bringing the share of coal in the US electricity market down from 50 percent to 39 percent, while gas-fired plants account for about 32 percent of the electricity basket, thereby contributing to a reduction in carbon emissions.

Strategic Benefits of US Gas Exports

Despite the robust opposition both from sectors of domestic industry as well as environmentalists, as the Energy section of the Economic Report of the President states, one of the biggest benefits of the shale revolution for the US is its fallout on its foreign policy. Without the increase in production and concomitant reduction in dependence on imports, it would not have been possible to have taken action against Iran by way of imposing sanctions, as it would have a deleterious impact on international oil prices and risk further destabilising an already beleaguered global economy. Moreover, it was thanks to the

10. Economic Report of the President, together with the Annual Report of the Council of Economic Advisers transmitted to the Congress, February 2015 at https://www.whitehouse.gov/sites/default/files/docs/cea_2015_erp.pdf
11. Ibid.

extra American oil and gas supplies that did not see prices escalate more steeply during the Arab Spring disturbances, although actual supplies were not affected as much as were expected.

Beyond economic benefits, the shale gas revolution has greater significance for the US' strategic goals. With several LNG cargoes meant for the US market now freed up for redirection to Europe and Asia, it set the course for a sea change in the world gas market. Without an over-supplied gas market, and potential alternative supply sources, it would not have been possible for Europe to free itself of Russia's proclivity to use its monopoly over its gas market as a political weapon.

For Asian countries, the largest LNG importers in the world, it has provided not only alternative sources of supply but has also provided alternatives to dependence on the West Asian energy producers. It has also provided the option of flexible and cheaper pricing models from the hitherto costly oil-indexed term deals they were dependent on. Now there is a real possibility of the gas market becoming a global market instead of the existing regional one. With 22 LNG import terminals in the US in the process of being converted into export terminals, the LNG market is set to expand, to rival the existing pipeline-dominated and regionally divided gas market to a more liquid and truly globalised market.[12] As of June 2016, the Federal Energy Regulatory Commission (FERC) had given final approval to 10 LNG export proposals, of which six are under construction, and four have not yet commenced with construction.[13] (see Map 2.1)

As American gas enters the global market, it will increase global supply and push global prices down. Lower natural gas prices around the world have a positive geopolitical impact for the US as it would reduce European dependence on Russian gas, particularly the Central and Eastern European nations, and prevent it from exerting political pressure on these nations. It would also allow many Asian nations which are highly dependent on imports from West Asia, to reduce their

12. Robert Manning, "The Shale Revolution and the new Geopolitics of Energy", Brent Scowcroft Center on International Security, Atlantic Council, November 2014 at http://www.atlanticcouncil.org/images/publications/Shale_ Revolution_ and_the_New_Geopolitics_of_Energy.pdf
13. "North American LNG Import/Export Terminals Approved", FERC at http:// www.ferc.gov/industries/gas/indus-act/lng/lng-approved.pdf

Map 2.1

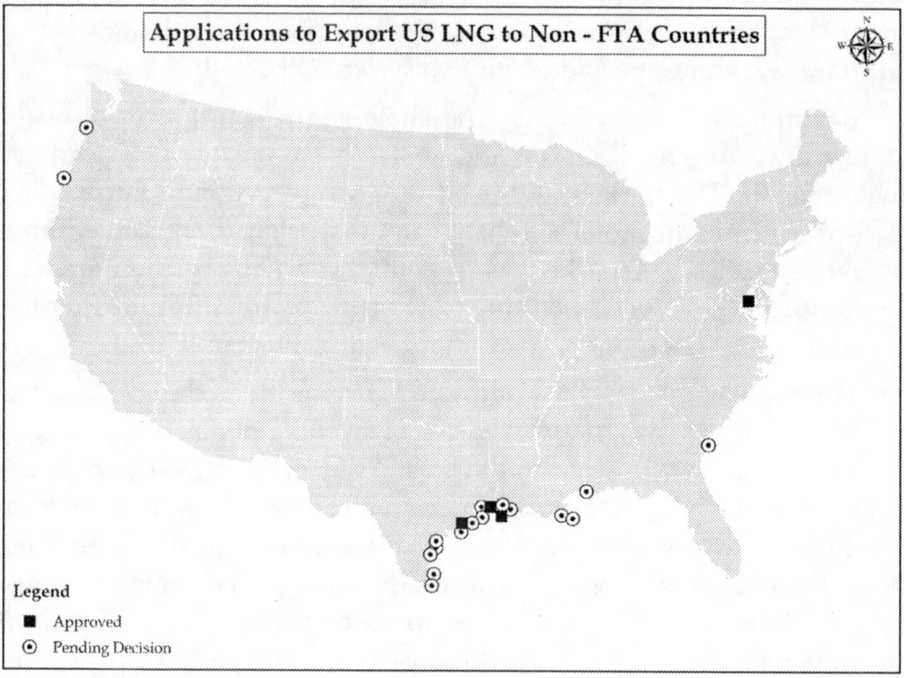

dependence on a region that is politically turbulent, and provide them the option of diversifying their supplies from a steadier and more reliable source of supply.[14]

At the same time, it would allow the US to strengthen ties with allies and trading partners around the world. Moreover, US LNG can also help the developing world by providing not only a source of affordable energy, but also one that is less carbon-intensive than the fuels that these countries are now using, and assist them in reaching their environmental objectives.[15] In effect, rising US gas exports would lead to rising American global influence.[16]

14. "Prosperity at Home and Strengthened Allies Abroad – A Global Perspective on Natural Gas Exports", The Policy Paper Series – Transforming Ideas Into Solutions, U.S. House of Representatives Committee on Energy and Commerce Chairman Fred Upton, Vol. 3, Issue 1, February 4, 2014, energycommerce.house.gov at http://energycommerce.house.gov/sites/republicans.energycommerce.house.gov/files/analysis/20140204LNGexports. pdf
15. Ibid.
16. Ibid.

Opportunities and Challenges for US Gas Exports

According to the President's Economic Report's section on energy, over the last decade, with US natural gas production increasing by roughly 40 percent, the US can produce more than enough natural gas to meet domestic demand affordably as well as support exports. However, while US LNG construction is scheduled to export large volumes over the next three years, Australian supplies are expected to come on line by 2017, raising concerns that a further saturation of the LNG market will drive prices down further.

However, in what could prove to be a game changer with the potential to catapult the US into the group of leading gas exporters, is the inauguration of the newly expanded Panama Canal on June 26, 2016. Following the deepening and widening of the Canal, which connects the Atlantic Ocean to the Pacific Ocean via the Caribbean Ocean, the US will now be able to handle around 90 percent of the world's LNG tankers – as against the current 6 percent – and a carrying capacity up to 3.9 bcf (0.1092 bcm) of LNG, besides shortening the travel time and transportation costs for US suppliers to key overseas markets. For example, the transit from the US Gulf Coast through the Panama Canal to Japan will now cut the voyage time to 20 days, compared to 34 days for voyages around the southern tip of Africa or 31 days if transiting through the Suez Canal. The voyage time to South Korea, China, and Taiwan too will be reduced, as will voyage time to South America, although it will not have any impact on voyages to India.[17] With about 9.2 bcf per day (0.2576 bcm per day) of liquefaction capacity either in operation or under construction by 2020, of which more than 4 bcf per day (0.112 bcm per day) under long-term (20 years) contracts with markets in Asia, and an additional 2.9 bcf per day (0.0812 bcm per day) capacity under construction and contracted to various countries, the US is set to become the world's third-largest LNG producer, after Australia and Qatar. And with advantages of time and cost-cuts following the expansion of the Canal, the US will have narrowed the advantage gap with Australia in terms of Asian markets.

17. "Expanded Panama Canal reduces travel time for shipments of U.S. LNG to Asian markets", Today in Energy, Energy Information Administration, US Department of Energy, June 30, 2016 at http://www.eia.gov/todayinenergy/detail.cfm?id=26892

The US will, however, have to deal with domestic opposition to LNG exports due to their impact on domestic prices. Those who favour exports are of the opinion that even if domestic prices do rise, some benefits to the US will accrue. According to EIA estimates, US residential retail prices would rise by 2 percent between 2015 and 2040. Nevertheless, with an increase in exports, the resulting price changes would have a number of beneficial effects on producers, besides attracting more investment, increasing employment, and most importantly, enhancing the country's geopolitical security.

A second set of challenges have also emerged against developing shale resources from the environmental lobby. Their argument rests on three issues. First, it damages the environment and endangers local communities. Moreover, it also impacts on drinking water resources by contaminating wells due to acquiring water to use in stimulating the well and mixing the fracking chemicals with the water to construct wells, inject the fracking fluid into the well, and handle fracking waste water that flows back up the well. Opponents of fracking maintain that at the end of the day, gas was a fossil fuel and therefore not much better than coal or oil when it comes to emitting greenhouse gases (GHG), and would require changes during the production process.

Third, with renewable energy now making so much progress, and with the US now one of the largest producers of renewable energy, these should lead the way for the transition to a zero-carbon future. On the other hand, use of natural gas would potentially stand in the way of developing renewables.[18]

Finally, there are doubts whether the US could become the world's dominant LNG player. Some experts are of the opinion that most of the gas liquefaction projects planned in the US would never get off the ground, mainly because of the drop in oil prices. Due to the linkage between LNG contracts and the price of crude, the price advantage of US LNG projects would be wiped out. In a paper, Leonardo Maugeri said that it was likely that not more than five or six LNG export plants, as against the 30 planned, would materialise in the US through 2020.

18. Michael Levi, "Fracking and the Climate Debate", *Democracy*, Issue 37, Summer 2015 at http://www.democracyjournal.org/37/fracking-and-the-climate-debate.php

Over the past few years, US natural gas prices have been about $4 per 1000 cubic feet, with oil around $100 a barrel, giving US gas a price advantage. But with crude prices falling over the last six months to under $50-60 a barrel, the oil-to-gas price ratio has shrunk, as natural gas in the US is hovering near $3 per 1000 cubic feet. Moreover, falling natural gas prices in Asia have further complicated the situation. The price has dropped by some 50 percent less than a year ago, which has eroded the advantage US exports had earlier. Given the huge costs involved in LNG infrastructure, several projects are likely to be delayed.[19]

To address these concerns, the Obama Administration released a much-delayed draft assessment issued by the Environmental Protection Agency (EPA) on the effect of the production technique on "specific instances" when fracking "led to impacts on drinking water resources, including contamination of drinking water wells." Although, earlier, the EPA had maintained that there was no evidence that fracking had contaminated drinking water, the study confirmed that fracking had indeed done so, albeit with the caveat that the number of contamination cases was not as widespread compared to the number of hydraulically fractured wells, and that the allegations of contamination were not confirmed as there was insufficient pre- and post-hydraulic fracturing data on the quality of drinking water resources.[20]

Moreover, as the Energy section of the Economic Report of the President states, natural gas has played a central role in the transition to a clean energy future as fuel switching, including replacing coal with natural gas as well as renewables like solar and wind energy, almost halved CO_2 emissions in the power sector from 2005. It also stated that unconventional (shale) natural gas development has opened a vast resource and had increased quantities of natural gas production, which

---

19. Ted Griggs, "Plans for export facilities in doubt", *The Advocate*, February 7, 2015 at http://theadvocate.com/news/business/10650285-123/falling-oil-prices-put-proposed
20. "Assessment of the Potential Impacts of Hydraulic Fracturing for Oil and Gas on Drinking Water Resources", Executive Summary, US Environment protection Agency, June 2015 at http://www2.epa.gov/sites/production/files/2015-07/documents/hf_es_erd_jun2015.pdf

had benefited the economy. It also states that the Administration had taken steps to ensure that natural gas and oil production would be undertaken in a responsible manner with environmental safeguards and that the current development of natural gas generation infrastructure "prepares the Nation for future widespread deployment of wind and solar generation." Given that high market penetration of wind and solar energy would benefit from either storage or backup generation capacity, developing natural gas infrastructure today would facilitate its use tomorrow for peak demand and renewable backup generation.[21]

Can LNG Exports Achieve US Geopolitical Strategic Goals?

Traditionally, the US has exported gas, primarily by pipeline, to Mexico and Canada. It has also exported LNG from Alaska to Japan, although in small volumes. Now, shored up by huge volumes of gas being produced from shale reserves, the US is poised to become a major player in the gas market. According to EIA estimates, domestic consumption of natural gas from 2015 to 2040 would be 31.6 percent of their resource estimates, and with consumption comprising only 17 percent of resource estimates, exports would not threaten America's supply of natural gas.

Apart from the economic benefits accruing from revenue earned and lowering imports, the prospect of becoming a major gas exporter could have effects that go beyond energy markets. For example, LNG exports would be able to support American allies in two regions, viz., Europe and Asia, by helping them diversify their energy sources and reducing the political clout of some producers by expanding the supply pool. In fact, in 2012, some former US Secretaries of Energy, viz., Bill Richardson and Spencer Abraham, stated that LNG exports can buttress US geopolitical leadership and trade, while at the same time, continuing to support low domestic natural gas prices and a renaissance in domestic manufacturing.

21. "The Energy Revolution: Economic Benefits and the Foundation for a Low-Carbon Energy Future", 2015 Economic Report of the President, Chapter 6 at https://www.whitehouse.gov/administration/eop/cea/economic-report-of-the-President/2015

The most vulnerable region to such energy-based pressure was Europe, particularly the Central and Eastern European states like the Czech Republic, Hungary, Bulgaria and Greece, because of their high dependence on Russia for natural gas. Russia has demonstrated its willingness to use energy as a political tool, cutting off natural gas supplies to European consumers several times over the years – in 2006, 2009 and more recently in 2014-15, when Gazprom halved supplies through the Nord Stream[22] – to maximise Moscow's political influence. Despite attempts by the EU to lessen their dependence on Russian gas through diversifying sources of supply, they have met with only moderate success thus far. Therefore, the shale gas revolution in the US has led to the expansion of US LNG exports to Europe which could help these countries reduce Russian influence.[23]

With respect to its Asian allies, particularly Japan, which is the top importer of LNG, the post-Fukushima incident led to a steep rise in LNG demand to replace nuclear energy, thereby pushing up prices and impacting the Japanese economy. This could be capitalised by Russia, which is considering building LNG export terminals in the Far East to service Japan. South Korea, the second largest LNG importer after Japan, is also in a similar situation. Hence, US LNG exports would serve to create a more liquid Asian market for LNG and lower prices.[24]

An even greater benefit accruing from the addition of US LNG to global markets than providing new supplies to its allies would be hastening the decline of the oil-indexed pricing formula. The gas market being regional in nature, LNG suppliers are able to dictate prices. As a result, consumers in Europe and Asia pay a huge premium for oil-indexed gas. However, with the influx of more LNG into the market, the market is becoming more liquid, putting pressure on oil-indexed prices as more and more consumers are turning to the spot

22. Jack Farchy, Kathrin Hille, Roman Olearchyk and Christian Oliver, "Russia cuts off gas supplies to Ukraine", *Financial Times*, June 16, 2014 at https://www.ft.com/content/db64d8f8-f522-11e3-afd3-00144feabdc0
23. Nick Cunningham, "The Geopolitical Implications of U.S. Natural Gas Exports", *Perspective*, American Security Project, March 2013 at https://www.americansecurityproject.org/ASP%20Reports/Ref%200116%20-%20The%20Geopolitical%20Implications%20of%20U.S.%20Natural%20 Gas%20Exports.pdf
24. Ibid.

market which is based on hub-based pricing formulae. It may eventually lead to a decoupling of oil and gas pricing. Already, Asian and Russian gas exporters are being forced to accept spot prices instead of oil-indexation. Greater spot market liquidity would also mean fewer destination-restricted vessels, which have cramped the LNG market's ability to respond to changing market conditions.

Finally, by improving energy efficiency and taking advantage of shale gas as a transitional fuel and thereby reducing its carbon emissions, the US would be able to provide international leadership to address climate change. According to EIA 2012 data, from 2005 to 2012, the US reduced its total CO_2 emissions more than any other nation. Revenue earned from gas exports, and reduction in imports would allow more R&D funding for the development of clean energy. Moreover, while at home, replacing coal in the power sector and oil in the transport sector would cut emissions, by making more gas available in the global gas market; it would also assist other countries to cut emissions by replacing gas with other more carbon-intensive fossil fuels.

Impact of Energy Independence on US Foreign Policy

Prior to the shale revolution, the US, which had been severely affected by the 2007-08 financial crisis, was being perceived as a descendant power, unable or unwilling to deal effectively with the many crises emerging in various parts of the world, most notably in West Asia. Given its status as the world's largest reservoir of conventional oil and gas, the free flow of resources from the region was a key imperative of the US' foreign policy, although the US per se was not a major market for West Asian oil and gas. Now, with the revolution wrought by its shale reserves and fracking technology, the US is poised to become a potential oil and gas exporter, as well as the largest energy producer, concerns over supply disruptions no longer hold the same critical importance. Hence, removed from such concerns, Washington will be able to take foreign policy decisions based on its interests alone, without energy supply pressures weighing in.

Several Western writers have hailed the advent of a new era of energy independence that will allow the Western world to free itself from the shackles of Arab oil and gas. On the other hand, the Gulf regimes are concerned that an energy-rich US will no longer be as engaged as before in the region, devoid of the security umbrella that the US had provided. Although the US has denied shifting its attention away from the West Asian region, and in fact, according to a Department of Defense report on its budget priorities, the US plans to "rebalance its force structure and investments toward the Asia-Pacific and the Middle East regions while sustaining key alliances and partnerships in other regions",[25] there is a perception that a strategic shift is imminent. Moreover, following the signing of the nuclear deal with Iran and the P5+1 and the potential strategic changes that may take place in Iranian-American relations resulting in the rise of Iranian influence in the region, the Arab regimes' concerns are understandable.

However, the major long-term regional threat is a rising China with its rapid economic growth and desire of its leaders to restore what they see as Beijing's rightful dominance, not only in East Asia, but also beyond. With the fast build-up of China's military, including a blue-water navy and upgraded nuclear strike force, Beijing has already signalled its intention to assert its claim over territory in the East and South China Sea, building new islands on shoals in international waters and establishing air and naval bases to project Chinese power, but is also extending its influence in West Asia. It has built strong ties with Israel, and is currently its third-largest trading partner, while Israel is China's second-largest source of military technology.

On the other hand, Chinese companies have invested heavily in infrastructure, engaged in arms sales, and invested heavily in the energy sector of the Arab and other Muslim countries in the West Asian region. Given that more than half of its oil and a large portion of its gas imports come from West Asia, the ties with the region are expected to be strengthened further.[26]

More importantly, with the fate of the dollar largely tied to oil, can the US afford to see the dollar replaced by other currencies? Trading

25. "Defense Budget: Priorities and Choices", Department of Defense, January 2012 at http://www.defense.gov/news/Defense_Budget_Priorities.pdf

26. David Lai and Noah Lingwall, "China: A Solution in the Middle East?", *The Diplomat*, June 18, 2015 at http://thediplomat.com/2015/06/china-a-solution-in-the-middle-east/

oil and gas in dollars since the 1945 agreement with the Saudis in return for US military security and protection, has kept the demand for US dollars by all nations who needed to trade hydrocarbons constant, and thereby allowed Washington to become a financial hegemon. However, since 2013, Russia began selling its hydrocarbons in Rubles and in the currencies of its trading partners, like China and other BRICS countries. Currency swaps between Russia and China have already been implemented, while similar swaps are underway between these two countries on the one hand and other countries which are members of the Shanghai Cooperation Organisation (SCO), including prospective members like Iran, Pakistan and India, as well as Mongolia.[27]

By becoming an energy superpower in the same genre as Russia and Saudi Arabia in terms of gas and oil respectively, the US can to some extent avoid, or at least stave off, the potential economic disaster that the demise of the petrodollar would bring, as well as gain a geopolitical advantage. It would allow Europe to reduce – perhaps end– its dependence on Russian gas, as well as deny Russia the revenue that it acquires from the sale of gas. It would encourage investments in the American energy sector, including those from West Asian energy producers as political turmoil in the region makes the region unattractive for further investments, thereby strengthening ties with these states. With more liquidity in the gas market, it would accelerate the move towards a more global gas market, and forestall any attempt by Russia, Qatar and Iran to form a gas cartel.

It would allow its Asian allies like Japan and South Korea, as well as India, the independence to not only diversify their LNG import sources, but also have access to hub-based spot price index. As Singapore's Ambassador to the United States Ashok Kumar Mirpuri, said at a forum hosted by the US Subcommittee on Energy and Power entitled "U.S. Energy Exports: Geopolitical Implications and Mutual Benefit", in October 2013, "Increased LNG exports (to Asia) would further anchor the US economic presence and further contribute to enhancing the region's energy security. In doing so, the US would

27. Peter Koenig, "Russia and China: The Dawning of a New Monetary System?", *Global Research,* January 9, 2015 at http://www.globalresearch.ca/russia-and-china-the-dawning-of-a-new-monetary-system/5423637

strengthen its partnerships in the region, serving regional stability and its global interests."[28]

However, all the above would be contingent upon the ability of US producers to maintain production at high levels. And here lies the dilemma. With Saudi Arabia and Russia fighting back to retain their market share by retaining production levels and keeping prices at a level that will hurt high-cost output, including shale production, US shale producers are finding it difficult to keep up with production in the face of falling prices. Till 2015, the EIA's figures indicated that after four years of record supply, natural gas output in the US has been declining as drillers curtail gas output from reservoirs to prevent further price declines.[29] But after prices started picking up following the November 2016 OPEC deal, there has been signs of some rig activity again.

Moreover, with Iran now back in the picture as a potential oil and particularly gas producer – and a potential exporter in the not too distant future – the global gas market, already over-supplied, runs the risk of seeing prices dropping once again. The new US Administration's 'America First' policy, which has removed regulations on oil and gas drilling, may hasten the fall, as huge supplies are expected to enter the market from 2017 through 2025. Apart from the LNG export terminal at Cheniere Energy's Sabine Pass, which began shipments in 2016, additional LNG export terminals are planned within the next several years, including the Cove Point facility in Lusby, Maryland, which is scheduled to open by end-2017. More than half of the LNG export capacity that is scheduled to be online by 2020, has been contracted to Asia, as the expansion of the Panama Canal cuts travel time to the region.[30]

---

28. "Transforming Ideas Into Solutions Prosperity at Home and Strengthened Allies Abroad – A Global Perspective on Natural Gas Exports", no. 14.
29. Christine Buurma and Naureen Malik, "Shale Gas Supply Held Hostage by Oil to Drop by Most in a Year", *Bloomberg*, July 14, 2015 at http://www.bloomberg.com/news/articles/2015-07-13/accelerating-shale-gas-declines-show-supply-held-hostage-by-oil
30. "U.S. Becomes a Net Energy Exporter in EIA Forecast", Institute for Energy Research, as reported by Canada Free Press, January 14, 2017 at http://canadafreepress.com/article/u.s.-becomes-a-net-energy-exporter-in-eia-forecast

While domestic considerations will have to be weighed against larger geopolitical goals, there is no doubt that the entry of the US as a gas producer and exporter has changed the energy landscape. The biggest beneficiaries from an energy perspective are the large Asian consumers who were held hostage by the traditional producers. According to US government estimates, production– particularly from shale gas– will continue to expand till 2035, despite depressed prices. In such a scenario, it is almost certain that the US will once again be in a position to call the shots in the energy markets.

3

RUSSIA – MASTER OF THE (ENERGY) GAME

Since the czarist period, the energy sector has been an important part of the Russian empire. Realising its lack of access to technology as well as capital to exploit its energy assets, the Russian monarchy allowed foreign companies to invest in the development of the Baku and Volga oil fields. By the turn of the century, the Russian Empire was producing 31 percent of global oil exports.[1] On the other hand, the roots of Russia's gas industry were created in 1965 when the USSR decided to place greater emphasis on gas production and consumption.[2] During the Soviet era, the Kremlin leveraged its energy resources to expand its power across its immediate neighbourhood in order to create buffers against other powers, and energy exports accounted for half of Soviet export earnings.[3] This influx of capital was, and continues to be, instrumental in helping Russia build its military and industrial basis, which is critical for maintaining its status as a regional and indeed a global power. Hence energy resources are viewed as both a tool and a means to achieve not only the governments' economic but also security and political goals. The revenues from oil and natural gas exports empowered the Kremlin to consolidate its hold over the Soviet Empire.

1. Lauren Goodrich and Marc Lanthemann, "The Past, Present and Future of Russian Energy Strategy", *Stratfor Global Intelligence*, February 12, 2013 at https://www.stratfor.com/weekly/past-present-and-future-russian-energy-strategy
2. Roman Kupchinsky, "Russia: Gazprom –A Troubled Giant", Radio Free Europe Radio Liberty, January 05, 2006 at http://www.rferl.org/a/1064448.html
3. Lauren Goodrich and Marc Lanthemann, no. 1.

The Russian government has control of developments in the energy sector through commanding stakes in key energy companies.

The energy sector also contributes to Russia's ability to expand its influence to its immediate neighbourhood. Moscow's use of energy as leverage varies from controlling regional energy production (as it did in former Soviet states) to subsidising cheap energy supplies to these countries as well as controlling the energy transport infrastructure. With its low cost of labour, Russia was able to sell its oil at subsidised rates to its Soviet satellite states and from thereon to Western European countries, which also strengthened its position in its own periphery.

After the break-up of the Soviet Union and the loss of status as a superpower, Moscow continued to use its vast energy resources, mainly to earn revenues. However, it was not until Vladimir Putin took over the helm of the government in 2000 that energy became a major strategic factor in Russia's foreign policy. After re-nationalising some strategically important sectors of the economy, including the oil and gas companies that had been privatised during the post-Soviet Yeltsin era, Putin focused on the nation's energy policy. It is interesting that although Putin wrote his dissertation on basing Russia's domestic and foreign policy on the development of its energy resources prior to becoming President, many of the policies that were followed subsequently reflect his theories on how to shape the country's energy sector, from extraction to development and export.[4]

Since then, Russia has been using its energy resources to further its foreign policy goals in by importing oil and natural gas from the former Soviet Republics at a discount and exporting them to other countries at higher prices; ensuring that the routes of the – mainly natural gas – pipelines go through its own territories or transit only friendly countries; and third, using this monopoly over its vast supply network to influence foreign policy decisions in these countries that are in Russia's national interests.

To a large extent, Russia succeeded in using its energy strategy

4. V. V. Putin, "Mineral and Raw Materials Resources and the Development Strategy for the Russian Economy", Putin's Thesis (Raw Text), translated by Thomas Fennell, The Atlantic, 2008 at https://www.theatlantic.com/daily-dish/archive/2008/08/putins-thesis-raw-text/212739/

effectively to further its national interest. For example, the gas sector was left out of the sanctions regime that was imposed on several other sectors of the economy – including the oil sector – after Russia's annexation of Crimea in 2014. However, both the former Soviet Republics, as well as Russia's European client states have been attempting to reduce their dependence on Russian energy supplies by pursuing gas infrastructure projects. In October 2014, Lithuania launched its Project Independence – a floating LNG storage and regasification unit, owned by Norway's Statoil – to be moored in the port of Klaipeda, and supplied with gas from non-Russian sources, including possibly American LNG in the future. Eventually, the project proposes to hold sufficient capacity to meet around 90 percent of the gas demand of the Baltic states of Lithuania, Latvia and Estonia. This is only the first step in the EU's list of projects to wean itself away from dependence on Russian gas supplies. Poland too opened its first import terminal in 2015, while Bulgaria, which also buys close to 90 percent of its gas from Russia, stating that supplies of US gas could arrive via Greek LNG facilities.[5]

However, following the US shale revolution, the subsequent price fall and the looming possibility of US LNG entering the European market has seen Russia facing the biggest threat since it re-emerged as an energy superpower post-2000. Today, Russia is scrambling to retain – and diversify – its markets, not only for economic reasons but also to retain its leverage in a region it considers vital for its survival and power.

The Russian Gas Sector

Russia has one of, if not *the* largest gas reserves in the world. According to the *Oil and Gas Journal*, Russia has 1,688 trillion cubic feet (tcf) or 47.7 trillion cubic metres (tcm) of gas reserves as of January 1, 2013, accounting for about a quarter of the world's total proven reserves.

5. Petrras Vaida, "LNG terminal – guarantor of Lithuania's energy security", *The Baltic Course*, October 23, 2014 at http://www.baltic-course.com/eng/energy/?doc=97991, and Georgi Kantchev, "With U.S. Gas, Europe Seeks Escape From Russia's Energy Grip", *The Wall Street Journal*, February 26, 2016 at http://www.wsj.com/articles/europes-escape-from-russian-energy-grip-u-s-gas-1456456892

The majority of these reserves are located in Siberia, with the Yamburg, Urengoy, and Medvezh'ye fields alone accounting for more than 40 percent of its total reserves, with other significant deposits located in the northern part of the country.[6]

The state owns the majority of the gas with the state-run Gazprom controlling more than 65 percent of reserves and additional reserves being controlled through joint ventures with other companies. The company produced about 74 percent of the country's total output. Although independent producers have gained importance recently, and are contributing increasing volumes to the country's production, upstream opportunities remain fairly limited for them. Gazprom's domination of the gas sector is further ensured by its monopoly on Russian gas exports through its vast pipeline network. Although the government has stated that it would allow independent producers to export by 2014 by allowing third-party access (TPA) to the domestic pipeline network, actual changes have not occurred.

There are currently 10 major pipelines in Russia, eight of which are for export. These include the Yamal-Europe I, Northern Lights, Soyuz, Bratstvo, and Nord Stream pipelines, all of which carry Russian gas to Eastern and Western European markets via Ukraine, Belarus, and across the Baltic Sea. Three other pipelines, viz., Blue Stream, North Caucasus, and Mozdok-Gazi-Magomed, connect Russia's production areas to Turkey and the former Soviet Republics in the east. Following the Ukraine crisis, Russia is now shifting focus to another pipeline – the South Stream pipeline – that envisages transporting 63 bcm of gas per annum under the Black Sea to Central Europe via Bulgaria and Serbia, avoiding Ukrainian territory. The project was abandoned by Russia in 2014 after the former Bulgarian government decided not to issue construction permits for its exclusive economic zone in the Black Sea, possibly under pressure from the EU. The Bulgarian government has said that it would revisit the project after elections scheduled to be held in March 2017.[7]

6. "Russia", US Energy Information Administration, Department of Energy, March 12, 2014 at http://www.eia.gov/countries/analysisbriefs/Russia/russia.pdf
7. "South Stream 'Could Be Revisited' after Bulgaria Election - Hungary FM", Novinite.com, *Sofia News Agency*, February 28, 2017, http://www.novinite.com/articles/179063/South+Stream+'Could+Be+Revisited'+after+Bulgaria+Election+-+ Hungary+FM

Russia also produces and exports LNG, the majority of which is exported to Japan and South Korea, as well as China and Taiwan under long-term supply agreements from Sakhalin. Although additional trains have been planned between 2017 and 2018, these would require other sources of gas in addition to the existing fields, some of which are in the environmentally, economically and technologically challenging Arctic region. There are a number of proposals in various stages of planning including the construction of new LNG terminals. Interestingly, these projects will include independent companies such as Novatek and Total as partners.[8]

Natural Gas Exports as a Strategic Tool

For Russia, while its oil is used mainly to earn revenue, its vast natural gas resources are used both as an instrument and a means to achieve economic as well as security and political goals. This became most evident in the mid-2000s, when Moscow terminated gas supplies to Ukraine after Kiev began becoming increasingly oriented towards the West following the Orange Revolution in 2005. As a key transit country for Russian gas exports to Western Europe, Ukraine's apparent leveraging of its position by demanding higher transit tariffs was seen as going against Russian interests. Moscow therefore demanded Kiev pay market-driven prices as against the subsidised gas prices offered earlier. The dispute reached a climax in January 2009 when Russia terminated gas exports to Europe for two weeks, thereby depriving south-eastern Europe of gas in the middle of winter. The issue was resolved after prices were renegotiated, but it impaired Russia's reputation as a reliable supplier.

In a similar case, in 2010, Russia also cut off gas to Belarus, after its President Alexander Lukashenko, refused to join a Belarus-Kazakhstan-Russia customs union being championed by Vladimir Putin, who was prime minister at the time, as well as demanding duty-free Russian oil as the price of further cooperation. He also gave refuge to Kyrgyz leader Kurmanbek Bakiyev, ostensibly against the Kremlin's wishes. However, once again the apparent dispute was over reviewing subsidised gas prices provided to Belarus by Russia. Eventually, the

8. Ibid.

dispute was settled after Russia acquired a larger share in the country's energy infrastructure, and thereby further control, in exchange for continued discounted gas.

Although couched under the garb of price revisions, the gas cut-offs were aimed at inflicting punishment for these countries' policies of trying to move closer to the West. Although both disputes were settled on Russia's terms, they served to impair Russia's credibility as a reliable supplier, hastening the resolve of European customers to diversify their energy supplies away from Russian dependence.

More recently, Russia's surprising involvement in the Syrian conflict has also been attributed to its strategy to prevent rival producers from providing European customers with alternative gas supplies. Since 2009, following Qatar's proposal to build a pipeline to send its gas to Europe through Turkey and Saudi Arabia transiting Jordan and Syria, Russia imposed pressure on President Assad to reject the same. Similarly, an Iranian proposal in 2011 to construct the Iran-Iraq-Syria pipeline, which was slated to be finished in 2016, has also been held up, first due to the 'Arab Spring' and now due to the conflict in Syria. Although Moscow is more amenable to the Iranian proposal, Qatar's involvement in Syria is believed to have been a factor in its decision to enter the Syrian conflict.[9]

According to European Parliament data, in 2013 Russia provided 43.2 percent of the European Union's gas imports, 31.38 percent of its oil imports, and 26.7 percent of its coal imports.[10] However, according to other data, Europe's dependence on Russia is much lower now with Russia supplying 27 percent of the overall European natural gas market and supplying over 90 percent of the gas consumed in Eastern Europe.[11] Be that as it may, as the Russian government became dependent on

9. Mitchell A. Orenstein and George Romer, "Putin's Gas Attack: Is Russia Just in Syria for the Pipelines?" *Foreign Affairs*, October 14, 2015 at https://www.foreignaffairs.com/articles/syria/2015-10-14/putins-gas-attack

10. Tara Shirvani, "The Dash for Gas How Iran's Gas Supply Can Change the Course of Nuclear Negotiations", *Harvard International Review*, Vol. 36, Issue 3, Spring 2015.

11. Amy Myers Jaffe, Kenneth B. Medlock III and Meghan L. O'Sullivan, "China's Energy Hedging Strategy: Less than meets the eye for Russia Gas Pipelines", *NBR Energy Security Program*, February 9, 2015 at http://www.nbr.org/research/activity.aspx?id=530

energy revenues, it also became a liability, as with oil and gas exports to Europe accounting for almost 52 percent of Russia's federal budget income, Russia is as dependent on the European market as the Europeans are on Russian supplies. Moreover, although its monopoly over Europe's gas supplies facilitated Moscow to develop a sphere of influence, it came at a cost as low revenues did not allow it to develop its depleting fields as efficiently as was required. Many of Russia's older and larger fields are in long-term decline and production is coming mainly from smaller and more expensive and less accessible fields. As a result, maintaining oil production in Russia would require an infusion of new technologies, without which oil production in Russia will begin to decline from 2016-2017.[12] Moreover, Russia is facing a financial crunch due to the drop in oil prices since mid-2014, along with the Western-imposed sanctions over the Ukraine crisis. Between June 2014 and January 2015, the price of Russian oil fell from $113.70 a barrel to $46.05 per barrel – a drop of nearly 60 percent. Gas prices too have dropped, albeit not as much as oil.

Policies to Retain Markets

Global and regional circumstances have changed to the point that Moscow has had to prioritise one of the two uses of its energy industry – and it has unequivocally decided to maintain its revenue-generating capability. The Kremlin has begun crafting a set of policies designed to adjust the country to the changes that will come in the next two decades.

According to the Russian State Energy Strategy (which sets out the country's energy policy), "the creation of oil and gas industrial complexes in the east of the country that should allow the regions not only to become independent of outside energy and hasten their development but diversify exports flows to Asia-Pacific countries" has become an important pillar of Russia's energy policy.[13]

12. James Henderson and Ekaterina Grushevenko, "Russian Oil Production Outlook to 2020", The Oxford Institute for Energy Studies, Energy Insight 3, February 2017, https://www.oxfordenergy.org/wpcms/wp-content/uploads/2017/01/Russian-Oil-Production-Outlook-to-2020-OIES-Energy-Insight-benefactor-advance-copy.pdf
13. Tatiana Mitrova, "Looking East Amid a Crisis to the West: Russia's Export Strategies," interview by Laura Schwartz, National Bureau of Asian Research (NBR), September 9, 2014 at http://www.nbr.org/research/activity.aspx?id=483

The next decade will be critical for the Russian natural gas industry with its future prosperity depending to a large extent on the government's pricing and policies. *However, it is the gas sector which is crucial as Russia is bound to the European gas market due to its pipeline network which cannot be re-routed to other markets* due to the lack of necessary infrastructure. With the domestic market being over-supplied due to increased competition and demand stagnation, frozen regulated prices, and Rouble depreciation because of sanctions imposed by the Western countries following the annexation of the Crimean peninsula, the investment climate has been rendered unattractive. The situation has been exacerbated further as a result of depressed oil and gas prices. Moreover, with weak demand in Europe and the Commonwealth of Independent States (CIS), and traditional export markets (Europe) looking to diversify their supply sources in a bid to reduce their dependence on Russia, the industry faces a bleak future, and will affect revenue earnings. For example, in Europe, Gazprom's exports came down by 15 percent in the third quarter of 2014 compared to third quarter of 2013 – from 40 billion cubic metres to 34 billion – which translated into a decline of $2.2 billion from the European market.[14] Nevertheless, Gazprom remains the largest single gas supplier to Europe, and supplies about 30 percent of its needs; on the other hand, Europe comprises 76 percent of Russia's gas market. Hence, although the European market is crucial for the Russian economy, it needs to capture new markets to compensate for stagnating demand in Europe, as well as withstanding political pressure and Western-led sanctions emanating out of the Ukraine crisis. Despite the recently signed $400 billion gas supply deal with China, the project can only pay dividends – if at all – in the medium term, and depends on several factors which will be discussed below.

First, Russia plans to retain its position in the face of the growing threat from the US shale revolution by increasing its gas extraction significantly by developing new fields. Although the short and long-term forecasts are much more modest than those made in 2009, Russian

---

14. Paul Roderick Gregory, "Russia's Natural Gas Sales Plummet: Is Russia Captive To European Buyers?", *Forbes*, December 24, 2014 at http://www.forbes.com/sites/paulroderickgregory/2014/12/24/russias-natural-gas-sales-plummet-is-russia-captive-to-european-buyers/

gas production is planned to increase to the level of 739-770 bcm per year within five years, to 785-842 bcm by 2025, and to 860-936 bcm after 2034 from 444 bcm in 2014.[15] Furthermore, the IEA expects an increase in gas production, from more than 660 bcm per year by 2020 to more than 800 bcm after 2035. However, maintaining a high level of production and significant growth in forthcoming years will be a key challenge given the rate of depletion in its older fields.

Second, given its recent contentious relations with transit states particularly Ukraine, Russia is moving to find alternative routes bypassing these states. Moscow dropped its $40 billion South Stream pipeline project via Bulgaria to Europe in December 2014, on the grounds that it was blocked by EU regulations, and had opted for the Turkish Stream project instead. After it offering Ankara a price cut, Moscow announced that the Turkish Stream would replace the South Stream project. Although the negotiations were suspended, due to the crisis in bilateral relations following the downing of a Russian jet by Turkey in Syria in November 2015, a decision was made to resume the project after talks held between Turkish President Tayyip Erdogan and President Putin in August 2016. According to a Gazprom release, a contract to build the second string of the Turkish Stream's offshore section, was signed on February 20, 2017.[16]

Third, although it intends to retain its lucrative European market share by expanding natural gas discounts formerly reserved for strategic partners such as Germany or Italy to other customers, it is looking at diversifying its market eastwards by developing linkages with the growing East Asian energy markets.[17]

---

15. Zuzanna Nowak, Jaros³aw Cìwiek-Karpowicz and Jakub Godzimirski, "The power to influence Europe? Russia's grand gas strategy", *Natural Gas Europe*, March 12, 2015 at http://www.naturalgaseurope.com/the-power-to-influence-europe-russias-grand-gas-strategy-22678 and Caroline Copley and Vladimir Soldatkin, "Russia's Gazprom warns EU over gas, Ukraine", Reuters, April 13, 2015 at http://www.reuters.com/article/2015/04/13/us-russia-crisis-gas-europe-idUSKBN0N41ED20150413
16. South Stream Transport BV, Allseas Group sign construction contract for second string of offshore section, New Europe, February 22, 2017, https://www.neweurope.eu/article/russia-inks-second-turkish-stream-pipe-offshore-construction-contract/
17. Note 1.

Fourth, with its mature oil and gas fields in decline, Russia urgently needs to develop new reserves, including those in the Arctic, to not only retain its market share but also to meet supply agreements signed recently with China.

Finally, it is reviewing its earlier plan to expand LNG exports to Asia due to the fall in oil prices. Given that Russian gas prices are indexed to oil, this would have an impact on not only LNG prices and is once again focusing on increasing pipeline exports, including to Asian clients, including the pipeline to China, and is negotiating with India for piping gas through China.

The US and EU sanctions, limiting the availability of finance for Russian energy companies and threatening the possibility of an embargo on LNG technology, have accelerated both a move into the Asian market by Russian companies and a shift away from Russian LNG to pipeline gas projects. The signing of the 38 bcm per year pipeline contract with the Chinese company CNPC in 2014, with the possibility that a second contract could be signed in 2015 for 30 bcm per year via the Altai pipeline, would mean that – adding in existing LNG deliveries from the already operational Sakhalin LNG project – Russia could be delivering over 80 Bcm/year of (mainly pipeline) gas to Asia (but mainly to China) by the early 2020s.[18]

Diversifying Markets

Europe Still a Coveted Market

Russia's energy market diversification policy has two strands – one to seek pipeline export routes to Europe avoiding Ukraine, and the other to non-European markets, particularly towards the growing Asian gas market.

Within Europe, in order to diversify away from Ukraine, which is now perceived as an unreliable transit route, Russia built Nord Stream,

18. Jonathan Stern, Simon Pirani, Katja Yafimava, "Does the cancellation of South Stream signal a fundamental reorientation of Russian gas export policy?", Oxford Institute for Energy Studies, January 2015 at http://www.oxfordenergy.org/wpcms/wp-content/uploads/2015/01/Does-cancellation-of-South-Stream-signal-a-fundamental-reorientation-of-Russian-gas-export-policy-GPC-5.pdf

a pipeline carrying Russian gas under the Baltic Sea to Germany. Another line – South Stream – which was proposed to carry Russian gas under the Black Sea to Bulgaria and onto central Europe, has been shelved after the European Commission expressed regulatory concerns (the EU is now promoting a rival project – the Southern Gas Corridor – which seeks to bring Azeri gas through Georgia and Turkey to Europe). Russia responded by announcing Turkish Stream, which would also bring gas across the Black Sea to Turkey for delivery to Europe at the Greek border. (see Map 3.1)

During the 1990s, a pipeline across Poland to Germany was built to cut Ukrainian transit dependence, albeit from 100 percent to 80 percent. This was relinquished in 2001 in favour of a submarine pipeline (called the Nord Stream) across the Baltic Sea to connect with Germany directly, as it was Russia's largest gas market. However, after the 2006 Ukraine-Russia gas crisis, Russia intensified its diversification strategy and announced the building of the South Stream project across the Black Sea, thereby further reducing its dependence on Ukraine. Following the 2009 crisis, Russia rapidly advanced this project. In November 2012, the first phase of Nord Stream was commissioned. At the same time, in December 2012, Gazprom and the other South Stream partners announced the construction of the first string of the South Stream project,[19] which envisaged transporting up to 63 bcm of natural gas across the Black Sea into Bulgaria, after which the pipeline would have been split, with one stream supplying the Balkans and Austria, and the other eventually supplying northern Italy. However, after the imposition of sanctions following the 2014 Ukraine-Crimean crisis, Russia announced in December 2014, that South Stream would now be abandoned and instead a Turkish route to supply southern Europe may emerge.[20]

However, despite attempts, there is limited scope for Europe to find alternative supply sources before the mid-2020s. Countries in the Baltic region and south-eastern Europe which are highly dependent on

19. Manfred Hafner, "Russian Strategy on Infrastructure and Gas Flows to Europe", POLINARES Working Paper No. 73, December 2012.
20. Tim Boersma, "The Cancellation of South Stream is a Pyrrhic Victory, At Best", Brookings, December 18, 2014 at http://www.brookings.edu/blogs/up-front/posts/2014/12/18-south-stream-pipeline-boersma

Map 3.1

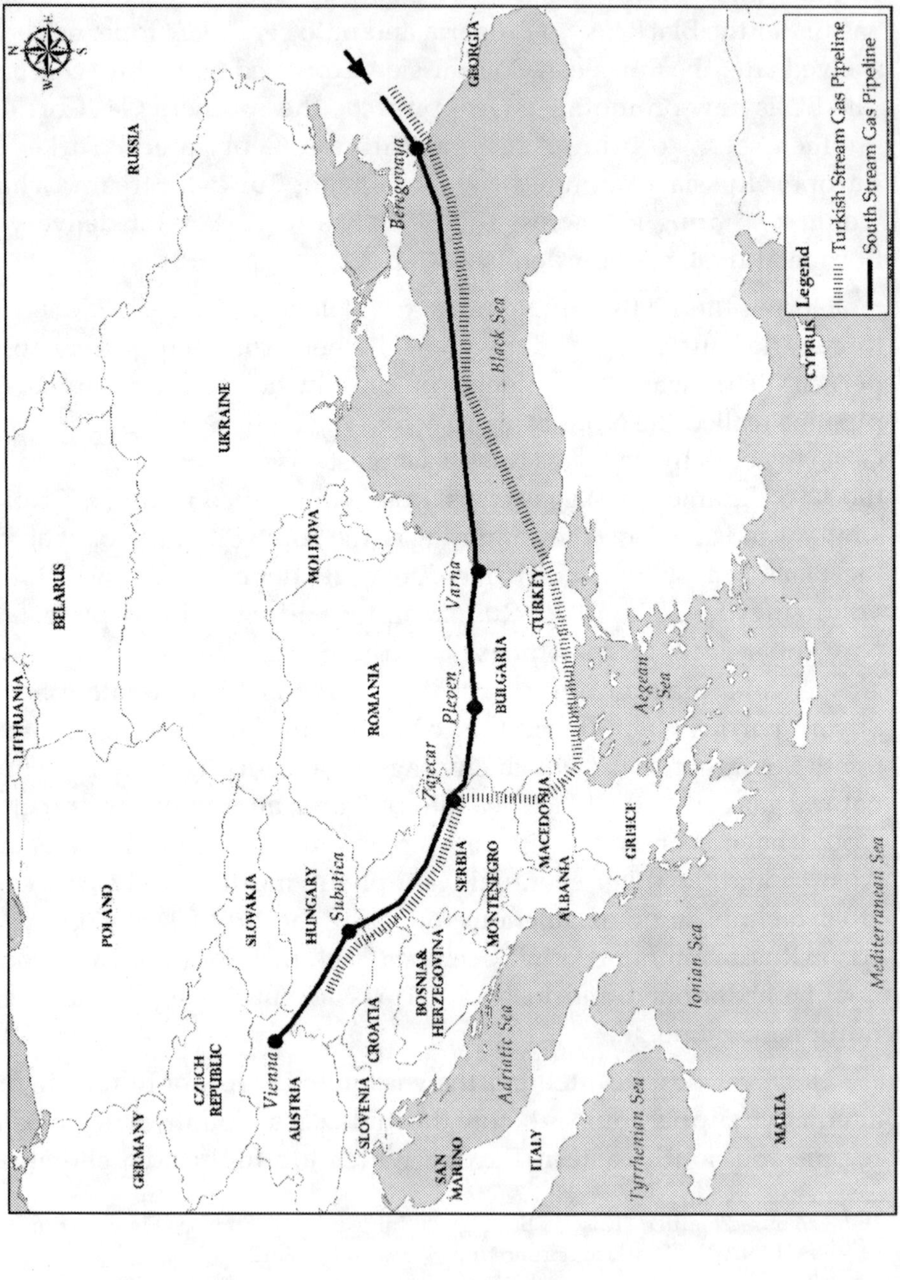
Legend
Turkish Stream Gas Pipeline
South Stream Gas Pipeline
RUSSIA
BELARUS
LITHUANIA
POLAND
GERMANY
CZECH REPUBLIC
SLOVAKIA
UKRAINE
MOLDOVA
ROMANIA
HUNGARY
AUSTRIA
SLOVENIA
CROATIA
BOSNIA& HERZEGOVINA
SERBIA
MONTENEGRO
MACEDONIA
ALBANIA
BULGARIA
TURKEY
GREECE
GEORGIA
CYPRUS
ITALY
SAN MARINO
MALTA
Beregovaya
Varna
Pleven
Zajecar
Subotica
Vienna
Black Sea
Aegean Sea
Adriatic Sea
Ionian Sea
Tyrrhenian Sea
Mediterranean Sea

Russian gas, are extremely vulnerable to interruptions, and the only alternative option available for them to reduce imports of Russian gas is through a combination of LNG supplies and pipeline gas from Azerbaijan. Central Europe and Turkey could also adopt similar measures to reduce, but not eliminate, their dependence on Russian gas. However, it is doubtful whether LNG imports will be able to replace Russian pipeline supplies. Re-gasification capacity of nearly 200 bcm a year at European LNG terminals was less than 22 percent utilised in 2013, and although imports may have risen slightly in early 2014, most terminals have substantial spare capacity. The reason for this is the difficulty of transporting LNG to many of these countries as well as their competitiveness with respect to Russian gas.[21]

Although since the early 1980s, North Africa has emerged as Europe's second-largest supplier of natural gas, with total exports to Europe of 44 bcm in 2013, in the short to medium term, an increase in North African gas exports to Europe appears bleak. Given the region's deteriorating investment climate in the aftermath of the political turbulence in 2010-11, and the surge in domestic gas demand, attracting new upstream investment will be an uphill task over the coming years. Hence, even if North Africa does succeed in emerging as a viable alternative to Russian supplies, it is unlikely that this will happen before 2020.[22]

Moreover, till the mid-2020s, European companies are contractually obliged to import at least 115 bcm per year of Russian gas – which is around 75 percent of the 2013 import level –with a slight reduction to around 65 bcm by 2030. Even if long-term contracts are terminated, projections indicate that a requirement of at least 100 bcm a year of Russian gas will be required up to 2030, and in some cases, double that amount. Countries with strong geopolitical reservations about Russian gas dependence will need to either terminate, or not renew their long-term contracts with Gazpromon expiry, given that the vast majority of Russian gas exports to Europe are sold on long-term contracts varying

21. Ralf Dickel *et. al.*, "Reducing European Dependence on Russian Gas: distinguishing natural gas security from geopolitics", Oxford Institute for Energy Studies, October 2014, OIES Paper, NG 92 at http://www.oxfordenergy.org/wpcms/wp-content/uploads/2014/10/NG-92.pdf
22. Ibid.

from 10-35 years. These contracts, which are legally binding and subject to international arbitration, contain take-or-pay clauses which require buyers to pay for a minimum annual quantity of gas, irrespective of whether they take that quantity. In the post-2008 period, the take-or-pay level in many of these contracts was reduced from 85 to 70 percent. Moreover, any attempt to terminate these contracts will result in substantial additional infrastructure costs for LNG import terminals and pipeline connections, or investments in alternative energy sources and/or policies. Hence, European countries have little option other than carefully managing their relations with Moscow.[23]

Seeking an Asian Market

Nonetheless, Russia is taking counter-measures by promoting trade and investment to other regions, mainly Asia. The development of its energy market and positioning itself as a major energy supplier for the energy-hungry East Asian markets is a core piece of Russia's pivot to Asia. Concurrently, the cutting of Russia-Europe ties and the Ukraine crisis has been a major catalyst for certain relationships, namely, enhanced Sino-Russian strategic and bilateral cooperation.

In 2013, President Vladimir Putin announced the intention to pivot towards the Asia-Pacific region by turning to eastern markets and by developing the Siberian and the Far Eastern districts, which though underdeveloped, are rich sources of energy resources and raw materials. The Putin administration has acknowledged that the global focus towards the Asia-Pacific region and has made developing the Russian Far East a top priority of the nation. Russia's energy strategy for 2030 forecasts that the Asia-Pacific market will consume 22-25 percent of all Russian exports and 19-20 percent of Russian gas exports.[24] Accordingly, Russia has worked to broaden its energy outreach to various Asian partners, including Vietnam, Laos, South Korea, China and Japan. Significantly, China was not a Russian gas customer until 2013, whereas between 2000 and 2012, the share of oil and gas in Russian exports to Japan increased from 1 percent to 74

23. Ibid.
24. "Energy Strategy of Russia for the period up to 2030", Ministry of Energy of the Russian Federation, Institute of Energy Strategy, 2010 at www.energystrategy.ru/projects/docs/ES-2030_(Eng).pdf

percent. Moreover, in the wake of the Fukushima Daiichi disaster, Russia promised supplies of LNG, oil, coal and electricity and worked to accommodate Japan's high LNG demand. The Sakhalin-2 pipeline is being developed by Japanese trading companies Mitsui and Mitsubishi (which together own 22.5 percent) in collaboration with Gazprom (with a 50 percent plus one share stake) and Shell. The pipeline provides Japan with about 10 percent of its LNG needs – making it Japan's fourth-largest supplier of LNG – and has increased its exports to Japan exponentially over the past five years. The Japanese government and private corporations are evaluating importing more gas from Sakhalin to meet 17-18 percent of Japan's gas needs and in addition, Japan plans to build a $13 billion LNG plant in Vladivostok in collaboration with Gazprom and a group of Japanese companies known as the Japan Far East Gas Company, which is expected to begin LNG exports in late 2018 or early 2019 and could account for around 13 percent of Japan's gas imports. Both countries have also created joint working groups on issues such as oil and gas.[25]

However, with its alliance with the US being the centrepiece of Japan's security policy, the Ukraine crisis made it difficult for Japan to maintain relations with Russia at the level prior to the crisis. But although Japan did go along with the US and imposed sanctions on Russia, these were less harsh than those imposed by Washington and the EU, and the Abe government made it clear that it was still interested in continuing the dialogue with Moscow. In addition to the projects that are already underway in Sakhalin and Eastern Siberia, a consortium of Japanese companies has agreed to jointly pursue exploration, development and production of oil and gas in the Sea of Japan off Russia's coast. Japanese media also reported that major Japanese trading houses were also planning to invest in a $40 billion natural gas field project on the Gydan Peninsula near the Arctic Ocean with Russia's Novatek.[26]

25. Wrenn Yennie Lindgren, "Energizing Russia's Pivot: Japan-Russia energy relations, post-Fukushima and post-Ukraine", Norwegian Institute of International Affairs (NUPI), Policy Brief 4/2015, p. 4 at https://www.files.ethz.ch/isn/188197/NUPI%20Policy%20Brief%204-15-Yennie%20Lindgren.pdf

26. "Putin-Abe summit brings big Japan-Russia economic projects", The Associated Press, December 16, 2016 at http://bigstory.ap.org/article/9695c7bd712e435082e3 b95ee6db3e1b/putin-abe-summit-brings-big-japan-russia-economic-projects

However, the biggest move to capture the eastern market came in 2014 when after 10 years of negotiations, Russia's Gazprom signed a historic 30-year $400 billion gas supply deal named the 'Power of Siberia' project, with China's CNPC in May 2014, which would deliver 38 bcm per annum from 2018. If the deal comes through, and Russia succeeds in delivering on the deal, Russia would not only have accomplished its goal of acquiring a large chunk of the world's largest gas market, but would also succeed in forming a strategic alliance that would go far beyond commerce. But with the fall in prices three months after the deal was signed, may have put a spoke in the deal, as China will have to contend with paying more for Russian gas than its lower domestic prices. Although both sides contend that considerations of a deal of this size were based on long-term considerations that went beyond short-term market realities, such as pricing, doubts regarding the deliverability of the agreement persist. For Russia, a foothold in the Chinese gas market would compensate for any losses accrued from a reduced European market, while for China, it would strengthen its strategy to diversify its sea-based energy supply vulnerability. At the time the deal was signed, the volume of gas to be supplied amounted to around 20 percent of China's consumption and 60 percent of its gas imports.[27]

Caspian Reserves

Negotiations to establish maritime borders of this landlocked water body known as the Caspian Sea, have been on for nearly two decades, with all the littoral states, namely, Russia, Iran, Kazakhstan, Turkmenistan and Azerbaijan making many proposals and counter-proposals, with no solution that is agreeable to all five states in sight. The Caspian Sea's importance lies in the huge energy resources, which is projected to be around 48 billion barrels of oil and 8.7 trillion cubic metres of gas in proven or probable reserves, both in offshore deposits and in onshore fields, although many of these figures are disputed. Most of the natural gas fields are located onshore in Turkmenistan, Kazakhstan and Uzbekistan, as well as offshore Azerbaijan, although

27. Pierre Noel, "The Power of Siberia natural-gas project: commercial or political?" IISS, January 30, 2017 at https://www.iiss.org/en/politics%20and%20strategy/blogsections/2017-6dda/january-7f20/power-of-siberia-2a1d

Russia and Iran also have sizeable natural gas deposits. Till the break-up of the Soviet Union, the Caspian Sea did not emerge as a major arena of dispute, as any exports were dependent on the Soviet pipeline network.

But following the emergence of the Central Asian states in 1991, three of the former Soviet states, namely, Kazakhstan, Turkmenistan and Azerbaijan, also became littoral states bordering the Caspian Sea. Given the potential of the energy resources in the Caspian, the newly independent states also demanded a share of the resources. Encouraged by the US, which saw in the development of the Caspian's energy resources an opportunity for an alternative energy source from the Persian Gulf, as well as a means to wean the former Soviet states away from Moscow's influence the region, the newly independent states began asserting their stakes in the Sea. But under the 1921 Friendship Treaty signed between Iran and the USSR, which divided the Caspian between these two states, no changes could be made in the treaty without the agreement of all littoral states. While Russia and Iran consider this treaty valid, Azerbaijan, Kazakhstan, and Turkmenistan – none of which were signatories – did not feel bound to it. (see Map 3.2)

Another controversy over the Caspian was whether it should be classified as a lake or a sea under the United Nation's Convention on the Law of the Sea (UNCLOS). As a lake, each littoral state would be entitled to an exclusive zone for a given number of miles from its shore, but the centre of the Caspian would be a shared zone for all littoral states. On the other hand, if it was declared a sea, the entire Caspian would be divided according to each state's coastline. While Russia and Iran designated the Caspian a lake, the three new states defined it as a sea.

In the mid-1990s, the US proposed the construction of a project to import natural gas from Turkmenistan through a sub-sea pipeline. As a result, in 1999, the Turkmen government entered into an agreement with some American companies for a feasibility study on the proposed pipeline, and signed a number of agreements concerned with pipeline construction. However, opposition from Russia and Iran as well as a gas discovery on Azerbaijan's Shah Deniz field, shelved the project.

While some pipelines carrying oil from the Caspian, namely the

Map 3.2

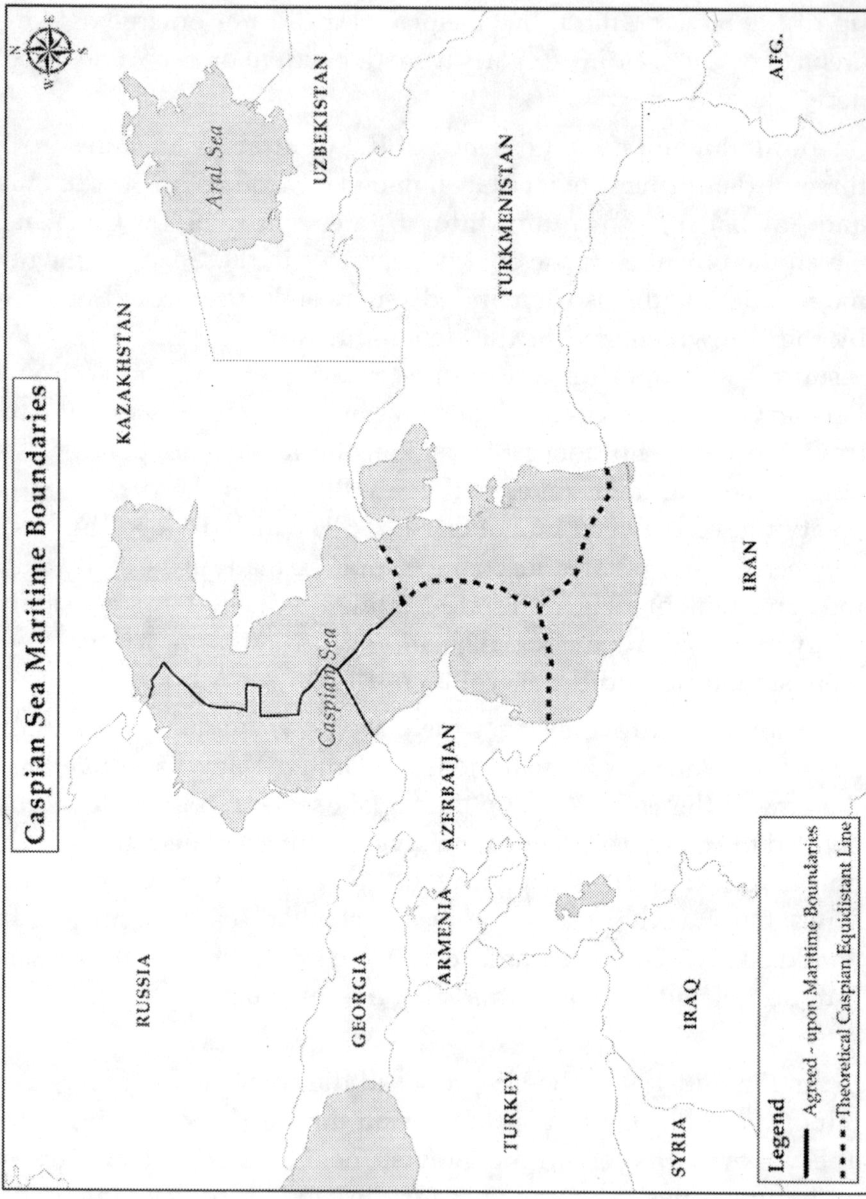
Caspian Sea Maritime Boundaries
N
E
S
W
KAZAKHSTAN
UZBEKISTAN
Aral Sea
TURKMENISTAN
AFG.
RUSSIA
Caspian Sea
GEORGIA
ARMENIA
AZERBAIJAN
IRAN
TURKEY
IRAQ
SYRIA
Legend
Agreed - upon Maritime Boundaries
Theoretical Caspian Equidistant Line

Caspian Pipeline Consortium and the Baku-Novorossiysk pipeline were constructed in 2001 and 2010 respectively, Caspian gas moved to Western Europe through a combination of Soviet-era and newly constructed pipelines.

The South Caucasus Pipeline (SCP) runs parallel to BTC and supplies natural gas to Georgia and Turkey from Caspian fields. The pipeline began operating in 2007 and has the capacity to transport about 280 bcf (7.9 bcm) of natural gas, according to IHS Global Insight. In 2010, the daily supplies of SCP averaged 180 bcf (5.00 bcm) of natural gas, according to BP.

Exports to South Asian Markets

India and Pakistan have also seen the energy demand rise, and for several decades a consortium of countries has planned to construct a pipeline that runs from Turkmenistan to India. This would allow Turkmenistan to supply to the growing South Asian markets and diversify its natural gas exports.

According to *Oil and Gas Journal*, the proposed Turkmenistan-Afghanistan-Pakistan-India (TAPI) pipeline would run approximately 1,050 miles – 90 miles will be in Turkmenistan, 460 miles in Afghanistan, and 500 miles in Pakistan, bringing it to the Indian border. The pipeline would have a 1 tcf (0.02 tcm) capacity. India and Pakistan will each get approximately 42 percent of natural gas pumped through TAPI, with the rest going to Afghanistan.

Despite the stalemate over the definition, all the states have undertaken oil and gas exploration and drilling. Russian and Iranian claims stemming from the treaty are becoming weaker and weaker with each passing year, though the issue is far from settled. In July 2001, Iran deployed a warship and two fighter jets to stop an Azeri research vessel exploring a gas field near the centre of the Caspian, but well within what Azerbaijan considers its territorial waters. Even though Russia agrees with Iran on the issue of Caspian ownership, it has not taken such drastic measures. Also, despite the Friendship Treaty, Russia has proven willing to make bilateral deals with other states, such as, the one in 2005 under which it signed a production sharing agreement with Kazakhstan for that country's Kurmangazy offshore oilfield, situated on the northern part of what is generally agreed to be Kazakhstan's Caspian sector.

Russia provides 90 percent of Western Europe's gas and the majority of its oil. Whereas gas and oil must currently flow through Eastern Europe to reach the West, Russia is in the process of constructing the Nord Stream, a gas pipeline that will extend from Vyborg (near St. Petersburg) under the Baltic Sea and into Greifswald, Germany. By bypassing Eastern Europe, Russia will be freed from transit fees, but more importantly, it will have full vertical control of its gas, from drilling to sales.

Russia considers Central Asia to be firmly in its sphere of influence, and would loathe losing any of its influence in the area and the benefits – especially the economic ones – which would accrue. Also, by combining the sizeable Central Asian reserves with its own, Russia could become a petroleum power to rival the Middle East. Just as in the 20th century, the USSR relied on its military for its superpower status, in the 21st century it will rely on its oil and gas.

Out of the four countries being discussed in this chapter, only Russia has a completed, operational pipeline – the Caspian Pipeline Consortium (CPC), which started transporting oil in 2001. It runs from Kazakhstan's Tengiz fields to the Russian Port of Novorossiysk and is the largest current export route of Caspian oil, carrying 34 million tonnes of oil every year. There is talk of almost doubling capacity to 67 million tonnes a year by adding 10 new pumping stations. An example of the complicated nature of the geopolitics of oil in the region is the fact that the CPC has varied shareholders: Russia holds 24 percent, Kazakhstan 19 percent, Chevron 15 percent, and Oman 7 percent. A variety of oil and gas companies make up the remainder.[28] In addition to Kazakh oil, the CPC also exports for major Russian producers such as Lukoil, Rosneft, Surgutneftegaz, and TNK-BP.

There is no major pipeline to export Caspian gas, and interestingly enough, Russia has shown no inclination to fill this need. Any Caspian

28. Alla Afanasyeva & Vladimir Soldatkin "CPC pipeline oil exports down 7 pct in Jan, m/m, Reuters, February 1, 2017, http://af.reuters.com/article/energyOilNews/idAFL5N1FM4TM

gas pipeline would also likely need to connect to Turkmenistan to take advantage of that country's massive gas reserves. However, President Niyazov proved himself an unreliable negotiating partner, evidenced in the planning of the American-sponsored Trans-Caspian Pipeline (TCP). Nevertheless, Russia's involvement in the region's natural gas markets would be a prudent move, since control of Caspian gas as well as its own, would cement Russia's position as the world's pre-eminent gas supplier. During recent talks concerning a possible Russian-led gas OPEC, one of the experts' criticisms of the idea was that Russia already has such massive reserves that forming such a cartel might be unnecessary. While this is debatable, by obtaining control over Caspian gas, Russia should be able to completely put itself in a position to effectively determine and manipulate the world's natural gas market as it sees fit.[29]

Challenge to Retain Leadership

Despite the unlikely scenario of Europe moving away from dependence on Russian gas, there have been some concerns that the advent of the US shale gas revolution and the resultant increase in gas, mainly LNG supplies, will have an impact on Russia's markets. Even if US LNG does not enter Europe in large quantities, it would nevertheless have an indirect impact on energy costs and security, as with US cutting down its gas imports, much of US-bound supplies have increased global supplies thereby pushing prices down in markets, including in Europe.

Any capacity addition would enable Europe to increase its leverage in future price negotiations with Moscow. A similar effect was seen when the US shale boom took place over the last decade.

Moreover, with the price of US gas being lower than those available to Europe and Asia since 2009, has seen an increase in short-term supply contracts and spot trade of LNG as they offer buyers the ability to fill supply shortfalls at competitive prices. Moreover, Washington

29. James Fishelson, "From the Silk Road to Chevron: The Geopolitics of Oil Pipelines in Central Asia", School of Russian and Asian Studies, December 12,2007 at http://www.sras.org/geopolitics_of_oil_pipelines_in_central_asia

has been *intensifying its efforts to enter the European market and replace Russia as one of the EU's largest energy suppliers, both for economic as well as geopolitical gains. Particularly, following the recent Russia-Ukraine conflict, the US and* Western strategists have been trying to find a replacement for Russian energy supplies to Europe.

However, in the long run, there will be only a marginal difference between US LNG export prices to Europe, making it difficult to compete with Russian pipeline supplies on price. Moreover, if the prices are too low, US shale gas will not be able to match the operational costs of traditional European suppliers, including Russia. With European gas prices indexed to oil prices, and no upward movement expected in the near future, hub-based US gas may not be as competitive as expected.

Meanwhile, Russia is fighting to retain its dominant position in its traditional market, besides diversifying to new ones. It is planning to increase its gas production significantly within five years by developing new fields in order to recapture its leading position from the United States. On the other hand, some projections indicate gas production will go up as Russia is pushing a number of multi-billion dollar oil and gas projects, particularly in its Far East and Arctic regions. Among its most promising projects are the new fields on the Yamal peninsula, which currently provides only small quantities, but are projected to produce more than 100 bcm per year from 2020 and 200 bcm from 2035. It is also planning to increase production from its Eastern Siberian and Far Eastern regions, where the annual increase is estimated to rise from the current 7 bcm and 30 bcm, to 89 bcm and 94 bcm, respectively, by 2035. While production from Yamal will be for the European market, gas from Eastern Siberia will be exported to Asian markets. Moreover, it plans to construct an LNG plant in Yamal, and the Altai pipeline that will help Russia redirect some of the gas from Western Siberia to China.[30] While there are doubts about Russia's ability to deliver given its current economic stress, partly due to the

30. Zuzanna Nowak, Jarosaw Æwiek-Karpowicz and Jakub Godzimirski, "Russia's Grand Gas Strategy – the power to dominate Europe?", *Energy Post*, March 25, 2015 at http://www.energypost.eu/russias-grand-gas-strategy-power-dominate-europe/

sanctions imposed after the Crimean crisis and partly due to the fall in oil – and gas – prices, the fact that its gas trade is not only linked to its energy security policy but has a strategic component, where its energy resources are viewed as both a tool and a means to achieve security and political goals, it is unlikely that Russia will give up its markets without a fight.

4

Iran Re-emerges as a Potential Gas Superpower

After more than two weeks of negotiations, Iran and the P5+1 namely, the US, Russia, China, the UK, France and Germany, announced on July 14, 2015 that they had reached a Long Term Joint Comprehensive Plan of Action (JCPOA) which would scale back Iran's nuclear capabilities for more than ten years. In return, the P5+1 committed to significant easing of the sanctions on Iran's energy (mainly oil) and banking sectors, albeit only after the IAEA issued its final report, scheduled for December 2015, verifying Tehran's compliance with the obligations under the JCPOA. Although Washington cautioned that the sanctions could be re-imposed if Iran went back on its pledge or did not adhere to the terms of agreement, the agreement set the ball rolling for unravelling of the sanctions that had taken a huge toll on the country's economy, signalling the return of Iran to the international community. Already, reports of contracts with European and Asian firms being signed are emerging, but even as some American companies were said to be getting ready to head back to Iran, the new US administration under President Donald Trump imposed sanctions on dozens of Iran-linked individuals and entities following an Iranian ballistic missile test, which include financial and banking sectors and will freeze the US assets of the entities, both Iranian and others, that have assisted Iran's programme, with threats of more sanctions to follow. However, the new sanctions did not mention the nuclear deal and therefore does not have a bearing – at least at the time of writing – on non-US companies interested in Iran's energy sector. However, Iran will have to overcome several challenges before it can resume its status as a leading energy producer and exporter. More importantly, Iran's return occurred at a time when the energy market is over-supplied.

Background

The experience of years of interference, political manipulation and military intervention by Western powers and the resultant deep resentment this generated towards foreign governments has, to a large extent, contributed to successive Iranian leaders – both pre- and post-revolution – mistrusting foreign entities. This in turn is reflected in political sensitivity in dealings with the energy sector, which is not only a symbol of national pride and sovereignty, but also a vital source of revenue for Iran. From the granting of the oil production concession to William Knox D'Arcy in 1901 in which the British government played a role by providing political support in order to prevent the Russians from acquiring it, and the subsequent sale of the concession to Burmah Oil, which was later incorporated into the Anglo-Persian Oil Company (later known as Anglo-Iranian Oil Company, then British Petroleum and eventually BP) in 1908, the British government, which held the majority shareholding, benefited more from the concession than did Iran.[1] This was followed by the signing of the Anglo-Persian Agreement in 1919, the negotiations of which were kept secret and which gave the Anglo-Persian Oil Company guaranteed access to Iranian oil fields, although in effect, it gave control to the British government control over the financial and military affairs of Iran, thereby turning Iran into a buffer state between Russia and British colonies in the Middle East and its "jewel in the crown", India. Following the overthrow of Ahmed Shah, the Persian ruler, by Reza Shah Pahlavi, the agreement, which was never ratified by the Majlis, was renegotiated in 1933, and was economically more in favour of Iran,

1. Daniel Yergin, "The Prize: The Epic Quest for Oil, Money & Power", *Free Press*, 2008, pp. 119-121.

but in reality extended the oil concession for another 60 years.[2] Finally, during the Second World War, the Allied forces forcibly occupied Iran in 1941, in order to prevent the country – and its precious oil – from falling into the hands of the Germans. Thereafter, following the abdication of Reza Shah and the succession to the throne by his son Mohammed Shah Reza, Britain's control over the country increased, which led to increased resentment by the Iranians against both the Shah and the Westerners.

However, the incident which perhaps reflected the deep anger and resentment of the people against foreign influence was the 1951 nationalisation of the oil sector under the aegis of the nationalist Prime Minister Mohammed Mossadegh, and the subsequent embargo placed on Iran by the Western powers. In action that was similar to the sanctions imposed in the 1990s by the US, purchase of Iranian oil was embargoes, the country's financial assets were frozen and all export of goods to Iran were banned. Eventually, in a coup engineered by Britain's MI6 and the US' Central Intelligence Agency (CIA) in 1953, Mossadegh was overthrown and Mohammed Shah re-instated. However, control over the country's oil sector passed on to the Americans under a new contract called the Consortium Agreement of 1954, which was perceived by the Iranians to be every bit as exploitative as its predecessor.[3]

Finally, in 1979, when the revolution took place, it was seen as an explosion against decades of exploitation, domination and above all, humiliation of the Iranian people by foreign powers and the country's rulers who were perceived as puppets in the hands of first the British and then the Americans, but who were equally culpable in looting the country's wealth at the cost of the people. It also provides an insight into the reason for the anti-West policies of the post-revolutionary government and the climate in which policies with regard to the energy

2. Maysam Behravesh, "Iran and Britain: The Politics of Oil and Coup D'état before the Fall of Reza Shah", e-International Relations, November 9, 2010 at http://www.e-ir.info/2010/11/09/iran-and-britain-the-politics-of-oil-and-coup-d%e2%80%99etat-before-the-fall-of-reza-shah/
3. Elham Hassanzadeh, "Politicization of the Petroleum Industry in Iran's Natural Gas Industry in the post-revolutionary period: Optimism, Scepticism and Potential", Oxford Institute for Energy Studies, 2014, pp. 53-57.

sector – which are often perceived as self-defeating – were framed. The stiff resistance towards private and foreign participation from conservative elements in the post-revolution political set-up and the greater state influence over sectoral operations that was initiated stemmed from the deep mistrust and fear of exploitation and manipulation by foreign or domestic forces.

However, while the prize coveted by the Western powers and the international oil companies were concentrated on Iran's oil riches, more recently it is the country's natural gas sector which has come under the geopolitical lens of the international community. Given that Iran has the world's largest natural gas reserves surpassing leader Russia's reserves in 2013 according to BP[4], the fact that the country's gas sector has not engineered the kind of excitement as the oil sector is due to a number of factors. These include the fact that natural gas has attracted the energy market's attention only in the last few decades as the demand for gas has increased worldwide, particularly in the developed countries; the country's fast depleting oil reserves; domestic opposition to the export of gas, and the difficulty and expenditure involved in transporting it over long distances, given that Iran does not have access to LNG technology.[5] However, this issue is being addressed with the Iranian national state company National Iranian Oil Company (NIOC) conducting negotiations with European and Asian firms to restart incomplete LNG projects, with NIOC officials stating that the goal is to complete the projects in the next two years. Russian, French, Chinese and East European companies are reported to have also shown interest in the LNG projects.[6]

More importantly, the sanctions imposed on Iran by the US and Western powers, which saw oil production dropping from a record 6 million barrels of oil a day (mbd) prior to the Islamic Revolution to 2.8 mbd now due to years of sanctions and underdevelopment of fields,

4. *BP Statistical Review of World Energy*, June 2016 at https://www.bp.com/content/dam/bp/pdf/energy-economics/statistical-review-2016/bp-statistical-review-of-world-energy-2016-full-report.pdf
5. "Iran in talks to complete LNG projects", Trade Arabia Business Information, February 1, 2017 at http://www.tradearabia.com/news/OGN_319981.html
6. "Iran shortlists 29 IOCs to bid for upstream oil, gas tenders", *Platts*, January 3, 2017 at http://www.platts.com/latest-news/oil/london/iran-shortlists-29-iocs-to-bid-for-upstream-oil-26630383

also saw the less developed gas sector starved of the requisite technology and investment required to capitalise on the vast reserves.

Potential Gas Superpower?

With the advent of shale oil from the US as well as from new sources, leading to an oversupply of the oil market and the resultant plunge in prices, the Iranian government has the option of turning to its natural gas resources to earn revenue, and position itself as a major energy power player. A section of the government, the moderate section, are of the opinion that establishing linkages through gas export pipelines with regional and international markets is a key foreign policy strategy in order to strengthen its bargaining power in the global political arena. By making importing countries dependent on Iranian supplies, Iran would be in a position to have the advantage in future negotiations.[7] In fact, one of the main reasons for pushing for the gas pipeline project to Pakistan and India (IPI) was to maintain its relevance as a major energy supplier in the international energy market.

Nevertheless, given the condition of the energy sector – both oil and gas – it will not be easy. Not only did the 1979 revolution as well as the eight-year long war with Iraq from 1980-88 damage the oil and gas fields, the contracts that were offered on payback terms were not sufficiently attractive for the international oil majors with the requisite technology to invest. Despite some reforms being introduced in the early 2000s, the sanctions remained a deterrent for IOCs to return to Iran.

According to some experts, the impact of political forces on the energy sector has proved as detrimental as the sanctions. Moreover, there is a tendency to treat all information about the country's energy resources as confidential.[8] As a result, the few contracts that were signed were either with domestic firms or with other state-owned oil

7. Elham Hassanzadeh, "Natural Gas Allocation Policy and Prioritization Challenges" in *Iran's Natural Gas Industry in the post-revolutionary period: Optimism, Scepticism, and Potential*, Chapter 6, Oxford Institute for Energy Studies, 2014, pp. 126-130.
8. Elham Hassanzadeh, "Politicization of the Petroleum Industry, Chapter 2 in "Iran's Natural Gas Industry in the post-revolutionary period: Optimism, Scepticism, and Potential", Oxford Institute for Energy Studies, pp. 62-63.

companies, rather than with international oil majors. As a result, while the sanctions starved Iran of investment and technology, the personnel with technical expertise needed to revive production to the pre-sanctions level were also not available, as many of the senior technical, engineering and commercial staff had left. Following the election of hardline President Mahmoud Ahmedinejad in 2005, political interference increased in the energy sector, while on the other hand, relations with the West deteriorated even further, particularly after the new regime, dominated by conservatives and hardliners, resumed the uranium enrichment programme in Natanz that had been handled more diplomatically by the previous reformist regime of President Mohammed Khatami. Soon after, the United Nations imposed a series of resolutions between 2006 and 2010 that included punitive sanctions, while the US and the EU imposed even tougher unilateral sanctions[9] which targeted almost every major area of the Iranian economy, including Iran's Central Bank and its ability to repatriate oil revenues as well as many transportation, insurance, manufacturing and financial sectors. More importantly, while the initial phase of the sanctions – between 1979-1995 and 1996-2005 – were imposed unilaterally by the US, the sanctions from 2006-2010 and again from 2010 till the present time, were imposed by the EU and the UN and included measures that were even more stringent than those imposed by Washington.[10] Prior to 2010, the EU was more conciliatory towards Iran and adhered to sanctions that were imposed by the UN since 2006. It was only after the fear that Iranian intransigence could cause an escalation of the conflict, including an Israeli attack on Iran's nuclear facilities, which in turn could cause greater instability in the oil market, that the EU had to adopt punitive measures. In a series of sanctions from 2010 to 2012, the EU imposed trade and investment restrictions on not only the oil and gas sector, but also on banking and financial transactions,

9. Shahram Chubin, "The Politics of Iran's Nuclear Program", The Iran Primer, US Institute for Peace at http://iranprimer.usip.org/resource/politics-irans-nuclear-program

10. Ali Vaez, "Iran Sanctions: Which Way Out?" The Iran Primer, US Institute for Peace, November 3, 2014 at http://iranprimer.usip.org/blog/2014/nov/03/iran-sanctions-which-way-out

shipping and insurance, and export of major equipment and technologies.[11]

But after the election of moderate leader Hassan Rouhani to the presidency in 2013, which facilitated the lifting of the UN sanctions in January 2015, the prospects for the return of IOCs into the country's upstream sector are looking up. To further attract foreign participants into its upstream sector, the oil ministry, in November 2015, replaced the previous buyback system with a new contract model known as the Iran Petroleum Contract (IPC), which offered better terms for investors, including improved cost recoveries and up to 25-year contracts. However, given that the Iranian Constitution clearly states that the nation's natural resource reserves cannot be owned by foreign entities, all foreign oil companies are required to partner with a domestic firm that is assigned by the ministry.

Despite the new – and improved– contractual terms that are on offer, only a handful of international energy majors have responded, albeit tentatively. These include France's Total, which has teamed up with China's CNPC and Iran's Petropars, Norway's DNO, and Royal Dutch Shell, all of which have signed non-binding letters of understanding with the NIOC. Some Russian companies, namely, Gazprom, Gazprom Naft, and Lukoil are also reported to have signed memoranda of understanding for seven oil and gas agreements, along with other projects such as the construction of a power station and renovation of a railway.[12]

Nevertheless, challenges remain. These include a lack of capital, renewed US sanctions imposed after the new American President Donald Trump took over office in January 2017, Iran's infamous bureaucratic red tape, and most importantly, the forthcoming presidential elections scheduled for May 19, 2017, wherein the current incumbent, Rouhani is a candidate, but there are reports that former president Mahmoud Ahmedinejad may also be in the running. The

11. Elham Hassanzadeh, "The Impact of US and International Sanctions, in Iran's Natural Gas Industry in the Post-revolutionary Period", Oxford Institute for Energy Studies, 2014, p. 74.
12. Mansour Kashfi, "Is A Full Recovery Possible For Iranian Oil And Gas?" Oil Price.com, January 6, 2017 at http://oilprice.com/Energy/Crude-Oil/Is-A-Full-Recovery-Possible-For-Iranian-Oil-And-Gas.html

outcome of the elections will be an indicator of whether Iran will continue on its current reformist agenda, or if there will be a return to the previous radical path. If Rouhani wins, then the return of foreign investments in Iran is almost assured. If not, then Iran will have to wait a while longer before it can gain its position as a leading gas producer and exporter.

Market Options

Europe

For years, the sanctions imposed on Iran had only a limited impact on the country as several countries continued to do business with the Islamic Republic. However, two factors eventually led Iran to the negotiating table to thrash out an agreement that would be palatable to both parties, viz., Iran and the Western countries led by the US – Iran's increasing economic problems due, in part, to decades of sanctions, and the over-supply of oil and gas in the energy market due to the shale revolution and the consequent fall in oil prices. On the other hand, for the US, the prospect of energy independence, and the return of Iran to the international community would allow Washington more leverage over Saudi Arabia. Moreover, for years, the EU has been looking for alternative supply options to Russian gas, and Iran has the wherewithal to become a reliable alternative to Russia as a gas supplier to Europe. In April 2015, the EU's Directorate-General for External Policies published a study of natural gas import options in light of the Ukraine crisis and concluded that "Iran is a credible alternative to Russia."[13] Although there is no pipeline network that currently fully connects the Iranian gas grid to Europe, several options already exist. It is already connected to Turkey via the Tabriz-Ankara pipeline. This section transports gas from the South Pars gas field to the city of Bazargan at the border of Turkey. Iran is strongly bidding for the continuation of the pipeline network with the construction of the 'Persian Pipeline': a 3,300 km network system which crosses Turkey

13. Brenda Shaffer, "A Nuclear Deal with Iran: The Impact on Oil and Natural Gas Trends", *Policywatch* 2362, The Washington Institute, January 27, 2015 at http://www.washingtoninstitute.org/policy-analysis/view/a-nuclear-deal-with-iran-the-impact-on-oil-and-natural-gas-trends

before reaching Italy where it splits into a northern and southern section, transporting gas to Germany, Austria, Switzerland, France and Spain. The capacity of the Persian Pipeline is estimated at around 37-40 bcm per year and would require foreign investments of around $7 billion. The route would bypass Russian territory and allow the EU to import 25-30 bcm per year, that is, equal to Russian gas export to Italy and Germany. Another long-term energy delivery option for Iran to Europe would be via LNG at an estimated export capacity of up to 10 bcm a year with supply being transported through a pipeline system to the Omani LNG hub and then shipped via cargos to the Mediterranean seaports.[14]

For Iran, entering the European gas market is important. Huge gas reserves exist in the Iranian sector of the Caspian Sea, which however, are located in the deepest point of the Caspian and Iran does not have the required advanced technology for extraction. Therefore, Iran is eager to attract European energy companies into its energy sector.

Some of the potential routes that are being considered are through a pipeline that would pass through Turkey which imports about 9 bcm a year. Iranian gas supplies could be connected with Turkey's Trans-Anatolian Pipeline (TANAP) to Europe, although negotiations with the TANAP consortium have not been held. Russian firms have also expressed interest in Iran's gas development projects, with reports that Gazprom has recently signed a letter of intent with NIGC. Iran too has welcomed Russian participation in the $2.5 billion construction of a pipeline known as IGAT-9, a 35 bcm a year line that plans to supply gas from the South Pars field to Europe via Turkey.[15] At the same time, Iran is also looking at LNG shipment to Europe once they acquire the technology.

For both sides, this could become a win-win situation. Establishing

14. Tara Shirvani, "The Dash for Gas How Iran's Gas Supply Can Change the Course of Nuclear Negotiations" *Harvard International Review*, Vol. 36, Issue 3, Spring 2015 at http://www.naturalgasasia.com/harvard-business-review-the-dash-for-gas-how-irans-gas-supply-can-change-the-course-of-nuclear-negotiations-15325
15. "Iran hails Russia in Europe gas transfer plan", *Neftegaz RU*, January 25, 2017 at http://neftegaz.ru/en/news/view/157581-Iran-hails-Russia-in-Europe-gas-transfer-plan

itself as the EU's long-term gas supplier would be a highly lucrative avenue worth exploring, particularly as the recent fall in oil prices is having an impact on the government's budget. On the other hand, for the EU, decoupling from Russia's gas supply monopoly would be possible by obtaining Iranian gas, thereby solving its main energy supply dilemma. According to a study by the European Parliament, Iran's export capacity is more than 150 bcm per year, which could eventually rival Gazprom's export volumes of 140 bcm per year to the EU.[16]

Another long-term energy delivery option for Iran to Europe would be via LNG. Iran is planning to construct smaller LNG production, including floating LNG (FLNG) units, and hopes to export gas to Europe, either through Oman or directly as LNG. France's Total is reportedly in talks to buy a stake in Iran's partly-built LNG export facility and is planning to commit $2 billion to develop the 11th phase of the South Pars field by the summer of 2017, provided that no new US sanctions are imposed.[17]

West Asia

However, the most promising market for Iran is in its own neighbourhood, viz., the Gulf Cooperation Council (GCC) member-states. It is one of the fastest growing gas markets and is within pipeline-reach. Over the years, Iran has been negotiating with several of its Arab neighbours for the supply of gas. For example, in 2007, it signed a MoU with Bahrain for the supply of around 10 bcm per annum of gas starting 2010, through a pipeline across the Persian Gulf. However, political tensions between the two countries, Bahrain's close relations with Iran's regional rival Saudi Arabia, and the unrest during

16. Tara Shirvani, "The Dash for Gas How Iran's Gas Supply Can Change the Course of Nuclear Negotiations", *Harvard International Review*, Vol. 36, No. 3, Spring 2015, April 30, 2015 at file:///C:/Users/shebonti/Desktop/book/The%20Dash%20for%20Gas%20How%20Iran%E2%80%99s%20Gas%20Supply%20Can%20 Change%20the% 20Course%20of%20Nuclear%20Negotiations%20_%20 Harvard%20 International %20Review.html
17. Oleg Vukmanovic and Bate Felix, "Total in talks to buy Iranian LNG project: sources", Reuters, February 27, 2017, at http://in.reuters.com/article/us-total-iran-lng-idINKBN1661NM

the "Arab Spring", which Manama accused Tehran of supporting, scuttled the negotiations.[18]

Iran and Kuwait have also discussed the possibility of gas trade on several occasions, with both sharing an oil and gas field, which the Iranian side refers to as Arash, and the Kuwaitis calling it Dorra. Although a MoU was signed in 2010 to export around 8 million metric cubic metres per day (mmcmd) of gas from the Iranian side of the field, negotiations broke down following differences over pricing. Again in 2012, Iran repeated the offer. However, the discovery of gas reserves by Kuwait as well as hostile relations between the two made any agreement unlikely.[19]

Similarly, attempts at signing an agreement with the UAE have also been unsuccessful, mainly over pricing differences. Moreover, both countries share strained relations due to a dispute over ownership of three islands in the Persian Gulf. As a result, an agreement on gas sales appears remote.

Nonetheless, in March 2014, Iran signed a gas supply deal with Oman, with whom it shares comparatively warmer relations than with the other Gulf States. The deal was signed in 2014 after several previous attempts failed to deliver results, following differences over pricing and routing of the sub-sea pipeline, stated that Iran will export 10 mcmd of natural gas over 25 years. According to reports, Oman and Iran have yet to agree on the route of a 260 km sub-sea pipeline which will carry Iranian gas to Oman. Moreover, Oman produced about 85 mcmd, while consumption was only 39 mmcmd in 2013. It also imports 5-7 mmcmd of gas through the Dolphin system. However, given that its gas demand is expected to rise over the next few years, and given that it exports about 10.4 million tonnes of LNG per year (around 39 mmcmd), it may encounter shortages in the future.[20] Hence, despite the delay in commencing operations due to disagreements over price and American pressure on Muscat to find other suppliers, after the

18. David Ramin Jalilvand, "Iran's Gas Exports: Can past failure become future success? Oxford Institute for Energy Studies, NG 78, June 2013.
19. Ibid.
20. Dalga Khatinoglu, "Oman's gas deal with BP not to undermine Iranian gas import", *Trend News*, April 22, 2015 at http://en.trend.az/business/energy/2386443.html

sanctions on Tehran were lifted, both countries renewed efforts to implement the project. According to recent reports, the two countries have now agreed to change the route of the undersea pipeline in order to avoid waters controlled by the UAE. The planned pipeline, which is expected to be constructed soon and completed in two years, would connect Iran's gas reserves with Omani consumers as well as with LNG plants in Oman that could re-export the gas.[21]

Another Arab neighbour with which Iran shares warm relations since the overthrow of Saddam Hussein is Iraq. The two countries signed an agreement to supply Iranian gas to Iraq in 2013 which was expected to commence supplying 4 mcmd of gas exports from South Pars to Baghdad from May 2015, going up to 35 mcmd over the next two years.[22] However, the project had been suspended over security risks as a result of insecurity in Iraq; but recently, Iran said that it was ready to start the export of gas once Iraq was ready to pay. Earlier, Iran had cut electricity supply to Iraq due to late unpaid expenses.[23]

The South Asian Market

After 2008, following the signing of the civil nuclear deal with the US, several projects with Iran, including the gas pipeline via Pakistan (IPI) were put on hold or dropped altogether, ostensibly over differences over the size of the pipe, pricing and security issues. Instead, India decided to focus on the US-supported Turkmenistan-Afghanistan-Pakistan-India (TAPI) gas pipeline project. Now, with the removal of sanctions looking increasingly possible, that is expected to change. India's petroleum and natural gas minister, Dharmendra Pradhan met with his Iranian counterpart Bijan Namdar Zangenah in the first week of June 2015 and discussed the possibility of building a gas pipeline

21. "Iran, Oman reaffirm gas export project, change pipeline route to avoid UAE", Reuters, February 7, 2017 at http://in.reuters.com/article/iran-oman-gas-idINL5N1FS2ZK
22. "Iran to start gas exports to Iraq in a month: Official", *Iran Daily*, June 25, 2015 at http://www.iran-daily.com/News/118584.html
23. Mahmoud Eskaf, "Iran to start gas pumping to Iraq on Tuesday", *Middle East Observer*, January 22, 2017 at https://www.middleeastobserver.org/2017/01/22/iran-to-start-gas-pumping-to-iraq-on-tuesday/

Map 4.1

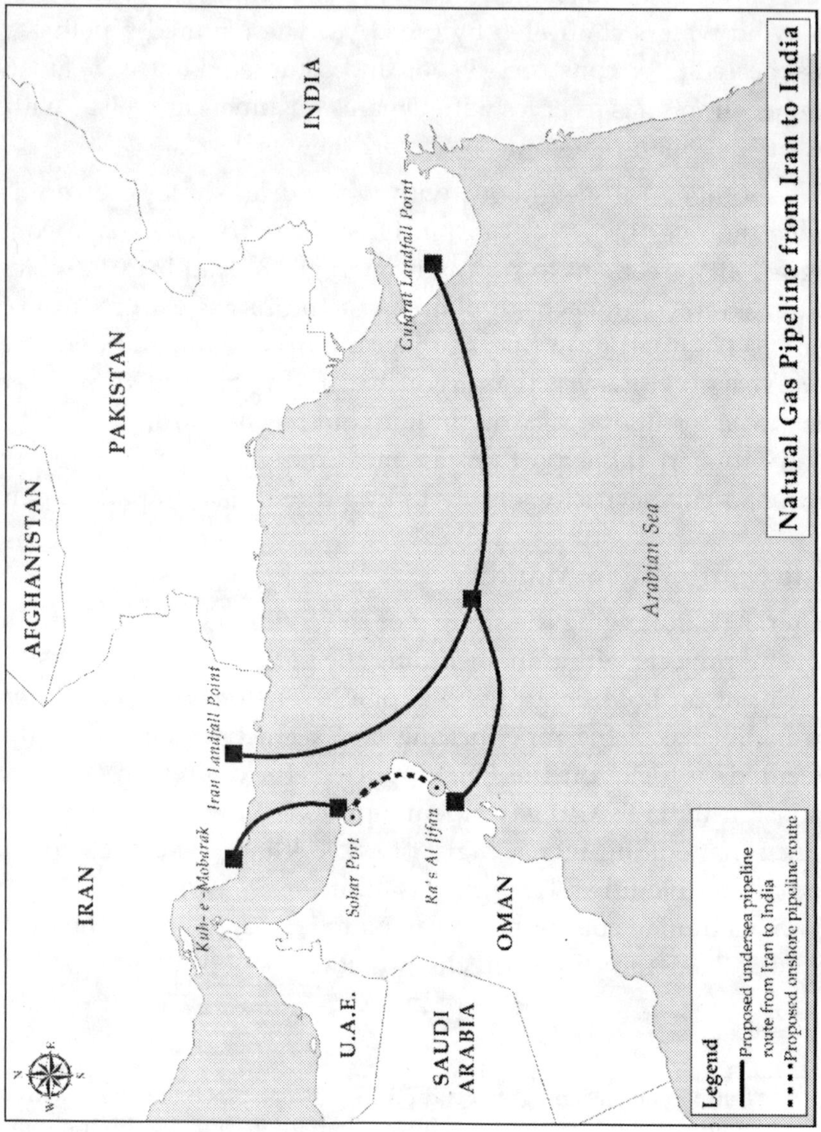
Natural Gas Pipeline from Iran to India
AFGHANISTAN
PAKISTAN
INDIA
IRAN
U.A.E.
SAUDI ARABIA
OMAN
Kuh-e -Mobarak
Iran Landfall Point
Sohar Port
Ra's Al Jifan
Gujarat Landfall Point
Arabian Sea
Legend
Proposed undersea pipeline route from Iran to India
Proposed onshore pipeline route

from Iran to India through various alternate routes.[24] Earlier, the possibility of direct gas exports to India through an under-sea pipeline, via Oman, were also being discussed, as well as future LNG exports to India. However, these are all in the planning stage and the implementation of such deals will depend largely on the pricing of gas as well as the demand for gas in India. (see Map 4.1)

Similarly, Pakistan, which despite claims that it would give in to US pressure, had also put its portion of the IPI project on hold, is now looking to resume the project – although not necessarily with India. During Chinese President Xi Xinping's visit to Pakistan in April 2015, the possibility of linking the gas pipeline from Pakistan to China was discussed. According to reports, once the planned project, namely the China-Pakistan Economic Corridor (CPEC), which aims to connect the Chinese city of Kashgar in Xinjiang's Uighur Autonomous Region with the deep water Chinese-built Gwadar Port at the mouth of Straits of Hormuz, becomes operational, it can link with the Iranian pipeline after the sanctions on Iran are lifted. India would be given the option to come on board as well.[25] However, there have been some reports that Pakistan was delaying the project under pressure from China as Beijing was of the view that its CPEC project was sufficient to meet Pakistan's gas requirements. Similarly, Iran too is reported to have said that it may cancel the project due to construction delays by Pakistan.[26]

Nevertheless, some of the projects that Iran is planning for the export of gas include the Iran-Iraq Pipeline, which is expected to commence supply soon. Initial exports are expected to be about 50 bcf per year (1.4 bcm per year) and are expected to increase in the future; the Iran-Oman Pipeline, for which an agreement was signed in March 2014, although construction may be delayed due to pricing agreements; the Iran-Pakistan Pipeline, for which construction on the Iranian side

24. Utpal Bhaskar, "India in talks with Russia, Iran on transnational pipelines", *Livemint*, June 5, 2015 at http://www.livemint.com/Industry/lTBSa05Fk3Wlyrj9c6pthP/India-in-talks-with-Russia-Iran-on-transnational-pipelines.html
25. Sajjad Ashraf, "China link-up an opportunity and a challenge for Pakistan" *East Asia Forum*, June 2, 2015 at http://www.eastasiaforum.org/2015/06/02/china-link-up-an-opportunity-and-a-challenge-for-pakistan/
26. Damir Kaletovic, "Iran May Cancel $7B Pipeline Project With Pakistan", Oil Price.com, January 27, 2017 at http://oilprice.com/Latest-Energy-News/World-News/Iran-May-Cancel-7B-Pipeline-Project-With-Pakistan.html

Map 4.2

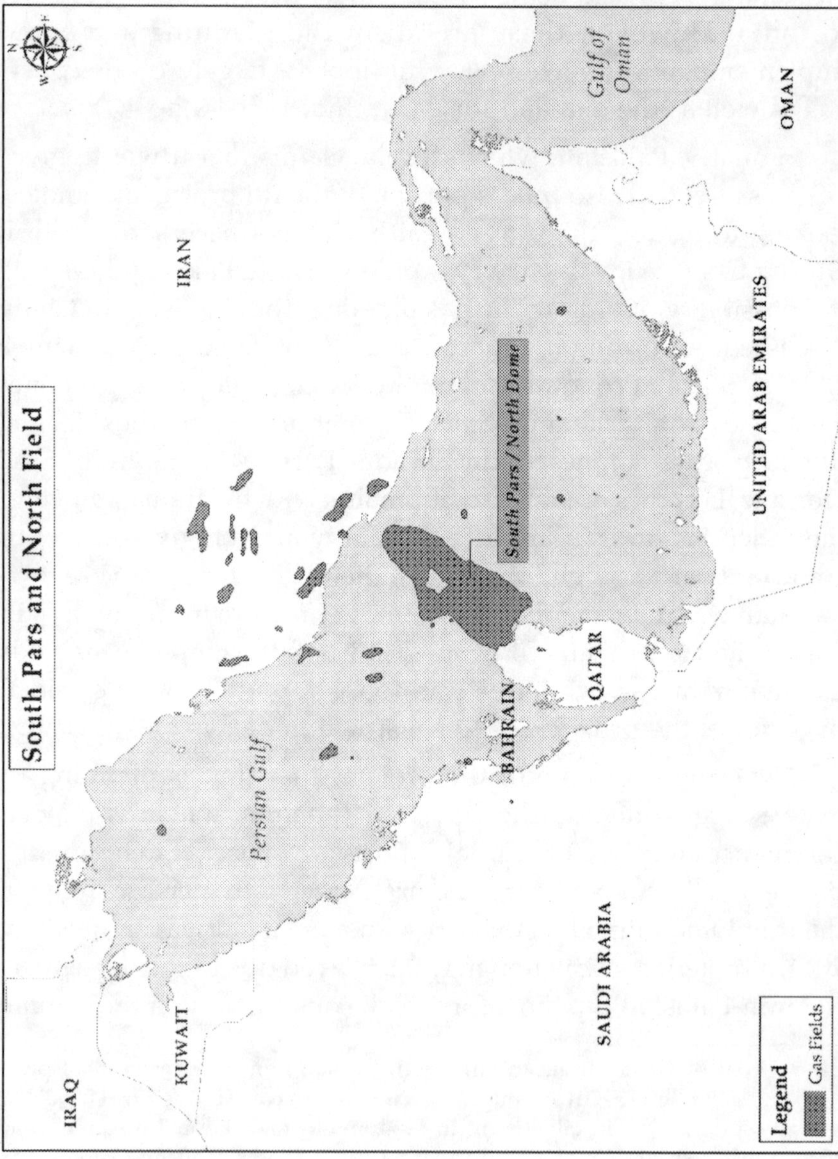
South Pars and North Field
IRAN
IRAQ
KUWAIT
Persian Gulf
SAUDI ARABIA
BAHRAIN
QATAR
South Pars / North Dome
UNITED ARAB EMIRATES
Gulf of Oman
OMAN
Legend
Gas Fields

is almost complete, although construction on the Pakistani side has been delayed, and the Iran-UAE Gas Contract, which however is facing hurdles over pricing and volumes. Currently, the contract has been referred to international arbitration.[27] (see Map 4.2) Therefore, despite the fact that Iran has the world's largest natural gas reserves, it is unlikely that it will be in a position to rival current leaders like Qatar, and future ones like Australia, as a major exporter.

The Challenges

Iran sees gas as the main fuel for the next 20-30 years for a world that is scrambling to replace coal and oil to meet carbon emission goals, and sees gas as the bridge fuel that will take their place. But there are several challenges that will have to be met before Iran can take its place among the leading gas market leaders.

First, it will need $100 billion to rebuild its gas industry. More importantly, it will need the technology to not only get the long-neglected fields to ramp up production above the current 173 bcm, but also to construct LNG liquefaction plants. Currently, Iran has only a half-built LNG export plant. Moreover, Iran lacks the pipeline network required for exports.

In the fourth 5-Year National Develop Plan (2005-2009), the country had plans to produce 70 million tonnes of LNG from the South Pars, North Pars, Ferdosi and Golshan gas fields by launching six LNG production facilities. However, all of these projects were cancelled after the withdrawal of several international oil companies, including France's Total, Spain's Repsol, the UK and Holland's Royal Dutch Shell, Malaysia's Petronas and Petrofield LNG Co., China's SINOC group and CEPA as well as Poland's PGNiG. However, with the departure of the Western firms, the inability of Iranian and Chinese contractors, who had agreed to provide the requisite technology, were unable to complete the projects and, as a result, Iran's LNG projects were delayed.[28] Now, with Total reportedly in talks to buy a large stake in Iran's partly-built LNG export facility in South Pars, Tehran is hopeful that the ability to produce and export LNG will be possible in the near future.

27. See Note 6 (EIA).
28. See Note 10 (Washington Institute).

No doubt there is strong support for the entry of Iranian gas into the market, particularly from Europe, which sees Iran as a viable alternative to Russian supplies. As the EU's energy commissioner, Miguel Arias Cañete, said, if all concerns over Iran's nuclear programme are fully addressed, there could be growing cooperation between the EU and Iran, including on energy matters, which would allow investments in Iran by EU firms, which in turn, would open up additional sources of energy supply. Nevertheless, it is unlikely that Iranian gas will be flowing to Europe anytime soon.[29]

A lifting of sanctions on the Iranian oil and gas industry would also have a number of geopolitical ramifications. Despite Russia's apparent support for Iran, many issues of strategic competition between Tehran and Moscow may resurface, including in the sphere of gas markets, with Moscow taking steps to block Tehran's entry into European markets, as it had done in 2007, when Tehran inaugurated gas supplies to Armenia, prompting Gazprom to build the pipeline project within Armenia with a small circumference to pre-empt its future use for transiting gas to European markets.

Moscow and Tehran could also find themselves competing for gas market share in Turkey, which is currently Russia's second largest gas export market, and a critical factor in Russia's gas export strategy following the proposed route change of the South Stream export pipeline from Bulgaria to Turkey. Another potential conflict that may emerge is with Qatar over the delimitation of their shared South Pars/North Field (see map below), given its status as the main source of Qatar's massive LNG and condensates – which are a low-density mixture of oil or gas that are present in gaseous form but condenses into liquid when pumped to the surface – exports, and an area which Iran has targeted for development.[30]

29. Rakteem Katakey, Anna Shiryaevskaya and Isis Almeida, "Iran Seeks $100 Billion for Gas as World Fixates on Nation's Oil", Bloomberg, June 12, 2015 at http://www.bloomberg.com/news/articles/2015-06-12/iran-seeks-100-billion-for-gas-as-world-fixates-on-nation-s-oil

30. Brenda Shaffer, "A Nuclear Deal with Iran: The Impact on Oil and Natural Gas Trends", *Policywatch* 2362, the Washington Institute, January 27, 2015 at http://www.washingtoninstitute.org/policy-analysis/view/a-nuclear-deal-with-iran-the-impact-on-oil-and-natural-gas-trends

However, the biggest obstacle to Iranian exports comes from within the country. Some members of the Parliamentary Energy Committee, mainly belonging to the conservative camp, have opposed gas exports on the grounds that they do not serve the long-term interests of the country. According to them, gas resources should be reserved for domestic use, given that Iran's demand for gas was growing along with its population, and for re-injection into oilfields to ramp up falling production and to prevent further decline. According to Iranian gas industry estimates, some 70-110 cubic metres of gas has to be re-injected into an oilfield to get an additional barrel of oil. If a comparison is made regarding the profitability of exporting gas or using it to increase oil production for export, the latter will be more profitable than the former. On the other hand, gas exports, particularly through pipelines, would have more strategic value.[31]

According to Azizollah Ramazani, international affairs director at National Iranian Gas Company, once the sanctions are lifted or eased, Iran plans to increase gas exports seven-fold to 200 mcmd in four years and to 1.2 bcmd in five years, from the current 800 mcmd now.[32] However, exporting gas will be challenging. Two main obstacles could, however, hamper Iran's entry into the international gas market: Iran's ability to produce more gas for export and two, the need to build infrastructure to transport it. For the former, although Iran holds nearly 17 percent of the world's natural gas reserves,[33] and owns South Pars, which is the largest natural gas field in the world, holding almost 40 percent of Iran's total proved natural gas reserves and accounting for about 40 percent of Iran's GDP in 2013, it is a net gas importer and accounts for less than 1 percent of the global natural gas trade. It imports gas from Turkmenistan and Azerbaijan, and exports only a small amount to Turkey, Iraq, Armenia and Azerbaijan, the latter through a swap deal, through pipelines.[34] Moreover, the country

31. Hassanzadeh, see note 7, p. 138.
32. Rakteem Katakey, Anna Shiryaevskaya and Isis Almeida, "Iran Seeks $100 Billion for Gas as World Fixates on Nation's Oil", Bloomberg, June 12, 2015 at http://www.bloomberg.com/news/articles/2015-06-12/iran-seeks-100-billion-for-gas-as-world-fixates-on-nation-s-oil
33. Ibid.
34. Iran, International energy data and analysis, Energy Information Administration, US Department of Energy, June 19, 2015 at http://www.eia.gov/beta/international/analysis.cfm?iso=IRN

consumes a larger proportion of natural gas than any other country in the world, partly due to low domestic gas prices.

Moreover, even if Iran did succeed in attracting and obtaining the technology for liquefaction, it would be difficult to attract the investments, given that with new LNG projects coming up, the market is currently over-supplied, and Asian importers, the largest buyers of LNG, are becoming increasingly sensitive to high prices.

In order to attract the huge investments required to ramp up production to levels that would once again establish Iran as a major energy player, the country's investment regime has to be drastically revamped. In fact, a major factor that contributed to the departure of international oil majors from Iran was the country's unattractive investment climate. Based on memories of exploitation and dominance of the petroleum sector by foreign entities, the post-revolutionary government had adopted severe restrictions on foreign companies and investments. Moreover, the buy-back contracts that were first introduced in 1993 and extended in subsequent deals, not only prohibited foreign companies from acquiring equity, but any costs incurred by a foreign company which went beyond the stipulated ceiling would not be reimbursed. As a result, most international oil companies, who were earlier ready to risk sanctions, backed out and left the country.[35]

However, realising the need to attract the vast sums of investment and technology required to rehabilitate the oil and gas sector, the current Rouhani government has now announced that the terms that will be offered to investors will not only be different from the earlier regime, but would be far more attractive than other countries. In February 2014, a new generation of upstream investment contracts, called the Iran Petroleum Contract (IPC) were unveiled, which made claims to have done away with most, if not all, of the earlier buy-back contracts' shortcomings. In essence, the new terms include the integration of all three stages of exploration, development and production under a single contract, increasing the duration of the contract to 25 years as against the earlier 5-7 years and 8-12 years

35. Elham Hassanzadeh, see note 8, pp. 85-92.

offered, a more flexible rate of return for oil companies depending on the risk and complexity of the project, offer of alternative fields in the event of failure to make commercial discoveries, and most importantly, the opportunity to book reserves in some high risk projects. The latter is a major reversal of Iran's constitutional rule prohibiting ownership of energy reserves by foreign companies.[36]

In fact, according to some analysts, the new contracts are more competitive than other oil producers as they provide higher potential profits and lower investment risks as well as favourable rates of return and long-term joint venture options with local Iranian firms. Hence, although the investors will have no rights over the reserves, after exploration is completed, they can report output they receive as payment.[37]

The new IPC has succeeded in generating renewed interest from international oil companies in the country's energy sector. In early June, representatives from some of the top oil majors, including Eni, Shell, Total and Lukoil, met with Iran's Oil Minister, Bijan Zanganeh in Vienna during an OPEC seminar and evinced their interest in returning to Iran, provided the sanctions were lifted.[38]

President Rouhani has also taken steps to reduce the influence and control of the Iranian Revolutionary Guards Corps (IRGC) which had taken over a number of firms during the second term of President Ahmedinejad (2009-2013), and was a major deterrent for potential investors. The IRGC, despite having little experience or expertise in the oil industry, was given the charge of maintaining the country's oil and gas production, as well as the development projects that international firms had abandoned because of the sanctions. The IRGC replaced several hundred managers of the Iranian oil companies, including the NIOC and affiliated companies, in the gas and petrochemical industry. However, corruption and poor management and technical skills of the IRGC, together with financing difficulties,

36. "Iran goes the extra mile with new Oil Contracts", *Middle East Economic Survey* (*MEES*), Vol. 58, No. 25, June 19, 2015, pp.2-3.

37. Parisa Hafezi and Jonathan Saul, "Iran sweetens oil contracts to counter sanctions and price plunge", *Reuters*, Feb 3, 2015 at http://uk.reuters.com/article/2015/02/03/uk-iran-oil-sanctions-exclusive-idUKKBN0L70G620150203

38. "Iran goes the Extra Mile with new Oil Contracts, no. 36.

led to a decline in the overall state of the sector, including in the South Pars, leading to a drastic fall in production.[39]

After Hassan Rouhani took over the presidency, with the support of the Supreme Leader Ali Khamanei, he reinstated Bijan Namdar Zangeneh, who had served as oil minister during the Khatami presidency, brought back the dismissed management personnel, and had the Supreme Leader issue a directive to have them step aside or reduce their involvement in the oil and gas sector.[40] Despite the support of the Supreme Leader, and the IRGC's accession to the directive to step aside, the fact that the energy sector is closely linked to the economic interests of the IRGC make it unlikely that the IRGC will willingly give up its control. Moreover, there is severe opposition from several conservative factions in the political set-upto the reforms that are being implemented, given that the oil and gas sector is perceived as a symbol of national pride and sovereignty.[41]

Finally, there is no guarantee that the sanctions will be lifted in the near future. Although the sanctions were lifted in January 2016 after Iran dismantled significant elements of its nuclear programme, Iran is not completely out of the woods. After Iran tested a ballistic missile at the end of January 2017, the current US administration under Donald Trump, enacted new sanctions on Iran a week later. Some 25 individuals and companies connected to Iran's ballistic missile programme and those providing support to Iran's Islamic Revolutionary Guard Corps linked to the programme were slapped with bans on banking transfers. However, the new sanctions strike at specific companies and arms traders from Iran to Lebanon and China, and despite Mr Trump's declaration that he was considering scrapping the JCPOA or the nuclear deal itself, it continues to stand, although the US has hinted that it may impose more sanctions.

39. Ariane Tabatabai, "Where does the Islamic Revolutionary Guard Corps stand on nuclear negotiations?" *Bulletin of the Atomic Scientists*, March 11, 2015 at http://thebulletin.org/where-does-islamic-revolutionary-guard-corps-stand-nuclear-negotiations8084
40. Nader Habibi, "Can Rouhani Revitalize Iran's Oil and Gas Industry?", *Middle East Brief*, No. 80, Crown Center for Middle East Studies, Brandeis University, June 2014 at http://www.brandeis.edu/crown/publications/meb/MEB80.pdf
41. Ibid.

Therefore, as of now, Iran is gearing up to increasing its natural gas (and oil) production to pre-sanctions levels, with several European oil and gas companies showing interest in doing business with the Islamic Republic. But the prospect of millions of barrels of Iranian gas entering the market at a time when the market is over-supplied could stave off a price recovery for a longer time. Hence, Iran would, in all likelihood, be able to develop significant export capacity only in the long term, that is, beyond 2020, while LNG exports could take even longer.[42]

However, Iran's limited gas exports are not the problem. In fact, from a macro-economic point of view, it may be more valuable for Iran to export gas and energy in other forms, such as electricity or products of gas-based industries such as petrochemicals, steel, cement and aluminium. The main problem is with Iran's domestic pricing regime and low energy efficiency. Although Iran has attempted some price correction through subsidy reforms with some success, residential and also industrial consumption remains high. Therefore, in order to achieve its potential, the government will have to draft a comprehensive strategy for the gas sector and related industries. An appropriate gas pricing strategy will be one of the success factors. Furthermore, Tehran has to attract the latest technologies to all sub-sectors of the gas value chain (from upstream to midstream and downstream), gas-based industries and most importantly, energy efficiency.

If all of the above are addressed, Iran will be on its way to becoming a significant hub for energy production and energy-related exports on an international scale, provided it succeeds in overcoming the challenges of meeting domestic requirements and an over-supplied market.

42. Elham Hassanzadeh, Note 7, pp.140-150.

5

QATAR – LNG LEADER, BUT FOR HOW LONG?

What Saudi Arabia is to the oil market, Qatar is to the gas, specifically the LNG, market. Nonetheless, being one of the smallest states in the Persian Gulf, with a population that is outnumbered by a foreign workforce, and sandwiched between powerful neighbours – Saudi Arabia and Iran – Qatar has successfully transformed itself from a traditional tribal society and a British protectorate till the early 1970s, into an economic powerhouse. Under the ruling al-Thani family, and more specifically Sheikh Hamad bin Khalifaal Thani, the son of Emir Khalifaal Thani, from whom he took over in a bloodless coup in 1995, the tiny kingdom has managed to position itself as a major political player in a region by playing a mediatory role successfully among varying factions, backed by immense wealth. It has one of the highest per capita incomes exceeding $ 105,829 and an enviable GDP growth rate, which however, has shown a decline over the last three years from a high of 26.2 percent in 2006 to 3.6 percent in 2016. Over the last decade and a half, Qatar has acquired valuable and prestigious assets around the world, including strategic shares in major companies, which has allowed it to gain the potential to influence economic and political decisions in the countries in which they are made.

On the political front, it has increasingly being acquiring the reputation of an international player. Apart from being a member of important organisations, including OPEC, the Gulf Cooperation

Council (GCC) and the Arab League, it has befriended the US by allowing it to use its air bases to supply American forces in Iraq and Afghanistan, although it has several differences with Washington. At the same time, it also facilitated non-state organisations like the Taliban to open a political office in its territory; it supported the forces involved in ousting Libyan strongman Muammar Gaddafi; it backed the Muslim Brotherhood in Egypt and the Islamist rebels in Syria and it mediated disputes among Palestinian factions as well as factions in Lebanon and Sudan. It owns the al Jazeera TV channel – the most important media outlet in the region – it hosts satellite campuses of American universities. Moreover, the Emirate has been acquiring strategic shares in major companies throughout the world, which gives it the potential to exercise some influence in policy making. As a result, Qatar is perceived as an important and influential player in the region.

Qatar's ability to punch far above its weight would not have been possible without its huge hydrocarbon reserves – particularly natural gas – which accounts for 15 percent of global reserves.[1] Since the discovery of the massive North Field, which is the largest non-associated gas field in the world, which held 40 trillion cubic metres, in 1971 – the year it gained independence, Qatar has positioned itself as the world's largest liquefied natural gas (LNG) exporter and more importantly, a critical "swing supplier" of gas. Although its LNG exports commenced only in December 1996, they have grown six-fold in the last 10 years.[2] Given that the North Field's reserves contain non-associated gas reserves, that is, the gas is not linked to that of oil, it is not fettered by Organisation of Petroleum Exporting Countries (OPEC) quotas, and more importantly, free from the possibility of Saudi domination.

However, recent events in the international gas market could force Qatar to surrender, or at the very least, downgrade its position as the undisputed leader of the LNG market. With new gas – including LNG–

1. Jim Krane and Steven Wright, "Qatar 'rises above' its region: Geopolitics and the rejection of the GCC gas market", Kuwait Programme on Development, Governance and Globalisation in the Gulf States, No. 35, London School of Economics and Political Science, March 2014, p.9.
2. Bassam Fattouh, Howard V. Rogers, and Peter Stewart, "The US Shale Gas Revolution and its Impact on Qatar's position in Gas Markets", Center on Global Energy Policy, Columbia University, March 2015.

producers and exporters entering the market, coupled with the prevailing low gas prices which may extend for a while leading to a fall in Qatar's revenues, Qatar has been fighting to retain its position. Most importantly, with the availability of more supplies of LNG poised to enter the Asian markets as new LNG production comes on line from Australia and the US, the emergence of a strong spot market is inevitable, which, in turn, will not only allow consumers to bargain harder for lower prices in future deals, but could also precipitate the formation of a regional pricing regime, as against the current system based on oil indexation. More importantly, Qatar may lose its status as the sole "swing producer" of gas, thereby removing Doha's strategic importance at the international level.[3]

Qatar's Energy Policy

In the early decades of oil production, natural gas was considered a near-worthless by-product and provided to domestic markets at low prices. Over time, however, natural gas came to be valued as a key domestic resource that could be deployed to substitute for more valuable oil in the domestic economy, assisting states in maintaining oil exports in the medium and longer term. Gas demand has risen within the power generation and industrial sectors, as well as in enhanced oil recovery applications, where it is re-injected into depleting oil reservoirs. The Gulf States have recently exhibited a new willingness to invest in gas-specific exploration and production and to pay much higher prices for gas imports. These states have also begun to invest in expensive marginal increases in domestic gas production.

Price distortions are thus a key factor behind shortages in the Gulf. Low prices drive demand as well as the inability to meet demand, through development of large but under-utilised reserves in most of the 'gas-short' monarchies. The GCC-5 states (i.e. not including Qatar) consume nearly all the gas they produce.

Natural gas reserves in Qatar were first discovered in 1971 in the huge North Field, although it took 20 years before its potential could be exploited, both because of its location at a distance from major gas

3. Naser al-Tamimi, "Navigating Uncertainty: Qatar's Response to the Global Gas Boom", Brookings, Doha Center, March 2015.

markets as well as investment challenges. As a result, production began only in the early 1990s. Qatar soon realised that apart from fulfilling domestic demand, it would be necessary to find export markets, particularly outside the region, if it had to monetise its resources due to low regional prices and unsuccessful plans to expand pipeline networks apart from the Dolphin project. However, it took a decade of perseverance to overcome constraints and tie-ups with international oil companies before Qatar's first shipment of LNG to Japan was contracted. Since then, Qatar has not looked back and over the next 15 years, it built a LNG chain and a reputation of a reliable supplier that has, so far, kept competition at bay. Today, Qatar is the largest exporter of LNG and gas-to-liquids (GTLs) in the world, with a supply chain that spans the globe.[4] Due to its strategic location which is roughly equidistant between the major energy-consuming centres of Asia and Europe, Qatar's strategy is to establish itself as a swing producer – which is quite different from Saudi Arabia's status as the swing producer of oil – in that, it can supply gas to markets in both the Atlantic and the Pacific Basins, and perform the role of arbitrageur between these regions. In other words, by taking advantage of a price difference between Asian and European markets, Qatar is able to sell LNG into Europe when prices in Asia are low, and direct LNG to Asia when prices in Asia are high.[5]

Although Qatar's reliance on gas exports, the decoupling of gas and oil prices in the aftermath of the Japanese earthquake of 2011, suggest that it is likely to be one of the best placed GCC nations to weather the current fall in oil prices. That said, Qatar is not immune from the changes that are taking place in the international gas market. According to medium-term projections for global gas supply, downward pressure on prices is very likely, given the entry of supplies from Australia, the US and African countries. Yet, Doha has not announced any increase in production from existing fields in its own territory, and in fact imposed a moratorium on increasing output from

4. Ibrahim Ibrahim and Frank Harrigan, "Qatar's Economy: Past Present and Future", QScience Connect, September 17,2012 at http://www.gsdp.gov.qa/portal/page/portal/gsdp_en/knowledge_center/Tab2/Qatar%20economy%20past%20present%20and%20future.pdf
5. Bassam Fattouh, Howard V. Rogers, and Peter Stewart, no. 2.

its North Field – which it shares with Iran's South Pars – till 2015, ostensibly to monitor the health of the reservoir to assess its longevity, but more likely to gauge market demand. Hence, apart from its $10.3 billion Barzan gas project, which is mainly dedicated for serving growing domestic demand, no further gas projects have been sanctioned. Instead, it plans to increase its LNG production by improving the efficiency of its LNG production plants and may also expand its production capacity of gas-to-liquids (GTL) and LNG fuel for the shipping industry.[6] (Map 5.1)

Moreover, in order to retain its dominant position as LNG supplier, it is pursuing a strategy of "buying up the competition", somewhat akin to Russia's policy, by forming joint ventures with international oil companies, including ExxonMobil, where its investment in the Golden Pass LNG terminal in Texas is expected to reach over $10 billion with over 20 bcm in annual export capacity. Clearly, despite the current dismal projections on the LNG front, Qatar is intent on remaining a long-term player.

However, with the advent of new LNG players entering the market and more importantly, with US exports offering hub-based pricing, Qatar has initiated reforms in order to retain its leadership role in the LNG market. Moreover, following the (partial) lifting of the sanctions, Iran has the potential to become a major rival for Qatar, both within the region as well as in the larger global market, provided it can overcome domestic opposition to gas exports and acquire liquefaction technology.

Regional Policy

Despite the presence of substantial gas reserves in the region, barring Qatar, the Arab states in the Persian Gulf, suffer from domestic shortages in gas demand. Ironically, although the demand for gas is growing in the region, the regional gas market is not a priority for Qatar, which exports 20 billion cubic metres a year (bcm/y) through the Dolphin Pipeline, which transports gas from Qatar's North Field to the UAE and to Oman, which is far less than the pipeline's capacity of 33 bcm/y. This is partly because the GCC states were unwilling to

6. Naseral Tamimi (see note 3).

Map 5.1

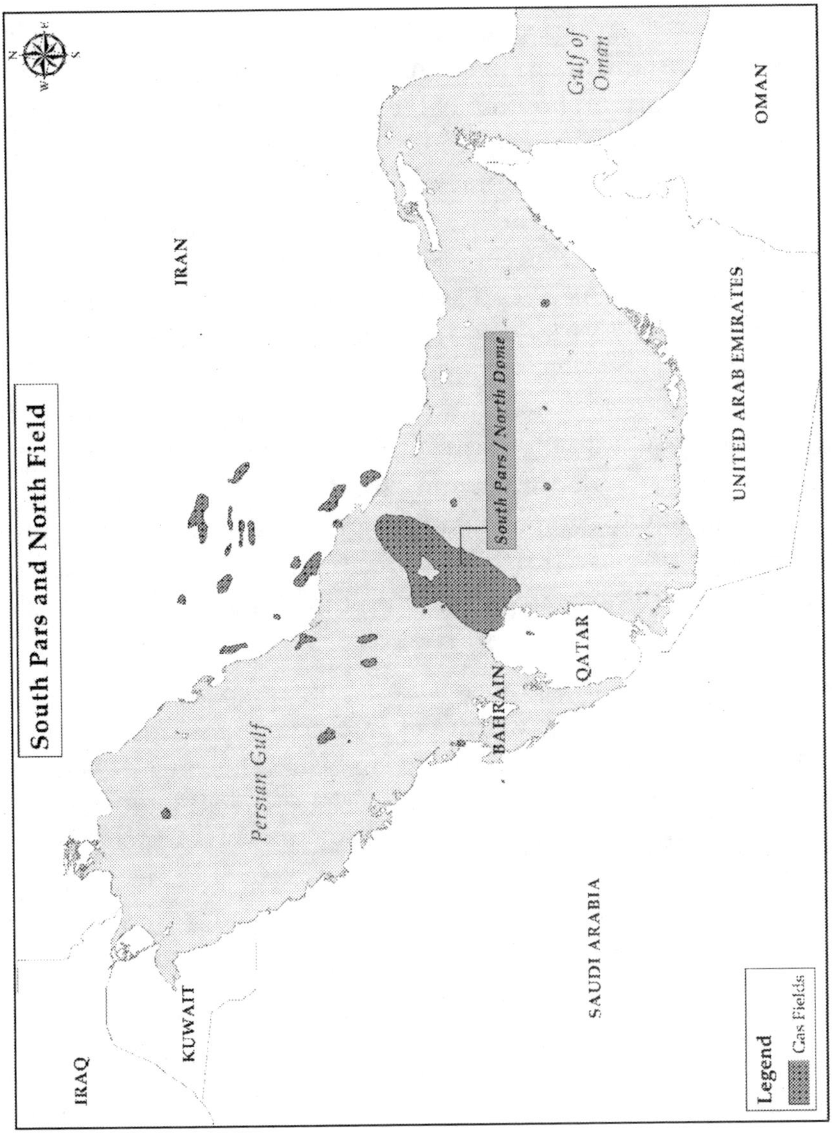
South Pars and North Field
IRAN
IRAQ
KUWAIT
SAUDI ARABIA
BAHRAIN
QATAR
UNITED ARAB EMIRATES
OMAN
Persian Gulf
Gulf of Oman
South Pars / North Dome
Legend
Gas Fields

pay what Qatar considered a reasonable price for its gas, and partly because of disputes between Qatar and its neighbours. Qatar's gas marketers, RasGas and Qatar Gas, demand that regional buyers pay prices that are equivalent to the netback value of global LNG exports, that is, all importers should pay the same price, whether it is exported to Japan or to neighbouring countries.[7] As a result, Qatar decided to go for constructing liquefaction plants in the late 1990s, albeit reluctantly, as the investments required for LNG plants were double that of pipelines, and sought instead to export its gas to customers far beyond the region. As gas prices were contractually linked to oil prices – which started to increase from 2002 – Qatar earned far higher revenues from LNG sales than those from fixed prices in the GCC. It also sold surplus production on the spot market. By so doing, Doha has attained not only the status of the world's largest LNG exporter, but has also succeeded in forming linkages with powerful importing states, who have become stakeholders in the security of continued Qatari supply. This strategy has facilitated it to expand its global influence, which not only allows it to punch far above its weight but also improve its national security.[8]

However, the only significant cross-border gas pipeline in the region is the Dolphin Pipeline, which began carrying gas from Qatar to the UAE in 2007. From 2008, an extension began delivering Qatari gas to Oman. But plans to expand the network to Kuwait and Bahrain were blocked by Saudi Arabia, as it was unwilling to allow new pipelines to be constructed across its maritime borders. As a result, 62 percent of Qatar's LNG exports are directed to Japan, South Korea, India and China.[9] But with the demand for gas in the region is expected to grow due to a combination of fast-growing population, and rising concerns over climate change, Qatar may look at increasing its market share within the region as well. In October 2016, Qatar Petroleum signed a long-term sales agreement with Dolphin Energy, whereby QP will deliver more gas to Dolphin for export to the UAE through the existing subsea

7. Krane and Wright, see note 1, p.5.
8. Ibid., pp.2-3.
9. Ibid.

pipeline.[10] It has also brokered a four-year deal earlier this year to supply Kuwait with 0.7 bcm/y from March.[11] (see Map 5.2)

Energy as Strategic Tool for Foreign Policy

Following the 1990 invasion of Kuwait by Saddam Hussein's Iraqi forces, Qatar realised its vulnerability vis-à-vis its powerful neighbours. Therefore, it decided to hedge its bets by building strong ties with the US on one hand – it gave the US Air Force conditional use of its al-Udeid Air Base, availing of its military protection – and on the other, ensured that it maintained relations with non-state actors such as Hamas as well as "pariah" states like Iran, the aim being to expand its traditional role as a mediator between rival tribes in the region in the international arena.[12]

But without its natural resources, mainly natural gas as well as substantial reserves of crude oil, this would not have been possible. Qatar has the world's third largest gas reserves of 871.5 trillion cubic feet (24.7 trillion cubic metres), representing about 13.3 percent of global proven oil reserves. The country also produced 158.5 billion cubic metres (bcm) or 4.7 percent of global gas production, making Qatar the world's fourth largest gas producer in 2013 after Russia, the US and Iran, according to the *BP Statistical Review 2014*.[13] More than 84 percent of Qatar's gas exports are in the form of liquefied natural gas (LNG), more than two-thirds of which (71.4 percent) is shipped to Asia. Furthermore, Qatar has managed to contain domestic price pressures by setting over $300 billion of export revenues aside in its growing sovereign wealth funds and managing a proactive interest rate policy.

---

10. Shardul Sharma, "Qatar Petroleum, Dolphin sign new gas contract", *Natural Gas World*, October 6, 2016 at http://www.naturalgasworld.com/qatar-petroleum-dolphin-sign-new-gas-contract-32017
11. "Qatar taking 'aggressive' stance in Europe to mitigate LNG risks", *Hellenic Shipping News*, December 10, 2016 at http://www.hellenicshippingnews.com/qatar-taking-aggressive-stance-in-europe-to-mitigate-lng-risks/
12. Robert Siegel, "How Tiny Qatar 'Punches Above Its Weight", *WBUR News*, December 23,2013at http://www.wbur.org/npr/255748469/how-tiny-qatar-punches-above-its-weight
13. *BP Statistical Review of World Energy*, 64th edition, June 2015 at http://www.bp.com/content/dam/bp/pdf/Energy-economics/statistical-review-2015/bp-statistical-review-of-world-energy-2015-full-report.pdf

Map 5.2

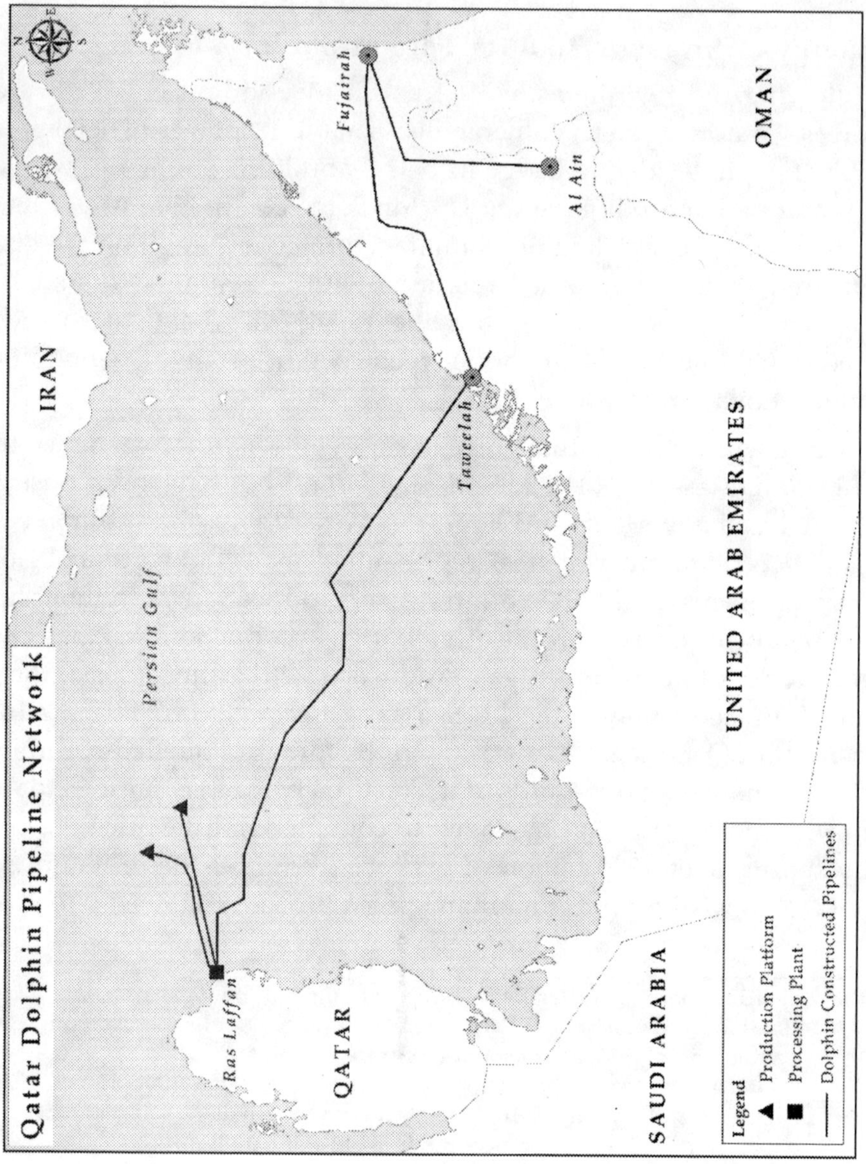
Qatar Dolphin Pipeline Network
IRAN
Persian Gulf
Fujairah
Al Ain
OMAN
Taweelah
UNITED ARAB EMIRATES
Ras Laffan
QATAR
SAUDI ARABIA
Legend
Production Platform
Processing Plant
Dolphin Constructed Pipelines

This strong gas revenue-base allowed Qatar to improve its regional autonomy, particularly with respect to Saudi Arabia. It also allowed it to diversify its security requirements beyond reliance on the US. Doha leveraged its energy linkages to build strategic relationships with several countries, and lessening its dependence on Saudi Arabia. As importing states grew more dependent on Qatari supply, they became stakeholders in Qatar's political stability and external security. Although Qatar continues to depend on the US' hard security umbrella, without which its energy lifeline would be vulnerable, Qatari policy of signing long-term contracts have allowed it to become less reliant on the US' diplomatic support. In other words, Qatar's foreign policy can be interpreted as maximising independence of action by leveraging its sovereign wealth investment strategy, through which it reaps further political influence, thereby augmenting national security. With the wealth that Qatar accumulated from its energy exports, enabled it to buy up prime real estate in the UK and Paris and invest in companies such as Barclays, LVMH and Xstrata. Economic power also allowed it to gain political influence.[14]

Impact of a Changing Gas Market

Although Qatar's main strength lies in its gas sector, it has traditionally earned most of its revenue from oil. Since the country's natural gas meets most of its energy demand, it exports most of its crude oil and petroleum products.[15] Hence, the changes that have taken place in the gas market with the advent of new supplies may have serious implications, not only for Qatar's economy but also for its role as a geopolitical actor.

Already, increasing supplies have wiped out premium for spot supplies in the East Asian markets, while the substantial fall in prices has seen several LNG export projects being delayed or cancelled. In fact, LNG prices began falling even before the crash in oil prices due

14. Anita Hawser, "Qatar Faces Geopolitical Risk", *Global Finance*, December 06, 2012 at http://www.gfmag.com/magazine/december-2012/report-qatar-faces-geopolitical-risk-
15. Qatar, *Country Analysis Briefs*, Energy Information Administration (EIA), US department of Energy, January 30, 2014 at http://www.eia.gov/beta/international/analysis_includes/countries_long/Qatar/qatar.pdf

to an increase in supply coupled with slow demand growth. Moreover, with the impending return of Iran to the energy – including gas – market following the signing of the nuclear agreement between Tehran and the P5+1 countries and eventual lifting of sanctions, possibly by December, Qatar may be facing even bigger competition in the longer term.

According to market projections, Australian supplies from 2015 onwards are expected to pose a serious challenge to Qatar's dominance, as it seems poised to overtake Qatar in 2018 as the top LNG exporter, while the US is expected to take the top spot by 2020. Some projections even indicate that Qatar may have to be content with sliding to the fourth position after Australia, Africa and the United States.

That Qatar needs to remain on top of the LNG suppliers' chart is imperative for the kingdom as the strategic importance it derives as the world's number one LNG exporter may also diminish concurrently. Given that more than 90 percent of Qatar's budget revenues and exports stem from activities associated with the energy sector, the fall in oil and gas prices are showing signs of impacting the country's economy, despite its large accrual of revenues earned from LNG sales. Continued lower oil prices could lead to a substantial deterioration of the fiscal and external balances, according to an IMF report, with the country's budget sliding into deficit and the current account surplus being largely eliminated.[16] In the case of gas, lowering of oil prices has also impacted on Qatar's revenue earnings, since Qatar prices its long-term LNG contracts on the Japanese Customs-cleared Crude or Japan Crude Cocktail (JCC) price index, which is usually between 14-15 percent of the JCC price.[17]

Most importantly, the leverage that Qatar enjoys as the main supplier for Asian LNG buyers may also be affected as new supplies enter the market. According to some reports, Qatar's LNG exports to Japan, South Korea dropped by 3.6 percent in 2016, while Australia increased its share in these countries by 8.4 percent. On the other hand, however, its exports to China and Taiwan have increased, albeit

16. Nicolas Parasie, "Qatar Risks Budget Deficit in 2016 Due to Low Oil Prices, IMF Says", *The Wall Street Journal*, April 2, 2015, http://www.wsj.com/articles/qatar-risks-budget-deficit-in-2016-due-to-low-oil-prices-imf-says-1427983369
17. Naseral-Tamimi, no. 3, p. 27.

modestly. Moreover, it has been seeking to increase its market share in Europe, and to some extent it has been successful by offering more flexible terms. Along with consortium partners in its QatarGas 3 joint venture, comprising Qatar Petroleum, ConocoPhillips and Mitsui, it will be exporting 1.5 bcm/y to Northwest Europe over the next seven-and-a-half years.[18]

However, some of Qatar's customers have been demanding that Qatar reduce its prices. Recently, India, which has a 7.5 million tonnes[19] a year contract with Ras Gas for LNG on a long-term 25-year contract, priced at around $12 per million British thermal units (mmBtu), has now succeeded in getting Qatar to bring the price down to $5/mmBtu. Citing the drastic fall in prices and using its growing leverage as a market, India had stated that if the prices were not cut, it would seek a 38 percent cut in import volumes for 2015. While Qatar agreed to the price cut, and also agreed not to seek damages for under-lifting supplies, it however, managed to get India (Petronet LNG) to sign for an additional import of 1 million tonnes per year for about 12 years with effect from January 1, 2016 at the prevailing market price.[20]

According to reports, other LNG exporters too have been cutting prices. QatarGas amended its long-term deal with PetroChina, signed in 2011 for 3 million tonnes per year, by allowing more deliveries during the peak winter period, as against the earlier system of delivering the same amount of LNG every month. In any case, Qatari volumes to China have come down by 77 percent year-on-year to just 92,000 m.t., levels that have not been seen since 2011.[21] Japan too has cut its imports.

Therefore, as Qatar's main buyers reduce their offtake, turning increasingly to the spot market, Qatar has three options. It can increase

---

18. "Qatar taking 'aggressive' stance in Europe to mitigate LNG risks" *Hellenic Shipping News*, December 10, 2016 at http://www.hellenicshippingnews.com/qatar-taking-aggressive-stance-in-europe-to-mitigate-lng-risks/
19. 1 million metric tonnes of LNG is equal to 1.38 billion cubic metres.
20. India renegotiates LNG agreement with Qatar: Indian minister", *The Peninsula*, May 4, 2016 at http://www.thepeninsulaqatar.com/business/qatar-business/380794/india-renegotiates-lng-agreement-with-qatar-indian-minister
21. Chinese April LNG imports reach 1.5 mil mt, significant cuts to Qatar volumes, *Platts*, May 26, 2015 at http://www.platts.com/latest-news/natural-gas/singapore/chinese-april-lng-imports-reach-15-mil-mt-significant-27449745

its spot sales or go for shorter term deals as against long-term contracts, reduce its price as per clients' demands, or adopt a flexible pricing regime.

With regard to the first, Qatar is already one of the top spot and short-term exporters, accounting for 38 percent of spot and short-term deals. But the fact that it is ready to show more flexibility is clear from its recent deal with Pakistan. In February 2016, QatarGas signed a deal with Pakistan for 3.5 m.t. per year, where under a take-or-pay deal, it has agreed to review the price 10 years after supplies commence, thereby giving Pakistan added flexibility in the contracts.[22]

In a bid to cut costs which will also allow it to lower prices even further, Qatar's number one and two LNG producers, Qatargas and RasGas, respectively, have announced recently that they will now operate under a single entity, named Qatargas. The integration process is planned to start immediately and is expected to be completed within the next 12 months. The two companies will merge their resources and capabilities to enhance their competitive position. The move is expected to save hundreds of millions of dollars.[23]

In fact, one of the factors that have allowed Qatar to adopt flexibility is the advantage it has in production costs. For example, RasGas can produce one mmBtu of gas at $1.60 – lower than US prices – which gives it a competitive edge vis-à-vis rival producers like Australian producers, whose production costs are around $13.50/mmBtu. Moreover, Qatar owns and operates a fleet of 60 LNG vessels, which provides it a huge supply chain coverage than many of its rivals, giving it a distinct competitive advantage.[24]

Nevertheless, Qatar is also diversifying its traditional market from Asia to Europe. In 2015, it sold an extra 3 million tonnes to European customers from a year earlier, offsetting the lower volumes to Asia.[25] However, given that the European market is saturated, and will have to deal with traditional and new suppliers like Russia and the US, both

22. Ibid.
23. "QatarGas and RasGas to merge", *LNG World News*, December 12, 2016 at http://www.lngworldnews.com/qatargas-and-rasgas-to-merge/
24. See note 21, *Platts*, 2015.
25. Ibid.

of who are ready to offer competitive rates, Qatar will not be able to bank on Europe to balance the loss of any Asian market.

Qatar's Options

In the face of emerging challenges, Qatar nevertheless has a few cards to play. Unlike its newer challengers in the LNG market, Qatar's cost of production is one of the lowest in the world, which, as in the case of Saudi Arabia in terms of oil production, leaves it in a more favourable position to withstand low prices. Production from emerging markets like Australia and some African producers, are much more expensive to produce.

Second, with climate change concerns increasingly taking centres tage, and renewable energy unlikely to deliver on the volumes required for increasing energy demand, particularly in Asia, the future for gas seems bright. According to the *BP Energy Outlook 2035*, global natural gas demand is expected to grow by 1.9 percent per annum, reaching around 490 billion cubic feet by 2035, driven by demand in non-OECD countries, as well as Asia and the Gulf states.[26] Given Qatar's geographical location, it is ideally positioned to serve both the Asian and West Asian markets.

Third, in order to further develop businesses in the global LNG arena, Qatar-owned companies are investing in production facilities outside the country. Using its huge sovereign wealth fund, the Qatar Investment Authority, plans to invest as much as $20 billion in Asia by 2020. Qatari energy companies are already collaborating with ExxonMobil through a joint venture to construct a liquefaction plant in Texas, which, pending approvals, could commence construction by 2016.

Fourth, Qatar can drive higher cost competition out of the market by increasing production and lowering costs. This was the plan when, despite the moratorium on North Field, it began work on the $10 billion Barzan project, a joint venture between Qatar Petroleum and Exxon-Mobil. The project was originally expected to come online in 2014, with

26. *BP Energy Outlook 2035*, February 2015 at http://www.bp.com/content/dam/bp/pdf/Energy-economics/energy-outlook-2015/Energy_Outlook_2035_booklet.pdf

plans to boost gas production by up to 2 billion cu ft per day (56633693.2 cu. metres per day) in the first half of 2017, with the bulk of the production going towards meeting rising domestic demand, leaving more supplies for export. However, the project has been delayed due to a leak in the upstream pipeline, dealing a blow to plans to increase production. Although the project was expected to commence operations in November 2016, there has been no news on the issue.

In the long run, the key for Qatar to retain market share would be to quickly adapt to changing market dynamics. Furthermore, it is also revisiting its regional policy, given that demand for gas in the region is projected to increase from 5.44 bcm in 2015 to 12.2 bcm by 2020, and 31.2 bcm by 2025.[27] It is well placed to meet most, if not all of the region's gas demand, both by pipeline as well as LNG, although pricing differences will have to be sorted out.

Therefore, in order to retain its premier position in the LNG market in the face of the impending competition, Qatar is now looking to diversify its market from its three main markets, viz., Japan, South Korea and India, and is not averse to including smaller markets, and more importantly, lower prices. Recently, it signed a contract to supply Pakistan with 2.2 bcm/y at a competitive price of $7 per million Btu and has also tied up contracts with Thailand's PTT for a 20-year supply from 2015 as well as Poland's PGNiG starting 2015.

It has also signed a joint venture with ExxonMobil and ConocoPhillips in the Golden Pass LNG export project, where it will be offering prices based on HH indexation to customers, thereby increasing its options to act as a swing supplier between Europe and Asia.[28] It has also signed an agreement with UK-based EDF to supply the new import terminal in Dunkirk with another 2.7 bcm/y over and above the current 11 bcm/y. It has also increased its market share in Europe by 3.3 percent year-on-year since 2015.

Recently, Qatar Petroleum (QP) signed a deal with Abu Dhabi National Oil Company to enhance supplies to the UAE via the Dolphin pipeline. Furthermore, QP has taken advantage of its domestic joint

27. Naseral Tamimi, note 3.
28. "Qatar looks to adapt amid shifting global LNG landscape", *MEES*, Vol. 58, No.9, February 27, 2015, pp.10-11

ventures to forge their first major foreign partnership with ExxonMobil, and their interest to purchase shares in both Mozambique and Egypt's Zohr field.

Qatar's ability to offer more competitively priced contracts ensures a steady stream of revenue, Apicorp said, adding at present, more than 80 percent of its production is committed for 2016-20, as part of supply purchase agreements, securing revenue stability.

Qatar is also expanding its non-oil and gas sector in order to reduce its dependence on the hydrocarbon sector. Using its huge wealth funded from decades of LNG sales, it has over the last year alone invested across the globe in assets as diverse as poultry farms in Turkey, Russia's Rosneft and the UK gas company National Grid Plc. as well as holdings in Hollywood, realty in New York and London, the Italian luxury sector and even a soccer team.[29] Furthermore, the government has established economic zones as part of its drive to expand local manufacturing and non-gas exports, and increase FDI into the country.[30]

Future Challenges for Qatar

In the not too distant future, the gas market may shift from a sellers' market to a buyers' market, with the onslaught of new supplies coming from Australia, the US, Canada, East Africa, Russia and the Levant. Moreover, with the sanctions on Iran lifted from 2016 following the nuclear deal, it will be only a matter of time before Iran, with its vast reserves of gas, will be in a position to rival Qatar. Iran has already begun focusing on increasing production from its giant South Pars (called North Field by Qatar) gas field, which it shares with Qatar. (See map) Since 2011 Qatar has placed a moratorium in place on further development of the North Field, ostensibly to conserve its gas resources. However, while South Pars is an important part of Iran's vast hydrocarbon reserves, the North Field, which also produces 700,000 barrels per day of condensate, is Qatar's largest source of gas,

29. Mohammed Sergei, "The Tiny Gulf Country With a $335 Billion Global Empire", Bloomberg, January 11, 2017 at https://www.bloomberg.com/news/articles/2017-01-11/qatar-sovereign-wealth-fund-s-335-global-empire
30. See note 28.

and Doha consequently takes a conservative view of reservoir management. For years, Iran has been accusing Qatar of siphoning off Iran's portion of gas. However, with the price of gas falling, Qatar is in a dilemma on whether to lift the moratorium. If it decides to lift the moratorium, and boost production, it will lead to depletion of the field earlier than the envisaged 100 years, which in turn would have a major impact on Qatar's plans to expand production in the long term.[31] On the other hand, if it delays lifting the moratorium, Iran will benefit. It has already signed a heads of agreement deal with Total to develop the Phase 11 of the South Pars gas field, the first to be signed under the new Iranian contract model.[32] For the time being therefore, Qatar is focusing on investing in overseas blocks, including in Cyprus and Morocco to sustain its share of the LNG market. (Map 5.3)

Secondly, Russia too is looking at setting up large-scale LNG projects aimed at generating at least 68 bcm/y of additional liquefaction capacity by the early 2020s, and a further doubling its LNG capacity from the current 4.5 percent, and further to 20 percent in the long term. If its Yamal LNG, which is already under construction and expected to produce 22.4 bcm/y of LNG by the end of 2017, as well as four other planned projects which are waiting in the wings, get off the ground, Russia would be in a position to compete with Qatar's LNG exports in European and Asian markets. It is with this in mind that it is studying the possibility of a tie-up with QatarGas. Russia's second largest gas producer Novatek has been talking with Qatar to jointly market LNG from its newly constructed production unit in Yamal peninsula, which it is building with France's Total and China's CNPC and Silk Road Fund.[33] However, given the present conflict over Ukraine and the sanctions imposed on Russia, it may be difficult for Russian

31. "Iran, Qatar face off over North Field, South Pars", Iran Review 2013, *Oil & Gas News*, Volume 32, Issue 14, April 6-12, 2015 at http://www.oilandgasnewsonline.com/Article/35647/Iran,_Qatar_face_off_over_North_Field,_South_Pars
32. Verity Radcliff, "Total eyes South Pars project FID in 3-6 months", Interfax, November 8, 2016, http://interfaxenergy.com/gasdaily/article/22729/total-eyes-south-pars-project-fid-in-3-6-months
33. Vladimir Soldatkin and Olesya Astakhova, "Novatek eyes cooperation with QatarGas in LNG marketing - Russian energy minister", *Reuters*, June 3, 2016 at http://af.reuters.com/article/commoditiesNews/idAFL8N18V2DF

Map 5.3 North Field/South Pars Field Shared Between Qatar and Iran

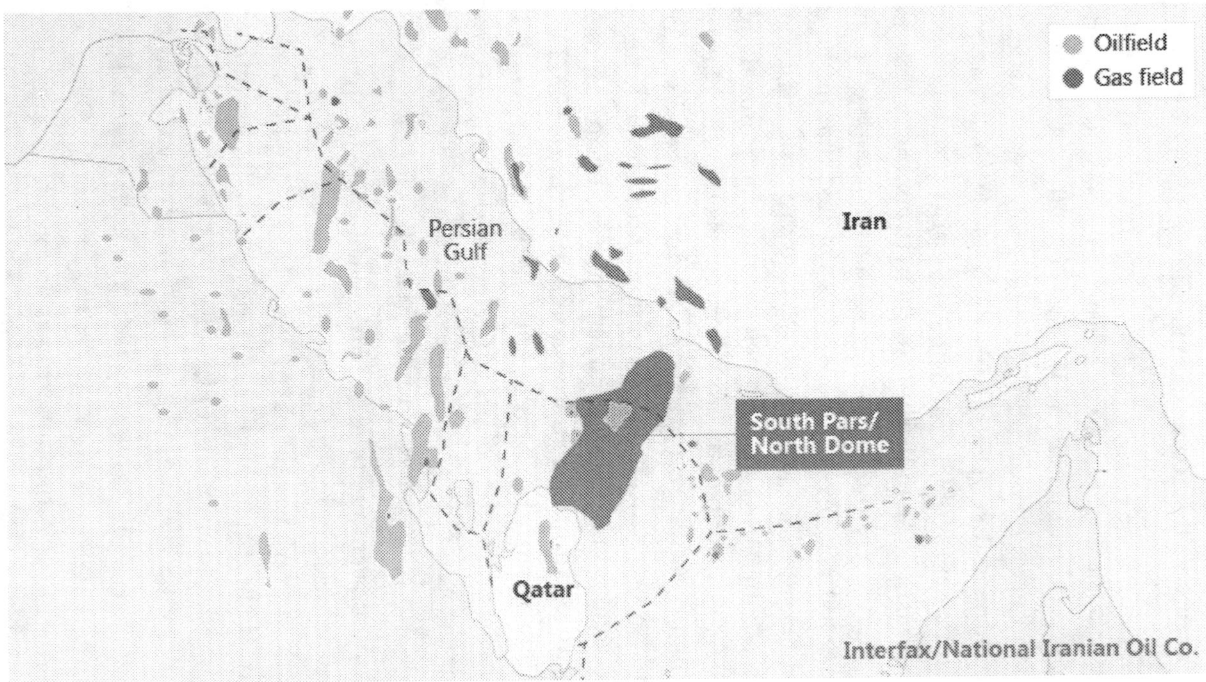

Source: Interfax (http://interfaxenergy.com/gasdaily/article/22729/total-eyes-south-pars-project-fid-in-3-6-months)

companies to move forward with these projects. Moreover, with Russia's economy being heavily dependent on oil exports and the decline in oil prices, the economic viability of many of these projects are in doubt.[34]

Qatar also has the option to do a Saudi Arabia and take advantage of its low-cost production to flood the market with LNG to lower prices, which could affect the bottomline of rival producers, particularly the high-cost producers like Australia as well as US shale gas producers as well as Iran, who will be requiring high prices to develop its long-neglected fields, making it difficult for them to compete. This, however, is a risky option as although, thus far, Qatar has managed to maintain its robust economic growth, the IMF has warned that in the medium term, growth is expected to come down due to a tapering off of public investment, due in part to lower revenues accruing from falling oil and gas prices.[35] At a time when the government has launched an ambitious infrastructure investment programme in order to diversify its economy, which would require around $210 billion through 2021, and despite attempts at diversifying its economy away from hydrocarbons, the oil and gas sector accounts for more than 50 percent of its GDP. Hence, Qatar needs a price that would foot the bill, as it were. If Qatar continues to use oil-indexed pricing, it would require, according to some estimates, a minimum oil price of around $78 a barrel, to avoid the possibility of running into a fiscal deficit.

Furthermore, as more buyers, particularly in Asia, are demanding a more flexible price indexation, there is a possibility of a new Asian gas hub emerging. Although this may not take place in the short term, particularly if the price of oil remains low which would make it beneficial for consumers to continue with oil-indexed pricing, the prospect of more US shale gas being made available to Asian consumers may pressure Qatar to offer more diversified pricing.

If any of the above changes occur, the impact on Qatar would be profound. Apart from economic stresses, its profile as a regional power which it has built up so carefully over the last decade, could be severely

34. Naseral Tamimi, see note 3.
35. "IMF warns Qatar of Budget deficit", *Middle East Economic Survey (MEES)*, April 17, 2015, p. 17.

affected; worse, its worst fears – of being subservient to its giant neighbours – may come true. Nevertheless, Qatar is in a better position than many of its rivals, mainly because of its low production costs and large monetary reserves which allows it the leverage to ride out this difficult period. It also got its LNG infrastructure constructed at an opportune time when it was flush with funds during a high-price regime, and therefore, does not have any major investments planned which require more capital expenditure. Moreover, with a fleet of 60 LNG vessels, almost half of which are the giant Q-Flex and Q-Max ships, it has an enviable supply chain that can transport supplies in any part of the world, giving it the advantage of infrastructure from start to finish, giving it a flexibility that is hard to match. Hence, if any gas exporter has the wherewithal to wait it out till the market balances out again, it is Qatar.

6

Turkmenistan – The Old Newcomer

A decade ago, few would have predicted that the former Soviet state of Turkmenistan would one day emerge as a serious contender in the gas market. Virtually closed to independent scrutiny, tightly restricted and monitored media and religious freedoms, and often criticised for human rights violations, Turkmenistan, with its huge energy reserves, particularly natural gas, has today emerged as a leading gas supplier, rivalling its regional, indeed global competitors as a contender for the world's leading gas markets. With a combination of low domestic demand given its small population of 5.4 million people, high economic growth at over 6 percent in 2016, Turkmenistan is well placed as an ideal natural gas exporter – albeit on paper as of now. With proven reserves reported at more than 17.5 trillion cubic metres (tcm) at the end of 2014, according to the *BP Statistical Review of World Energy 2015*, Turkmenistan ranks fourth in the list of gas-producing countries and the second-largest dry natural gas producer in Eurasia, after Russia. Moreover, recent discoveries are expected to offset the decline in mature gas fields. Onshore reserves are particularly concentrated at Galkynysh, in the south-east.[1] However, given the paucity and unreliability of official data, it is difficult to state with certainty whether the official figures are accurate.

---

1. Annette Bohr, "Turkmenistan: Power, Politics and Petro-Authoritarianism", Chatham House Research Paper, March 2016, p. 64 at https://www.chathamhouse.org/sites/files/chathamhouse/publications/research/2016-03-08-turkmenistan-bohr.pdf

Nonetheless, there is no doubt that a number of the world's largest natural gas fields, including the Galkynysh field, which is one of the world's largest natural gas fields, primarily in the Amu Darya basin in the southeast, the Murgab Basin in the south, and the South Caspian basin in the west. The country also has around 600 million barrels of proven oil reserves, and produces around 260,000 barrels per day (b/d).[2]

Despite being the leading gas producer in the region, the country has not made as large an impact on the international energy market. Despite the dependence of Turkmenistan's economy on gas and oil exports, which reportedly account for 31 percent of the GDP,[3] this has witnessed a decline recently. One of the reasons for this is, as in the case of the other Central Asian energy-rich countries, Turkmenistan is landlocked with the only viable outlets, apart from the Russian network and the recent pipeline infrastructure being constructed to export gas top China, is a pipeline through the Caspian Sea which can take Turkmen gas to the European market. But, with the dispute over the Caspian Sea's legal status unresolved, any offshore production and/or transport becomes the focus of conflict among the littoral states. For example, when Azerbaijan signed a production sharing agreement with Western oil companies in 1998 to explore the Alov offshore field in the Caspian, Iran objected to what it saw as Azerbaijan's unilateral decision, and demanded an end to such operations till the legal status of the Caspian Sea was settled. When Baku ignored the request, Iran sent a warship and two military aircraft to threaten the Azeri vessels assessing the field.[4]

Secondly, the government's policies have also been a factor in Turkmenistan's lack of success in developing its potential as an energy giant and to diversify its markets. Although President Gurbanguly Berdymukhamedov has attempted to increase his country's diplomatic

2. "Turkmenistan", Energy Information Administration, US Department of Energy, July 2015 at https://www.eia.gov/beta/international/analysis.cfm?iso=TKM
3. Paul Strionski, "Turkmenistan at Twenty-Five: The High Price of Authoritarianism", Carnegie Endowment for International Peace, January 30, 2017 at http://carnegieendowment.org/2017/01/30/turkmenistan-at-twenty-five-high-price-of-authoritarianism-pub-67839
4. LuçaZs Vasánczki, "Gas Exports in Turkmenistan", Institut Français des Relations Internationales (IFRI), November 2011, p.17.

outreach by engaging with several neighbouring countries, including state visits to Russia, India, Turkey, Kazakhstan, Iran and China among others, in order to gain greater international legitimacy, attract investments and to open up new markets for gas exports. He has retained the policy of denying access to upstream energy assets to foreign energy companies, with the exception of China.[5] This has contributed to the disincentive for potential partners in gas export projects.

As a result, till recently, Turkmenistan was almost entirely dependent on the Russian pipeline network infrastructure for transporting its gas exports. Although it also exports around 8 billion cubic metres (bcm) of gas to Iran annually, as well as some electricity to Afghanistan, Iran, and Turkey through the Central Asian electricity grid, these are small in volume. Hence, Ashgabat is keen to look for alternative routes and outlets to export its gas to other markets. Having adopted a foreign policy doctrine of 'permanent neutrality', this allows the country to strengthen its independence and develop transit routes and markets for hydrocarbons exports with a variety of states, without getting involved with the geopolitical ambitions of its neighbours, chiefly Russia.

The Russian Bearhug

Prior to its independence from the Soviet Union, Turkmenistan's energy relations were tied firmly to that of Moscow. However, being a victim of its geographical location, since its independence in 1991, although Turkmenistan has tried to shake off the shackles of its powerful neighbour, the Ashgabat-Moscow gas relationship has been fraught with several problems. Initially, most of its difficulties with regard to energy exports – mainly natural gas which was its main source of income – were related to the inability of Ukraine to pay for Turkmen gas, Russia did not hesitate to cut the flow of Turkmen gas westward to demonstrate its monopoly position as a conduit to foreign markets. Finally, in 1995, Moscow stopped allowing Turkmen gas to flow through its territory altogether, resulting in Turkmenistan's gas production falling drastically from 81.4 bcm in 1989 to 15.7 bcm in 1997.

5. Annette Bohr, note. 1.

Relations between the two countries worsened further following Ashgabat's involvement in the Trans-Afghan Pipeline, initiated by the Argentinian company Bridas in 1991, and subsequently taken over by Unocal in 1996 and renamed the CentGas project, which aimed to transmit gas from Turkmenistan's Daulatabad field through a $2 billion pipeline via Afghanistan to Pakistan, and with a possibility of extending the pipeline to India,[6] which Moscow viewed as unfriendly.

Other differences between the two countries included their varying positions on the legal status of the Caspian Sea, and Ashgabat's official withdrawal from the Commonwealth of Independent States (CIS). Nevertheless, by the beginning of the century, the two governments managed to resolve their differences, mostly because oil and gas prices had started to increase. Noting that Moscow had been gaining from buying cheaper gas from Turkmenistan and exporting it at a substantial profit from sales to European customers, Ashgabat demanded an upward revision of prices, to which Russia acceded, albeit after the Turkmens threatened to terminate supplies. Finally, in 2006, a new price was negotiated, with Gazprom agreeing to pay European prices. The agreement was probably reached after Russia realised Europe's proclivity in looking for alternative supplies from Central Asia bypassing Russia, and decided to base its strategy on (re)building strong relations with former Soviet energy-rich states.[7]

However, the rapprochement did not last long, as by 2008, oil prices had plunged again, and led to a massive drop in European demand, causing Gazprom to suffer economically. While domestic economic problems had caused demand for gas to drop, the EU's release of its *Second Strategic Energy Review* in 2008, which called for energy interdependence – which is an euphemism for Europe's attempt to reduce its dependence on Russian supplies in the aftermath of the Russia-Ukraine gas transit dispute – Moscow's requirement for costly imports from Turkmenistan have dropped drastically. But its contract with Turkmenistan saw Moscow continuing with the imports until April 2009, when the Daulatabad-Dariyalyk pipeline suddenly exploded near

6. Martha Brill Olcott, "International Gas Trade in Central Asia: Turkmenistan, Iran, Russia and Afghanistan", in *Natural Gas and Geopolitics: From 1970 to 2040*, Cambridge, 2006, pp. 217-219.
7. LuçaZs Vasánczki, no. 4.

the Uzbek-Turkmen border. Both sides accused the other of sabotage. While the Turkmen's blamed Gazprom for drastically cutting imports without prior warning allegedly to adjust the pipeline pressure, and accused it of violating the contract, Gazprom blamed the explosion on Turkmen negligence as well as the aging pipeline infrastructure. Some Russian analysts also saw a link between the timing of the explosion and the imminent Southern Corridor Summit scheduled for May 2009, implying that the blast was an example of Turkmen muscle flexing vis-à-vis Moscow. The general consensus, however, was that the "accident" was another example of Russian pipeline politics to stymie Turkmenistan's decision to build the East-West pipeline that would circumvent Russian territory. The fact that the explosion took place shortly after a meeting between Turkmen President Gurbanguly Berdymukhamedov and the then Russian President Dmitri Medvedev – wherein it was agreed that Russian companies would participate in the East-West pipeline's construction, but was followed soon after by Turkmenistan announcing an open tender for the construction of the pipeline – it was seen by Russia to be an indication that the project could eventually become an important part of the European Southern Corridor project, with Turkmenistan providing alternative gas exports to Europe via a non-Russian route. Eventually, at the end of 2009, after months of negotiations, both sides agreed to continue gas deliveries, albeit reduced, with President Berdymukhamedov stating that Russia was a long-term partner and his country was ready to boost gas exports to Russia.[8] However, relations between the two remained fractious, and finally, in September 2016, Gazprom, which had reduced Turkmen gas imports from 40 bcm in 2008 to 10 bcm a year in 2009, and further to 4 bcm a year in 2015, announced that it would halt imports completely till 2018, in what was seen as a bid to weaken Turkmenistan's position as a rival gas supplier.[9]

Turning Towards China

The move towards diversifying Turkmenistan's gas markets began in

8. Ibid.
9. Sergei Blagov, "Russia sees new opportunities in Central Asia", *Asia Times*, October 7, 2016 at http://www.atimes.com/article/russia-sees-new-opportunities-central-asia/

2006 with the signing of an inter-governmental framework agreement on gas and oil cooperation between President Hu Jintao and President Nyazov. The agreement outlined plans for joint exploration, gas purchases by China and the commissioning of the Trans-Asia Gas Pipeline (TAGP). In 2007 CNPC was also granted a licence to explore and produce gas in the Bagtyyarlyk area, making it the first and only foreign company to obtain permission to carry out onshore gas extraction activities in Turkmenistan along with a 30-year agreement for supplying upto 30 bcm/y, which formed the basis for a new eastern export route to China. Deliveries began in December 2009, making the TAGP the first major pipeline from Central Asia to bypass the Russian network. The first pipeline, known as Line A, carried gas from Turkmen fields through Uzbekistan, Kazakhstan and Xinjiang province, before joining up with China's pipeline grid. Then in 2010, Line B was initiated and together the two lines carried 30bcm/y. In 2012, China and Turkmenistan signed another agreement to increase total exports to China to 65 bcm/y by 2020, by adding another line – Line C – with a 25 bcm/y capacity which would run parallel to the one from Uzbekistan and Kazakhstan, and in September 2013, China and Turkmenistan agreed to launch yet another line – Line D – with a 25 bcm/y capacity, which would run through Uzbekistan, Tajikistan and Kyrgyzstan, to China. This line was scheduled to be ready by 2016–17, but has been delayed, reportedly due to slowing demand in China. Although the project experienced delays in production by 2011, by August 2013, Turkmenistan had delivered 60.645 bcm, which saw the total Turkmen gas delivered to China to 138.6 bcmby May 2016. Now, Ashgabat which had hoped that its volume to China would further increase to more than 75-80 bcm following the completion of the Line D, is now moving more actively on the TAPI pipeline to South Asia as well as looking at the trans-Caspian pipeline project.[10] (see Map 6.1)

Although the decision was apparently taken following the dispute with Russia,[11] a main reason for the success of the Sino-Turkmen deal

10. Ruslan Izimov, "China and Turkmenistan – a Regional Dimension", Central Asia Bureau for Analytic Reporting, August 29, 2016 at http://cabar.asia/en/ruslan-izimov-china-and-turkmenistan-a-regional-dimension/
11. Chemen Durdiyeva, "China, Turkmenistan, Kazakhstan and Uzbekistan launch Turkmenistan-China Gas Pipeline", Central Asia Caucasus Institute, January 20, 2010 at http://old.cacianalyst.org/?q=node/5254

Map 6.1

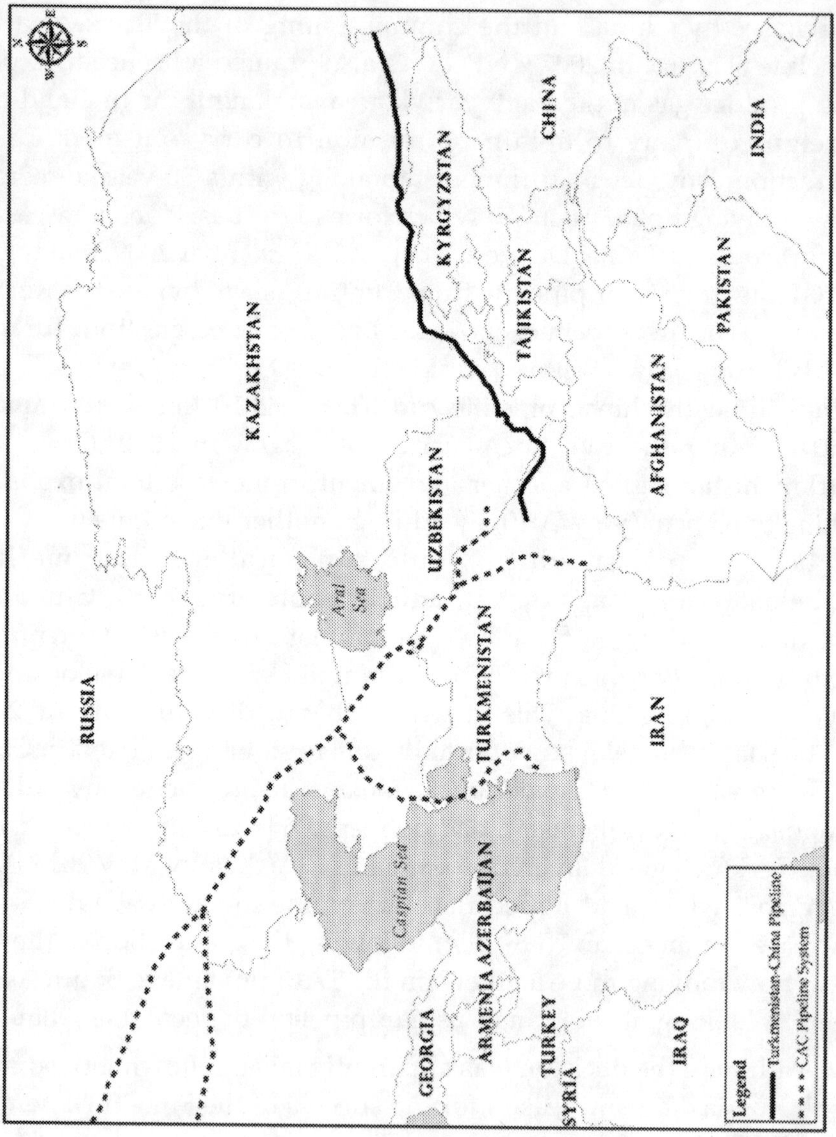
RUSSIA
KAZAKHSTAN
Aral Sea
UZBEKISTAN
KYRGYZSTAN
CHINA
TAJIKISTAN
INDIA
PAKISTAN
AFGHANISTAN
TURKMENISTAN
IRAN
Caspian Sea
AZERBAIJAN
ARMENIA
GEORGIA
TURKEY
SYRIA
IRAQ
Legend
Turkmenistan-China Pipeline
CAC Pipeline System

was China's policy of offering package deals in a manner that Western companies cannot emulate. Apart from offering credit lines on soft terms for gas complexes, including development of upstream projects, albeit developed by Chinese firms using Chinese equipment, it also offered billions of dollars in investment and built 'turnkey factories' at much lower rates than those offered by European firms. Moreover, China has also invested in other sectors including telecommunications, construction, light industry, pharmaceuticals, transport and chemicals. As a result, China has managed to connect the Central Asian countries via pipelines in record time, while Western firms have been waiting for almost a decade for a southern route.[12]

The Search for New Markets – South Asia

Despite the successful relationship with China, Ashgabat is wary of becoming overtly dependent on China due to a number of factors. Some officials have expressed concern about China's growing dominance and mercantilist approach. For example, Turkmenistan exports mainly raw materials to China, while China supplies manufactured goods, which has negatively affected local businesses. Moreover, the favourable conditions provided to Chinese workers has led to expressions of grievances by other workers, both local and foreign. Hence, in order to prevent ending up in a similar situation as that faced with Russia, Turkmenistan is keen to diversify and look for more export market options in the east to South Asia, and to the west to the lucrative European market. Apart from reaching out to Turkey, Japan and South Korea to develop projects in Turkmenistan for LNG, gas-to-liquids, and manufacture of fertilisers from natural gas, Ashgabat has been pursuing the TAPI (Turkmenistan-Afghanistan-Pakistan-India) project to tap the potentially lucrative South Asian market as part of its diversification strategy.

The project has its origins in the Trans-Afghan pipeline project, which later became the Unocal-led CentGas project in the mid-1990s following the signing of a memorandum of understanding between the governments of Turkmenistan and Pakistan for a pipeline project. Despite the demise of both projects due to the instability in

12. Annette Bohr, no. 1, p.78.

Afghanistan, the search for a project which would serve several economic and geopolitical goals was not given up. As Richard Boucher, former US Assistant Secretary of State for South and Central Asia, said in 2007, one of the US' goals was to stabilise Afghanistan and to link South Asia and Central Asia so that energy can flow to the south.[13] Moreover, Washington was keen to provide an alternative to the IPI (Iran-Pakistan-India) gas pipeline project in pursuit of its sanctions policy against Tehran.

In April 2008, the Asian Development Bank (ADB) outlined the details of a feasibility study of a project that was initially completed in 2005 at a meeting of the four participating countries, namely, Turkmenistan, Afghanistan, Pakistan and India. The ADB reported that the estimated capital cost was $7.6 billion and said it would consider financing for the project. The project was expected to transport 33 bcm of natural gas from Turkmenistan's Galkynysh field to South Asia, with Afghanistan receiving 14 million standard cubic metres a day (mmscmd), and India and Pakistan each receiving 38 mmscmd. But since then, a decade has passed, with no sign of the commencement of the project as it remains mired in problems associated with selection of a secure route, ensuring supplies, pricing, and most importantly, selection of a consortium. Initially, US oil majors Chevron and ExxonMobil had expressed their interest in assuming that role. However, after Ashgabat refused to allow them an equity stake in the Galkynysh field in exchange for assuming the risk of construction on the grounds that Turkmen policy of limiting production sharing agreements (PSAs) to its offshore reserves only, both companies withdrew from the project although Turkmenistan signed an onshore PSA with CNPC for its Bagtyýarlyk onshore natural gas project in the southeast, the only foreign company to be allowed one in Turkmenistan.[14] France's Total S.A., was considered thereafter as the

13. John Foster, "Afghanistan, the TAPI Pipeline, and Energy Geopolitics", *Journal of Energy Security*, March 23, 2010 at http://ensec.org/index.php?option=com_content&view=article&id=233:afghanistan-the-tapi-pipeline-and-energy-geopolitics&catid=103:energysecurityissue content&Itemid=358

14. Sarah Lain, "European Energy Security and Turkmenistan", *The Diplomat*, January 13, 2015 at http://thediplomat.com/2015/01/european-energy-security-and-turkmenistan/

leading candidate as was Russia's Rostec and CNPC, and there were reports that more than one consortium was also being considered.[15] However, to date, no consortium leader has been selected. In the meantime, the cost of the project has escalated from the original $7.7 billion to around $10-12 billion, making its future uncertain.[16]

Nevertheless, all the partners involved in TAPI, remain optimistic that the project, albeit delayed, would see the light of day. As India's external affairs minister Sushma Swaraj said, "Our energy needs are rising. Our needs in the agriculture sector and want for fertilisers are also rising. In both these areas, Turkmenistan can be our partner" and said that India was willing to build a fertiliser plant in Turkmenistan.[17]

However, there are several doubts regarding the project, including security concerns, gas pricing, transit fees and the refusal by Turkmenistan to give equity stakes in its hydrocarbon blocks, which saw several international oil firms opting out of the project.

Recently, despite Pakistani media reports stating that construction on the Pakistani portion of the project would commence in February 2017, and that a German project management consultant had been appointed, that a consortium of Japanese companies had being awarded the contract for developing the gas field in Turkmenistan and that a Chinese company had won the contract for laying the pipeline over Turkmen territory,[18] there have been subsequent reports regarding further developments.

Moreover, there are concerns that China may yet put a spoke in the TAPI wheel. Beijing wants to be the dominant market in Turkmen gas exports and the TAPI project does not fit into its strategy of energy

---

15. Micha'el Tanchum, "Turkmenistan Poised for TAPI Breakthrough", *The Central Asia-Caucasus Analyst*, March 18, 2015 at http://www.cacianalyst.org/publications/analytical-articles/item/13165-turkmenistan-poised-for-tapi-breakthrough.html
16. Ibid.
17. "Turkmenistan's rising gas production and international exports: A Guide", April 9, 2015, *ITE Oil & Gas* at http://www.oilgas-events.com/market-insights/turkmenistan/turkmenistan-s-rising-gas-production-and-international-exports-a-guide/801782978
18. Zafar Bhutta, "Japan, China companies win contracts for TAPI project", *Express Tribune*, August 24, 2016 at https://tribune.com.pk/story/1169388/energy-supplies-japan-china-companies-win-contracts-tapi-project/

and indeed, overall foreign trade in Eurasia, with Turkmenistan being an important part of its One-Belt-One-Road initiative, both in terms of energy supplies as well as a transportation and transit hub, through which China would like to access the Gulf markets. Furthermore, as far as China is concerned, the main beneficiary of the project will be the US, given that it was initiated by Washington as a counter to Iranian gas exports to South Asia, and would allow the US to enhance its influence in the region if the project was realised.[19]

To Europe

Another potential – and perhaps the most lucrative – market for Turkmen gas, is Europe. Since the mid-1990s, Turkmenistan has been looking for a western route to export its gas to the lucrative European market, and in fact, one of the reasons for its gas trade swap deal with Iran was the latter's location as the most direct and cost-effective route to Europe via Turkey. However, Western and US sanctions did not allow any project involving Iran and as an alternative, the US promoted the construction of the 2,000-km Trans-Caspian Pipeline (TCP), which envisaged transporting gas under the Caspian Sea to Azerbaijan, and on to Europe via Georgia and Turkey. While negotiations began to yield some results around 2000, differences between Azerbaijan and Turkmenistan developed following Baku's demand for a larger share of the pipeline's capacity, and after the then President Saparmurat Niyazov objected to the Azeri demand on the grounds that it would make the project unprofitable for Turkmenistan, the project was abandoned.[20]

Meanwhile, as concerns surfaced regarding the prospect of facing shortages after 2019, when the gas contract between Russia and Ukraine was expected to expire, the EU began to pursue its programme of identifying alternative supply sources, and increased negotiations over various gas pipeline initiatives under its Southern Corridor project – including the Trans-Caspian Pipeline – with the respective suppliers. Although the financial benefits were not its main concern, Turkmenistan, in the interest of gaining more markets, agreed to sign

19. Ruslan Izimov, no. 10.
20. Annette Bohr, no. 1, p.86.

on. Hence, in May 2015, along with Azerbaijan and Turkey, Turkmenistan signed the Ashgabat Declaration with the European Union, which stated that all the signatories supported the creation of favourable conditions necessary for ensuring reliable, stable and long-term international energy cooperation taking into account the interests of producers, transit countries and consumers of energy resources. (see Map 6.2) Significantly, the declaration recognised the importance of the equal and mutually beneficial cooperation in ensuring the supply of natural gas from Turkmenistan to Europe.[21]

In a further development, in November 2014, Turkmengaz signed a framework agreement with Turkey to supply the Trans-Anatolian Natural Gas Pipeline project (TANAP), which forms another section of the EU's Southern Gas Corridor project. The project proposes to transport gas from Azerbaijan's Shah Deniz II field in the Caspian Sea to Europe via Turkey.[22] But despite its potential to provide Europe with a supply source that would allow it to become less dependent on Russia, the TCP project presents several challenges, the chief being the legal status of the Caspian Sea and the conflict over ownership rights. Russia has opposed the project from the very beginning on the basis that the status of the Caspian Sea has to be first clarified. However, even several rounds of negotiations between the leaders and officials of the five littoral states have not succeeded in coming up with a consensus over how the Caspian – and its resources – should be divided. Moreover, Russia, with the support of Iran, has also expressed concerns about environmental consequences of a pipeline running across the Caspian Sea bottom, clearly to prevent its neighbours from constructing an alternative transport route, and has threatened to file a legal challenge to the construction of the TCP, which could hold up the project for years. Meanwhile, all five Caspian littorals have been building up their navies, although the Russian navy is the clear

21. Huseyn Hasanov, "Turkmenistan, Azerbaijan, Turkey sign energy declaration with EU", *Trendz News Agency*, May 1, 2015 at http://en.trend.az/business/energy/2390411.html
22. Catherine Putz, "Europe could be getting Turkmen gas by 2020", *The Diplomat*, May 5, 2015 at http://thediplomat.com/2015/05/europe-could-be-getting-turkmen-gas-by-2020/

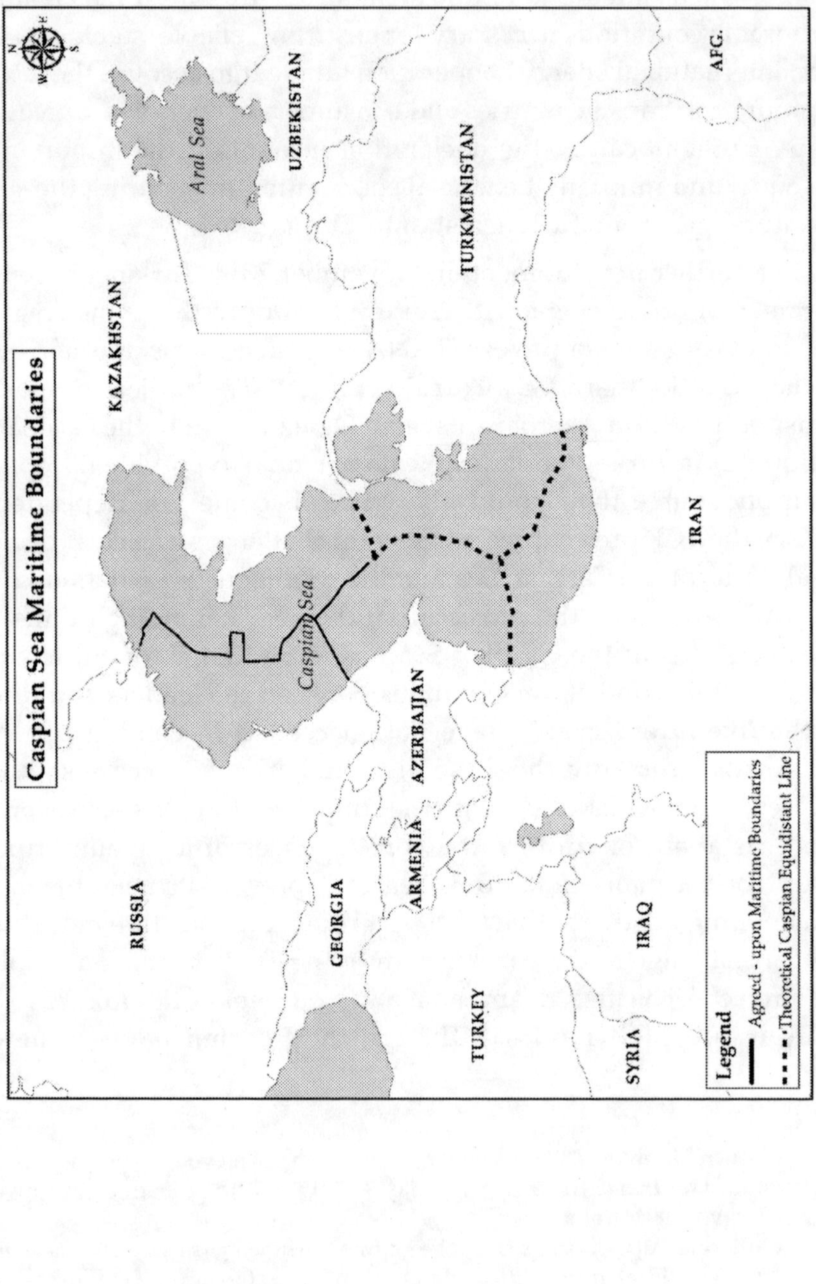

Map 6.2

Caspian Sea Maritime Boundaries

dominant power.[23] Not to be deterred, Ashgabat and the EU have been looking at other options. European Commission Vice-President Maros Sefcovic is also discussing other potential delivery options with Turkmenistan, including the possibility of transiting Turkmen gas via Iran. While a pipeline transporting Turkmen gas to Iran already exists, by building a 200-km pipeline from Tehran to Esfahan, Turkmen gas could be included. A pipeline from Esfahan to the Turkish border already exists and could be used to transport Turkmen gas as well.[24]

A third option is to build a cross-country pipeline from South Pars gas field towards Iran's north-eastern regions bordering Turkmenistan, known as the 11th cross-country pipeline. The pipeline has the capacity to transfer 100 mcmd of gas, and is aimed to make these regions self-sufficient instead of relying on Turkmen gas imports. Another Iranian project which is on the anvil, is a 1,860-km cross-country pipeline, projected to transfer 110 mcmd of gas from the South Pars gas field towards the Iran-Turkey border. If an agreement can be reached, Iran could sign a gas swap deal with Turkmenistan and Turkey by eliminating the 11th cross-country pipeline and accelerate the construction of the South Pars cross-country pipeline instead.[25] In fact, the prospects of Iran-Turkmen cooperation in supplying gas to Europe was one of the main issues discussed during Iranian President Rouhani's visit to Turkmenistan in mid-March. However, with a larger gas reserve base than Turkmenistan, Iran is more likely to emerge as a competitor rather than a trade partner to Turkmenistan. To make matters worse, Iran has, according to reports, recently declared that it may completely stop importing Turkmen gas in the near future following a dispute over payments, following a halt in gas exports by Ashgabat.

Meanwhile, around 2010, Turkmenistan had also begun constructing the East-West pipeline, with a projected capacity of

---

23. Qishloq Ovozi, "Still One Big Obstacle to Turkmen Gas to Europe", Radio Free Europe Radio Liberty, June 8, 2015 at http://www.rferl.org/content/turkmenistan-natural-gas-europe-trans-caspian-pipeline/26996003.html
24. "Potential routes for delivering Turkmen gas to EU", *Natural Gas Europe,* May 4, 2015 at http://www.naturalgaseurope.com/potential-routs-for-delivering-turkmen-gas-to-eu-23508
25. Ibid.

30 bcm/y. Once completed, it would allow gas from its eastern fields to the Caspian coast. At the same time, the pipeline could also allow supplies to be delivered to any customer, thereby increasing the country's supply diversification options.[26] Interestingly, the original plan was to feed gas into the Russian-backed Prikaspiisk pipeline, but after difference over pricing emerged with Gazprom, which was originally tasked with the construction of the pipeline, the project was scrapped, thereby freeing the gas that was dedicated for the project, for export elsewhere. At the time, it appeared that with Russia no longer interested in importing Turkmen gas, and with no additional volumes allocated to Iran, Ashgabat's intention to go ahead with the project was to prepare for gas exports via the TCP.[27] Whatever the intention, the pipeline was inaugurated in December 2015, with the potential to be linked with the TCP through a 300 km sub-sea pipeline under the Caspian Sea.

Despite these initiatives, Ashgabat does not display much urgency in either the TCP or any other project linked with the Southern Gas Corridor. Moreover, despite the very distinct possibility of Turkmen gas flowing into Europe, the prospect for this eventuality remains far from certain as both politics and logistics may get in the way. In order to hook into any pipeline associated with the Southern Gas Corridor, Turkmenistan will need to build a pipeline under the Caspian's disputed waters, which remains deeply contentious, with none of the five littoral states – Azerbaijan, Iran, Turkmenistan, Kazakhstan and Russia – showing any signs of compromising for the sake of a resolution. And as one of the central purposes of building the pipeline is to circumvent Russia, the most likely scenario is that Moscow will continue to play the spoiler in delineating the waters.[28]

However, with the fall in gas prices, high production costs and China's recent policy to develop its domestic shale gas resources, Turkmenistan is now looking for other alternatives. Moreover, the fourth phase of the pipeline to China – Line D – which runs through

26. Ibid. p. 81.
27. "The momentum for the trans-Caspian pipeline", *Natural Gas Europe*, July 14, 2015 at http://www.naturalgaseurope.com/the-momentum-for-the-trans-caspian-pipeline-24590
28. Catherine Putz, no. 22.

Uzbekistan, Tajikistan and Kyrgyzstan, is now facing several problems, raising concerns whether it will ever be completed. And now with the TAPI project too mired in problems over pricing in the current low price environment, selling to Russia, albeit on unfavourable terms, is looking like the only gas export option open to Ashgabat, at least for the time being.[29]

During Russian Foreign Minister Sergey Lavrov's visit to Turkmenistan in January 2016, President Berdymukhamedov extended an invitation to President Putin to make an official trip to the country. During the talks with Lavrov, the issue of reviving gas exports to Russia was discussed. The termination of gas exports to Russia has been detrimental to both countries, despite the increase in supplies to China. Given that the gas supplies to China are given as payment for the loans and other infrastructure assistance, and the Iran-Turkmen gas trade is also done under a barter deal, Turkmenistan requires hard cash, which Gazprom provided. On the other hand, Turkmen gas supplies comprised 30 percent of all Russian gas exports to third countries. Therefore, it would be in the interest of both sides to come to some understanding on gas prices and resume the trade. However, much will depend on Turkmenistan's flexibility on prices, as well as its willingness to consider Russian interests with regard to export routes and construction of pipelines.[30]

Representatives of Turkmenistan have also recently been to the UK to talk about expansion of bilateral cooperation between the two countries in order to import Turkmen gas. Currently, British companies such as Shell work in Turkmenistan, and relations between the nations are good.[31]

---

29. Qishloq Ovozi, "Russia Flexes Its Muscles In Turkmenistan", Radio Free Europe, June 29, 2016 at http://www.rferl.org/content/russia-flexes-muscles-turkmenistan-gas-exports/27793499.html
30. Arkady Dubnov, "A new Russian turn to Turkmenistan?". Carnegie Endowment for International Peace, February 18, 2016 at http://carnegieendowment.org/publications/?fa=62814
31. "Turkmenistan's rising gas production and international exports: A Guide", no. 17.

Ashagabat's Quandary

Turkmenistan certainly has the potential to become a serious player in the gas market, particularly after the announcement that more reserves had been discovered in the Galkynish field. However, despite the current leadership under President Gurbanguly Berdymukhamedov reversing some of his predecessor, Saparmurat Nyazov's, policies and investing substantially in developing the country's infrastructure, the principal aim of the regime continues to be self-preservation; one of the main tools of the leadership is to continue with its policy of complete state control of the state's energy resources and centralisation and control of revenues from hydrocarbon exports, which is used to finance security services and patronage networks. But despite falling global energy prices, the slump in the Russian Rouble and a slowdown in China's economy, Turkmenistan's leadership has not reversed its decision to review its longstanding policy of refusing to grant buyers equity stakes in upstream fields, and there are signs that Ashgabat may now be more open to other markets to increase its options.

First, while its dependence on China as a gas export market is poised to increase, following the 2014 deal with Russia, Beijing has other alternatives, making Turkmenistan more vulnerable to Chinese pressures with regard to prices, which in turn has impacted severely with the country's economy. Beijing already pays well below the European prices for its Turkmen imports, and may negotiate for even lower prices in the future. Second, despite the robust energy cooperation, Sino-Turkmen relations have their share of problems, with some Turkmen officials expressing concern about the growing dependence on China. Third, with the slowdown in the Chinese economy, China may cut its energy imports. The fact that there has been no movement on the fourth phase of the Turkmen-China pipeline is a clear indication. Finally, with deepening energy ties with Russia, as was evidenced by the slew of recent oil and gas deals signed between the two countries over and above the 2014 mega gas deal, Turkmenistan's plans to increase exports to China may be affected.

With Turkmenistan's economy substantially dependent on revenues accruing from hydrocarbon exports, the fall in prices has seen its economic growth rate come down from 10 percent in 2013-14, to 6.5 percent in 2015. The World Bank has predicted that it may fall further in 2016 to 6.2 and rise again to 6.5 in 2017.[32] Thus far, Ashgabat has not shown much interest in focusing on expanding its exports westwards, despite the EU's overtures. However, as most forecasts show that even if oil prices recover over the next few months, gas prices are expected to remain low over the next few years. As new producers enter the market concurrently with falling demand, Turkmenistan may well be more willing to cooperate with the other participants of the Southern Gas Corridor.

32. "Global Economic prospects: Weak Investment in uncertain times" Europe and Central Asia, World Bank, January 2017, http://pubdocs.worldbank.org/en/613131481727532936/Global-Economic-Prospects-January-2017-Regional-Overview-ECA.pdf

7

Arctic – The Last Gas Frontier

For years, the presence of large reserves of energy resources, particularly natural gas, in the Arctic region has been known and exploration activity has been carrying on intermittently since the 1920s. Various assessments of the reserves have been made, although the 2008 report of the US Geological Survey, which claimed that the Arctic is estimated to hold around 22 percent of the world's energy resources, with around 90 billion barrels or 13 percent of the world's untapped oil and 30 percent of natural gas reserves, besides vast quantities of mineral resources, such as rare earth elements, iron ore, and nickel, is deemed most accurate. But while some states like Norway and Russia had been exporting oil and gas from their fields, and Iceland and Greenland were actively pursuing exploration in their territorial waters, the harsh climate of the region and dense ice cover had made it difficult and economically challenging to prospect for energy in the region. As a result, the region had remained free from great power politics. But several events in the recent past have gradually seen the hitherto tranquil environment of the Arctic emerge as a geopolitical hotspot.

More than any action by a State, it is climate change that has emerged as the most effective actor that has changed the peaceful, almost languid pace of the region. The advent of global warming that has led to the melting of large swathes of the ice cover in the Arctic has rendered the region more accessible than ever before. Currently, the polar ice cap is 25 percent less than it was in the 1970s, and the summer ice in the Arctic Ocean has been decreasing at a rate of about 8 percent per decade, while the thickness of the sea ice has decreased by approximately 40 percent. As a result, while in the past, it was almost impossible to access the region due to thick year-round sea ice, today global warming has increased the navigability of the Arctic. In 2005, the Northeast Passage (or the Northern Sea Route) opened up along the Eurasian border for the first time while the Northwest Passage along Canada opened up in 2007.[1] These new sea lanes will substantially reduce maritime distances for commercial shipping. According to the US Navy, by 2030, the Northern Sea Route from the Kara Strait to the Pacific will see nine weeks of open water. This would cut the time taken to travel between European ports and East Asia by 35-60 percent as against the routes through the Suez or Panama Canals. At the same time, the Northwest Passage, which connects the Atlantic and Pacific Oceans through the Canadian Arctic Archipelago, which was completely non-navigable earlier, will have five weeks of open water by 2030, and will cut transportation time by 25 percent between Europe and the US than non-Arctic routes. The opening up of new passages has implications not just for trade in general but also for access to the vast energy resources in the region, seen as the last frontier of conventional energy reserves.[2] And it is not just the six littoral Arctic nations that are vying for extending their influence in the region, but some extra-regional states, are looking to raise their profile here as well.

Before the current drop in the price of oil and gas, fierce competition had broken out among the five Arctic states – namely, *Norway, Denmark (Greenland), Russia, Canada and the US – with each claiming rights not only to the resources in* the 200 nautical mile economic zone (EEZ) around their coasts under international *law, but also in* extending their territorial sovereign rights in order to exclusively exploit all natural resources within their economic zones. (See Map 7.1)

1. Heather Conley and Jamie Kraut, "U.S. Strategic Interests in the Arctic An Assessment of Current Challenges and New Opportunities for Cooperation", Center for Strategic and International Studies (CSIS), April 2010 at http://csis.org/files/publication/100426_Conley_USStrategicInterests_Web.pdf
2. Sohrab Ahmari, "The New Cold War's Arctic Front", *The Wall Street Journal*, June 9, 2015 at http://www.wsj.com/articles/the-new-cold-wars-arctic-front-1433872323

Map 7.1

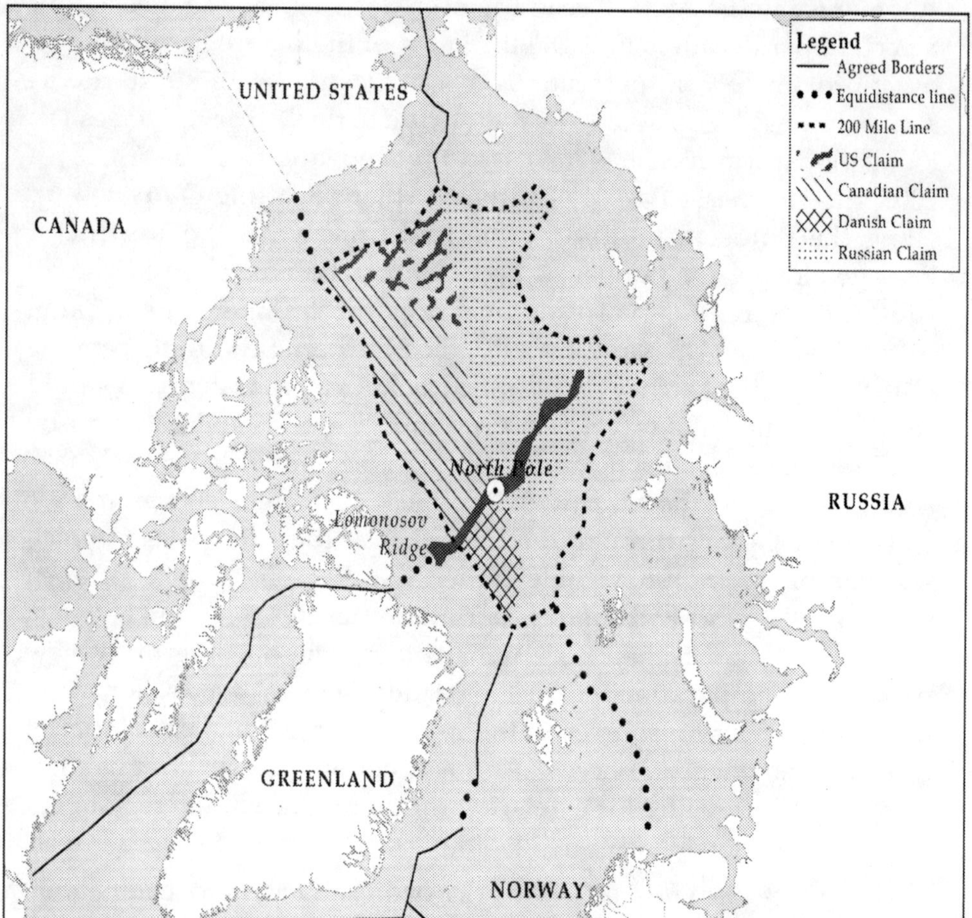

Russia Raising its Stakes

Despite its seemingly decreasing profile in the global theatre, Moscow has always perceived the High North as an important strategic domain, and has striven to strengthen and retain its hold over the region. In 2001, Russia made an official submission to the UN Commission on the Limits of the Continental Shelf (UNLCS), in accordance with the United Nations Convention on the Law of the Sea (UNCLOS), claiming an extension of territory beyond the 200-nautical-mile EEZ, namely the Lomonosov Ridge and Mendeleev Ridge on the grounds that the

Arctic Ocean seabed is a projection of the Siberian continental platform. But it was not till August 2007, when a steep rise was seen in the price of oil, that a Russian expedition called Arktika 2007, descended to the seabed at the North Pole and planted the Russian flag and took water and soil samples for analysis to be used as evidence to their claim to the mineral riches of the Arctic.[3] The Russian action sparked off a chain reaction of expeditions from other states. A few days later, the US sent a coast guard icebreaker to the Bering Sea, ostensibly to study global warming and its consequences for the region, while the Canadian government issued statements reiterating its sovereignty over the Arctic, and launched a "sovereignty operation" known as Operation Nanook, involving naval manoeuvres in the region. The Danish government too launched an Arctic scientific expedition around the same time, with instructions to gather evidence that the Lomonosov Ridge was an underwater extension of Greenland, not Russia, in order to support Denmark's territorial claims in the Arctic.[4]

Russia's action was no doubt set off by the fact that its existing energy assets were in decline and given its strategy of using its status as an energy superpower as a foreign policy tool, the need to ensure its hold on the Arctic's unexplored hydrocarbon wealth was seen as crucial. Concerned by the increasing human activity due to the ice melt and opening up of new sea routes and the growing ingress of more countries, including China, in the region, a major goal for Russia is to preserve its role as a leading Arctic power and transform the Arctic into a top strategic base for natural resources by 2020. Accordingly, in September 2008, the Russian government adopted a new Arctic strategy enunciated in a document, entitled "The fundamentals of state policy of the Russian Federation in the Arctic in the period up to 2020 and beyond", that was published on the 'Russian Security Council' website in the end of March 2009. The document emphasised the region's importance to Russia's economy as a major source of revenue, mainly

3. Shamil Midkhatovich Yenikeyeff and Timothy Fenton Krysiek, "The Battle for the Next Energy Frontier: The Russian Polar Expedition and the Future of Arctic Hydrocarbons", Oxford Institute for Energy Studies, August 2007 at http://www.oxfordenergy.org/wpcms/wp-content/uploads/2011/01/Aug2007-TheBattleforthenextenergyfrontier-ShamilYenikeyeff-and-TimothyFenton Krysiek.pdf.

4. Ibid.

from energy production as well as from maritime transport. It also states that defining the limits of the country's continental shelf by 2015 was a top priority and that Russia aimed to deploy a combined-arms force in the region by 2020.[5]

Although low oil prices since 2014, combined with Western sanctions imposed after Russia's annexation of Crimea saw new offshore projects being mothballed, Russian military presence did not see a slowdown, and in fact, strengthened its Northern Fleet defence forces to strengthen its Arctic position even further. It is building nuclear icebreakers to strengthen its existing fleet of around 40 breakers, which are used to clear channels for military and civilian ships.

In fact, for Moscow, establishing its dominance over the region has become even more important following its annexation of the Crimea and the subsequent imposition of sanctions. With only a handful of oil companies having the technological expertise and experience required to extract oil and gas from the harsh Arctic environment, and Russian state firms like Gazprom and Rosneft having limited experience with such challenging projects, Russia is looking beyond Europe and the US for investment and partnerships to develop its Arctic resources. Moreover, with many of its older fields depleting rapidly, Russia needs access to the Arctic's energy resources to ensure that it can deliver gas to China following the May 2014 $400 billion deal it has signed with China. More recently, in May 2015, the two countries announced more joint projects, including the development of shelf deposits in Russia's Arctic and Far Eastern regions.[6] Chinese energy company PetroChina has purchased a 20 percent stake in the Yamal LNG project for an undisclosed sum and in 2014, China and

5. Katarzyna Zysk, "Russia's Arctic Strategy: ambitions and constraints", *Geopolitics in the North*, June 15, 2009 at http://www.geopoliticsnorth.org/index.php?option=com_content&view=article&id=84:arctic-strategy-documents&catid=52&showall=&limitstart=2 and J. Michael Cole, "Militarization of the Arctic Heats Up, Russia Takes the Lead", *The Diplomat*, December 6, 2013 at http://thediplomat.com/2013/12/militarization-of-the-arctic-heats-up-russia-takes-the-lead/

6. Sergei Blagov, "Russia's partnership with China: An alliance of necessity", *Asia Times*, May 10, 2015 at http://atimes.com/2015/05/russias-partnership-with-china-an-alliance-of-necessity/

Russia issued a joint statement which included a note that Russia will facilitate the shipment of Chinese goods through the Northern Sea Route, as well as its railways and ports.[7]

Interestingly, Russia was also keen to cooperate with Japan in the Arctic. Although economic factors are a major consideration as diversifying the number of markets is in its interest, balancing China's increasing reach is also a factor pushing Moscow closer to Tokyo. In fact, Moscow supported Japan's candidacy for observer status at the Arctic Council. For Japan too, while balancing China is a factor in remaining engaged in the Arctic, the region's hydrocarbon resources and the Northern Sea Route (NSR) is important for Japan as it provides an alternative route for Japan to transport its energy imports from West Asia, reducing reliance on the Straits of Hormuz and Malacca. Japan has even appointed a special ambassador in charge of Arctic affairs. Currently, the three main areas of Russo-Japanese cooperation in the Arctic include research, the NSR and the Yamal LNG project, in which it has conveyed its interest to Russia.[8]

The US Turns to the Arctic

Russia's Arctic build-up has not gone unnoticed in Washington, with the new US Defense Secretary James Mattis stating at his confirmation hearing in January 2017 that it was not to the US' advantage to leave any part of the world to others.[9] Despite being an Arctic state, the US only began looking at the Arctic strategically during the latter years of the George W. Bush administration in 2009 when it released a presidential directive establishing a new US policy for the Arctic. The policy stated that the US had national security and homeland security interests in the region and discussed a number of issues related to the Arctic, including among others, maritime transportation and economic

7. Bree Feng, "China Looks North: Carving Out a Role in the Arctic", Asia Pacific Foundation of Canada, April 30, 2015 at https://www.asiapacific.ca/canada-asia-agenda/china-looks-north-carving-out-role-arctic
8. Mina Pollmann, "How Japan and Russia Cooperate in the Arctic", *The Diplomat*, March 10, 2016 at http://thediplomat.com/2016/03/how-japan-and-russia-cooperate-in-the-arctic/
9. Andrew Osborn, "Putin's Russia in biggest Arctic military push since Soviet fall", Reuters, January 31, 2017 at http://www.reuters.com/article/us-russia-arctic-insight-idUSKBN15E0W0

issues, including energy.[10] Thereafter, in May 2010, the Obama Administration released a national security strategy document that stated, among other things, that the US had broad and fundamental interests in the Arctic region, where it sought to meet the country's national security needs, protect the environment and responsibly manage resources.[11]

That the US is looking at the Arctic from a geopolitical perspective comes out clearly from a report that was published in March 2015 by the National Petroleum Council (NPC). In October 2013, following a request by the Energy Secretary, the NPC conducted a comprehensive study on the research and technology opportunities in the Arctic to enable prudent development of oil and gas resources. Among other things, the report stated that the US has large offshore oil potential, akin to Russia, and larger than that of Canada and Norway, and supported exploration in the region. The rationale was that despite the shale revolution in the country that had enhanced its oil and gas output, production from shale would decrease by 2040 according to the Department of Energy's Energy Information Administration's (EIA) 2014 estimates. Therefore, given long timelines for developing Arctic resources, exploration in the region now could add to US production in the future and enhance the US' energy security.[12]

It further adds that the other Arctic countries were pursuing oil and gas exploration in the region; hence to remain globally competitive and to position itself to provide global leadership and influence in the Arctic, the US should facilitate exploration in the offshore Alaskan Arctic now.[13]

Under these circumstances, Washington's overturning its January 2015 ban on developing some areas of the Arctic coast citing environmental reasons, and granting of conditional approval on May

10. "National Security Presidential Directives – NSPDs", The White House, January 9, 2009 at http://fas.org/irp/offdocs/nspd/nspd-66.htm
11. "National Security Strategy", The White House, May 2010 at https://www.whitehouse.gov/sites/default/files/rss_viewer/national_security_strategy.pdf
12. "Arctic Potential: Realizing the Promise of U.S. Arctic Oil and Gas Resources", Draft Report of the National Petroleum Council, March 27, 2015 at http://www.eenews.net/assets/2015/03/30/document_cw_01.pdf
13. Ibid.

11, 2015, to a plan by Shell Gulf of Mexico to begin exploratory drilling in the Chukchi Sea, is not surprising, given that the Arctic represents one of the last remaining unexplored energy frontiers.[14]

The US has limited international legal jurisdiction over exploration in the Arctic because it is not party to the United Nations Convention on the Law of the Seas (UNCLOS). UNCLOS establishes that the five nations bordering the Arctic are granted EEZ of 200 nautical miles off their coasts. However, without being a party to UNCLOS, Washington cannot secure international legal titles to sites more than 200 miles off the coast. If ratified, the US could gain recognised international rights to 600 miles of the extended Continental Shelf. Other countries, notably Russia and Canada, have submitted claims that reach to the North Pole.[15]

Growing Militarisation

In mid-December 2014, Denmark, together with Greenland, filed a submission to the UNCLCS, claiming ownership of around 900,000 square kilometers of the Continental Shelf in the Arctic Ocean, becoming the first country to attempt to claim outright ownership of the North Pole. Canada too made overlapping claims to the North Pole and large swathes of the territory, as did Russia, and Norway has been moving troops and equipment to the region, as well as moved its Coast Guard headquarters further north and based its largest active army unit above the Arctic Circle.[16]

In December 2014, Russian President Vladimir Putin signed a new military doctrine for the country. The new doctrine, while focusing on the threat emanating from the expansion of NATO, also mentioned the need for Russia to extend its influence in the Arctic region. According to some Russian media reports, Moscow believes that with

14. John Warrick, "One step closer to Arctic drilling? Obama administration grants Shell 'conditional' approval", *Washington Times*, May 11, 2015 at http://www.washingtonpost.com/news/energy-environment/wp/2015/05/11/one-step-closer-to-arctic-drilling-obama-administration-grants-shell-conditional-approval/
15. "The Arctic – America's Last Energy Frontier" at http://www.americansecurityproject.org/energy-security/the-arctic-americas-last-energy-frontier/
16. Elisabeth Braw, "Putin Makes His First Move in Race to Control the Arctic", *Newsweek*, January 6, 2014.

the increase in turmoil in West Asia, more and more countries will look increasingly to the Arctic. To this end, Russia has embarked on a spate of port constructions across the Arctic, and is upgrading its other military capabilities in the region as well.[17] In October 2014, the Russian defence minister, Sergei Shoigu, announced that military units would be deployed all along its Arctic coast, and construction of military facilities have commenced on Cape Schmidt in Russia's far east and on the country's Arctic Wrangel and Kotelny Islands. It also has plans to construct several airfields as radar stations, with an airport at Cape Schmidt – known as Mys Shmidta in Russian – which was reopened at the end of 2015. It has already reopened its northern Alakurtti military base near the Finnish border, and at the end of 2014, President Putin announced that Russia's Arctic command had become operational.[18] Meanwhile, the other Arctic littorals, including the US, Canada and Norway too, are developing surveillance sensors to provide for traffic-monitoring capabilities in the region.[19]

It is not only the Arctic littorals that are displaying interest in the region. Although the jurisdiction of the Arctic region falls under the Arctic countries, viz. Canada, Denmark (Greenland), Norway, Russia and the US (Alaska) as well as the Arctic Council (AC) members namely Sweden, Finland and Iceland, in 2013, six non-Arctic countries – China, India, Italy, Japan, South Korea and Singapore – were inducted as permanent observers, albeit with no voting rights. On May 15, 2013, the Arctic Council Secretariat adopted the Kiruna Declaration, which stated that the members:

> "Recognize the central role of business in the development of the Arctic, and decide to increase cooperation and interaction with the business community to advance sustainable development in the

17. Jeremy Bender, "Russia Is Militarizing the Arctic", *Business Insider*, December 3, 2014 at http://www.businessinsider.in/Russia-Is-Militarizing-The-Arctic/articleshow/45354606.cms
18. Elisabeth Braw, "Putin Makes His First Move in Race to Control the Arctic", *Newsweek*, January 6, 2015 at http://www.newsweek.com/2015/01/16/putin-makes-his-first-move-race-control-arctic-296594.html
19. John Keller, "Arctic surveillance is the result of East-West political tensions in the polar regions", Military & Aerospace, March 3, 2015 at http://www.militaryaerospace.com/articles/2015/03/arctic-surveillance-blog.html

Arctic...."[20] thereby acknowledging the central role of business, including the development of hydrocarbon resources, in the development of the Arctic.

China's Arctic Strategy

Of all the extra-regional countries, China has been the most proactive in the region. As far back as 2009 and 2010, China had disputed any claims of sovereignty in the Arctic waters beyond the twelve-mile zone granted to littoral countries who have signed the UNCLOS with Rear Admiral Yin Zhuo of the Chinese Navy, stating in May 2010, that the Arctic belongs to all the people around the world as no nation has sovereignty over it. He also went on to say that exploitation of the Arctic will become a future mission of the (Chinese) navy.[21]

China is also developing its bilateral, mostly commercial and economic relations with small Arctic states, particularly Iceland. In April 2012, Prime Minister Wen Jiabao toured Iceland as well as Sweden in a bid for gaining their support for permanent observer status after Denmark too stated that it would support China's position. In fact, taking advantage of Iceland's financial problems emanating from the 2008-09 crisis, China had increased its cooperation with Iceland, which had in turn allowed Beijing to increase its profile in the region. China is investing in joint energy, minerals exploitation and Arctic navigation projects with the smaller Arctic countries.

Officially, China claims that it does not covet the Arctic for its resources, but rather has a genuine interest in the future of the region. "China's activities are for the purposes of regular environmental investigation and investment and have nothing to do with resource plundering and strategic control," the state-controlled *Xinhua* news agency wrote in 2012.

However, the general perception is that China is eyeing the Arctic for three main reasons:

---

20. Arctic Council Secretariat, Kiruna Declaration, Kiruna, Sweden, May 15, 2013, Arctic Council (accessed on May 25, 2014).
21. Olga Alexeeva and Frédéric Lasserre, "China and the Arctic", Arctic Yearbook 2012, p.84 at http://www.researchgate.net/profile/Olga_Alexeeva/publication/259042084_China_and_the_Arctic/links/0c960529ce2575a172000000.pdf

Heavy dependence on exports, apart from the vast energy resource potential of the region and the opening up of a shorter sea route due to the melting Arctic sea ice that will save the country billions of dollars in transportation costs as well as time. For example, the distance from Shanghai to Hamburg is 2,800 nautical miles shorter via the Arctic than via the Suez Canal. Moreover, being the world's largest fishing nation, the Arctic may become a new and important fisheries frontier.[22]

Although some Arctic countries are wary of China's ambitions in the region, barring the US, many of them are working with China on developing resources; the rationale being that unlike the US, Canada and Russia, they supported the integration of the Arctic region into the global economy to prevent the Arctic Council from becoming too inward-looking.[23]

In fact, China's inclusion in the Arctic Council was partially due to strong support from the Nordic nations, and currently Russia. Beijing signed a free trade agreement with Iceland in 2013 and has built a new embassy there. Chinese resource companies have also invested $400 million in energy and mining projects in the Canadian Arctic and have committed to invest $2.3 billion in a mammoth, British-led mining project in Greenland. A Chinese mining company has taken over an iron ore mine in Greenland while talks are on between the government and two Chinese companies interested in mining in Greenland. Denmark too has stated that it is willing to work together with China to explore new Arctic sea routes, while Norway and Chinese state-owned oil company CNOOC are partnering in Iceland as well as considering the possibility of collaborating in offshore Norwegian oil exploration.[24]

More recently, Beijing has also increased its funding for Arctic research, set up a polar institute in Shanghai, and in 2012 sent the Chinese ice breaker *Xue Long* through the Northeast Passage above

---

22. Ed Struzik, "China signals hunger for Arctic's mineral riches", *The Guardian*, June 4, 2013 at http://www.theguardian.com/environment/2013/jun/04/china-arctics-mineral-riches
23. Kim Wall, "China seeks greater influence in Arctic region", *South China Morning Post*, June 25, 2013 at http://www.scmp.com/news/china/article/1268160/china-seeks-greater-influence-arctic-region
24. Bree Feng, "China Looks North: Carving out a Role in the Arctic", Asia Pacific Foundation of Canada, April 30, 2015 at https://www.asiapacific.ca/canada-asia-agenda/china-looks-north-carving-out-role-arctic

Russia and Scandinavia, to examine the suitability of using that route as a commercial waterway. It has also held several international symposiums, and invited foreign scholars onboard *Xue Long* during its polar voyages. In February, its third icebreaker, the Novorossiysk completed its first Arctic voyage.[25]

India's Interests

Even if India and China lack territorial contiguity with the polar region, healthy bilateral relations with the Council's permanent members and participation in research programmes will go a long way in gaining access to resources and transportation routes. But seasonal constraints, difficulty in navigation, high insurance costs, and poor infrastructure will impede the full economic potential of the NSR.

India's stated position is that it will contribute its scientific expertise, particularly the polar research capabilities, in advancing the goals of the Arctic Council. But beyond that, New Delhi will look at options to explore for hydrocarbons and diversify its energy basket. Geographically, Russia is best suited for exploration tie-ups. Half of the Arctic's population is Russian. The area accounts for 11 percent of Russia's GDP and over 20 percent of its exports. But to curry favour with Moscow, Delhi has to take a firm stand on the Russian contention that the disputed Lomonosov and Mendeleev ridges are extensions of its Siberian shelf. By toeing Moscow's line, New Delhi could get access to the rich mineral deposits and the NSR to ply trade. In a string of bids, New Delhi has lost out to Beijing in the battle for Russian energy resources. India got a major jolt when CNPC signed an agreement with Novatek, Russia's largest private gas producer, to acquire a 20 percent stake in a LNG project in the Yamal Peninsula in the Russian Arctic.

Though India's bilateral relations with the Nordic states are witnessing a spurt in trade and investments, the volumes are way behind that of China's. India is yet to firm up a multi-pronged approach as that of China to engage with the Nordic states, especially in the area of strategic interests which will invariably become the cornerstone in Indo-Nordic relations. While India has had a chequered past in the

25. Russia's newest Novorossiysk icebreaker completes first Arctic voyage, Tass, February 11, 2017, http://tass.com/economy/930329

area of defence and security cooperation with Sweden, Indo-Norwegian strategic ties had also suffered setbacks during the years of the Liberation Tigers of Tamil Eelam (LTTE) insurgency. On the economic front, Oslo has deplored Telenor's investment failures in India. Incidentally, India's Finance Minister recently paid a visit to Norway to iron out wrinkles in the bilateral relationship and further consolidate New Delhi's prospects in the Arctic. India is looking to woo Norway's $700 billion sovereign wealth fund, apart from bagging stakes in the offshore oil fields dotting the Barents Sea, recently opened up for development as per its New Exploration Licensing Policy. Though security issues did come up for discussion during the Finnish Foreign Minister's recent visit to New Delhi, the details of those talks remain under wraps. In Finland's 'Action Plan for India', trade and investment forms the core of Helsinki's vision document. Nehru's visit to Copenhagen in 1957 laid the foundation of Indo-Danish relationship. But ties between the two sides became frosty in July 2012 when India scaled down diplomatic ties with Denmark after its refusal to extradite Kim Davy, the main accused in the 1995 Purulia arms drop case. During the Icelandic Foreign Minister's visit to New Delhi in 2011, his counterpart S.M. Krishna broached the issue of Indian strategic interests in the Arctic. But it remains unclear whether the Indian Prime Minister picked up the threads from where S.M. Krishna left, in his talks with Iceland's President during his recent India visit.

According to the Multilateral Investment Guarantee Agency's 2009 survey of leading BRICS (Brazil, Russia, India, China and South Africa) "outward investors", Indian investors have been found to be more responsible and transparent than China in Africa, where several states are perceived to be "undemocratic" with weak regulations and lawlessness. According to the survey, Indian firms engage with local stakeholders and are sensitive to local concerns. If India is seen as a more trustworthy partner in Africa than China, then surely the Nordic countries can expect the same from Indian businesses if crucial sectors are opened up for Indian investments. Closer economic integration and confidence-building will pave the way for India's full membership in the Arctic Council along with China.

India has maintained that its interests in the region are scientific, unlike China and South Korea, which have been eager to dive into commercial activity in the environmentally sensitive region. In 2013, India scored a major diplomatic victory by managing to gain a seat on the Arctic Council as a permanent observer, along with China, Italy, Singapore, Japan and South Korea, which will give it the opportunity to be a part of what transpires in the region.

New Delhi has had good long-term relations with many of the Arctic Council members. However, with climate change being one of the top concerns of the Arctic Council, it may come under increasing pressure to do more on cutting emissions. Both India and China have been at odds with the European Union's environmental regulations that ask developing countries to cut levels of greenhouse gases (GHG). India's refusal to participate in many global programmes to cut GHG emissions over the past few years has seen it come under increasing pressure from several countries, although India has maintained that such demands are against its economic interests and will hurt its growth prospects. Its stand on emissions may also impinge on its Arctic interests. Now, following its inclusion as an observer in the Arctic Council, India may find itself placed in an awkward position while fulfilling its new role in the Arctic Council.

Regardless of its energy goals, India intends to be more active in the Arctic Circle. Plans are being drawn to send many more people to 'Himadri', India's research station in the Arctic, which was inaugurated in 2008. The station is located in the Norwegian archipelago of Svalbard at the International Arctic Research Base in Ny-Alesund. India has already spent \$3 million on developing Himadri and plans to spend up to \$15 million more on future development.[26]

India's interests in the region have been set out as the following:

- For domestic energy needs,
- Continuing the tradition of polar research from its permanent research station Himadri,
- Arctic shipping routes between Asia, America and Europe will be 40 percent faster than those in the Indian, Pacific and Atlantic Oceans,

26. Kabir Taneja, "India Arrives at the Arctic", *The New York Times*, May 20, 2013 at http://india.blogs.nytimes.com/2013/05/20/india-arrives-at-the-arctic/?_r=0

- India wants a stake in the Arctic Shelf, home to 10 to 30 percent of the world's undiscovered oil and gas reserves.

Former External Affairs Minister Salman Khurshid, who visited the remote island of Ny Alesund with his Norwegian counterpart, Espen Barth Eide, in 2013, announced that India is in the process of increasing its presence in the Arctic and at Himadri. The Indian and Norwegian delegations also examined other research facilities on the island that has been turned into the world's frontier post for research on the Arctic and houses 180 scientists from more than 10 nations.[27]

For the time being, Indian scientists stay for just 40 days at a stretch and the country's station is only manned during the winters. But that is set to change with New Delhi planning to spend close to $12 million over the next five years to enhance its presence there.

"What happens here has a direct bearing on the Monsoon and countries like India," said Manish Tewari, one of the lead scientists working at Himadri. "The Arctic is changing, ice melt is happening faster than anyone had anticipated, and that means higher sea levels across the world," he added.

But it is not just science that is driving nations to the Arctic. As the ice melt gathers speed, it is also exposing land which had earlier been inaccessible. "There [are] potentially substantial reserves of coal and oil trapped here and [have] sparked new global interest," adds Prasad Rao, lead scientist and PhD scholar at UNIS, the northernmost university on the planet located on the independently-governed island of Longyearbyen situated north of Ny Alesund.[28]

When asked if India was also planning to be part of the 'New Great Game' as several think tanks are calling the increased interest over potential energy resources in the Arctic, former foreign minister Salman Khurshid had said that India was interested in working with other nations in protecting the region.[29]

---

27. *Team Norway Newsletter*, at http://www.norwayemb.org.in/Global/SiteFolders/webdel/Newsletter%20June-Aug%2013.pdf
28. Sidharth Pandey, "India to expand engagement in the Arctic", *NDTV*, June 13, 2013 at http://www.ndtv.com/india-news/india-to-expand-engagement-in-the-arctic-525302
29. Ibid.

However, amongst Indian oil companies' agreements with their Russian counterparts include joint exploration for hydrocarbon resources, including in the Arctic region, and during President Putin's visit to India in 2014, he stated that Russia was ready to export LNG to India with the involvement of ONGC in Arctic projects.[30] Hence, while India's stated objective in the region appears to be more about scientific research, energy too may play a substantial role in its interest in the region.

In a follow-up to Putin's visit in 2014, India and Russia signed a number of agreements during the meeting between President Putin and Prime Minister Narendra Modi during the BRICS meeting in Goa in October 2016. Both countries stated their intent to expand their cooperation in Arctic energy along with other sectors. Around 20 deals were struck, including enhanced cooperation in Russia's Vankor oil project. A consortium of Indian companies, headed by Oil India Ltd, formalised a 23.9 percent acquisition of Vankorneft, the Rosneft-controlled company managing the huge Vankor oil field, located in Russia's northern tundra, to the west of River Yenisey.[31]

A New Great Game?

The Arctic Council is no longer defining itself in geographic terms and has factored in geo-economic elements. The economic rise of China and India is bound to impact on the Arctic region, both through global warming and their widening maritime footprint and interest in the Arctic's vast oil and gas resources.

The melting of the polar ice caps and the opening up of the yet unexplored mineral-rich Arctic frontier to navigation and subsequent exploration has compelled countries such as China and India to look northwards, and to seek observer status in the Council. The quest, however, has been far from smooth, as the Council is divided on whether to open its doors to geographical outsiders. While the Nordic countries were in favour of internationalising the Arctic, Russia and

30. Victor Prevost, "Arctic resources to boost Russia's pivot to Asia", *The Arctic Monitor*, February 4, 2015 at http://thearcticmonitor.org/tag/india/
31. Atle Staalesen, "A role for India in Russian Arctic", *The Independent Barents Observer*, October 18, 2016 at https://thebarentsobserver.com/en/arctic-industry-and-energy/2016/10/role-india-russian-arctic

Canada – which control more territory in the region – were opposed to the move. Interestingly, the Obama Administration did not have a clear stance, although according to some reports, the US was instrumental in brokering a compromise on the decision over the observer countries.[32]

China has aggressively made inroads into the region by approaching individual countries. Iceland has emerged as a partner of choice for China, whether through the ice-breaker *Xue Long* that journeyed from Shanghai to Iceland via the Northern Sea Route along the Russian coast (which cut the shipping time to northern Europe by up to two weeks) or former Chinese premier Wen Jiabao signing Arctic cooperation agreements with Iceland in 2012 and a free trade agreement that was signed between the two a year later, in addition to several commercial agreements with Denmark.[33]

Apart from the Arctic's natural resources and India's interest in shaping policies that would impact on climate change and glacier melting, the Arctic has a strategic relevance to India. China's increasing interest and presence in the Arctic would have implications for Indian strategy. With the opening of the Northern Sea Route, which is referred as the "Arctic Golden Waterway" in the Chinese media, China has an alternate route to its "Malacca syndrome", thereby negating India's strong presence and intervention capabilities in the Indian Ocean, as the Northern Sea Route allows Beijing the possibility of accessing an alternate route for its energy supplies.

A new 'Great Game' may be afoot in the Arctic, and India has now secured a toehold. In an interesting essay on the topic, the convenor of India's National Security Advisory Board and former Indian foreign secretary, Shyam Saran, argued that 'developments in the Arctic Ocean will redraw the geopolitical map of the world'. This, he argued, should compel emerging countries such as India and China to put the Arctic region on their international agenda. He also raised a pertinent

32. Steven Lee Myers, "Arctic Council Adds 6 Nations as Observer States, Including China" *New York Times*, May 15, 2013, http://www.nytimes.com/2013/05/16/world/europe/arctic-council-adds-six-members-including-china.html
33. Arthur Guschin, "China, Iceland and the Arctic", *The Diplomat*, May 20, 2015, http://thediplomat.com/2015/05/china-iceland-and-the-arctic/

question: 'There is currently a shift in the centre of gravity of the global economy from the trans-Atlantic to Asia-Pacific. Will there be a reversal of this shift back to the trans-Atlantic via the Northern Tier?'[34]

This question may well define the future actions of both the permanent members and the new observers of the Arctic Council. While Syed Akbaruddin, the official spokesperson India's Ministry of External Affairs, issued a statement welcoming Arctic Council observer status, 'affirming our commitment to contribute our proven scientific expertise, particularly in polar research capabilities, to the work of the Arctic Council and to support its objectives',[35] India needs to capitalise on the opportunity, and be an active participant in decisions not only on global ecology, but on global political economy and the distribution of political power.

While it is unlikely that the Arctic's energy and mineral resources will contribute to the global energy market till after 2025,[36] it makes economic sense to continue exploration for hydrocarbons in the Arctic, particularly following the recent recovery in oil – and gas – prices in the wake of the November 2016 OPEC deal. However, only those oil companies that have staying power will be able to exploit the Arctic's rich energy potential as exploration and exploitation of oil and natural gas in the region are daunting prospects. No doubt the region is covered in sea ice much of the year, and the environment is tougher than most other places where offshore production is concentrated. Moreover, it requires specialised equipment, including drilling rigs that can withstand rough seas and winds. The drilling season is much shorter and operations are located far away from local ports and airfields, making drilling more expensive. Despite the warming temperatures, exploration and development in the Arctic would still be subject to

34. Shyam Saran, "Why the Arctic Ocean is important to India", *Business Standard*, June 12, 2011 at http://www.business-standard.com/article/opinion/shyam-saran-why-the-arctic-ocean-is-important-to-india-111061200007_1.html
35. "India in Arctic Council with observer status", *Indian Express*, May 16, 2013 at http://archive.indianexpress.com/news/india-in-arctic-council-with-observer-status/1116294/
36. "Opportunities and Challenges for Arctic Oil and Gas Development", Eurasia Group Report for The Wilson Centre, Washington, D.C. January 2014 at http://www.wilsoncenter.org/sites/default/files/Artic%20Report_F2.pdf (accessed on May 22, 2014).

harsh conditions, especially in winter, which makes it costly and challenging to develop infrastructure necessary to produce and transport energy and mineral resources from newly discovered deposits. More importantly, the price of oil – and gas – will be a key factor, as producing in this environment requires the price of oil to be around $100 a barrel to be remunerative.

8

China – The Market Driver

China's phenomenal growth over the last two decades has been driven by a coal-based energy economy, which has not only taken a toll on the environment and placed China at the top of the list of carbon emitters, but has also opened China to international pressure on cutting its emissions. Two months after he took over the presidency in April 2014, at a meeting of China's top finance and economics body, Xi Xinping called for a sweeping energy revolution in China, where linking China's energy security to the country's economic prospects and goals, he focused on five areas: demand, production, technology, institutional governance, and global markets. Interestingly, although he emphasised the need for environmental goals and the deployment of cleaner energy in the country's economic reform policy that had already been stated at the Communist Party's Third Plenum in November 2013, he said that this would require a different approach as the impact of China's energy consumption and production patterns would to a large extent shape international energy and commodity markets. In fact, over the past decade, China's energy consumption has accounted for more than half of the global energy demand growth. As a result, today, it holds the dubious distinction of being the largest carbon emitter, producing a greater share of CO_2 emissions than both the EU and the US, with disastrous consequences on its own environment.

Driven by the need to see and be seen as a responsible power, able and willing to take on the mantle of global leadership, Xi Xinping declared at the Asia-Pacific Economic Cooperation forum that his country intended to achieve the peaking of CO_2 emissions around 2030 and to undertake efforts to peak early. Moreover, in a document to the UNFCC submitted to the UNFCCC ahead for the Paris talks in November 2015 outlining its intended nationally determined contributions and enhanced actions on climate change, China stated that it would aim to cut its greenhouse gas (GHG) emissions per unit of gross domestic product by 60-65 percent from 2005 levels by increasing the share of non-fossil fuels in its primary energy consumption to around 20 percent by 2030. The document, also declared that although by 2014, it had achieved a cut of CO_2 emissions per unit of GDP by 33.8 percent from 2005 levels and had increased the share of non-fossil fuels in primary energy consumption to 11.2 percent, it would, in keeping with its commitment to undertake nationally determined actions by 2030, aim to lower carbon dioxide emissions per unit of GDP by 60-65 percent from the 2005 level and increase the share of non-fossil fuels in primary energy consumption to around 20 percent.[1]

One of the strategies by which China plans to achieve its commitments is to move away from a coal-dominated economy where consumption accounts for around 66 percent of overall energy consumption. The government announced in 2014 that it would cap coal consumption by 2020 to 4.2 billion tonnes which would lead to coal accounting for around 62 percent for the period under consideration.[2] To fill the gap, it would increase the installed capacity of hydropower to 300 GW (2.57 times more than that of 2005); on-grid wind power to 95.81 GW (90 times that of 2005 levels) and installed capacity of solar power to 28.05 GW (400 times that of 2005) and an installed capacity of nuclear power to 19.88 GW (2.9 times more since 2005).[3]

1. "Enhanced Actions on Climate Change: China's intended nationally determined contributions", Department of Climate Change, National development and Reform Commission of China, June 30, 2015 at http://www4.unfccc.int/submissions/INDC/Published%20Documents/China/1/China's%20INDC%20-%20on%2030%20June%202015.pdf
2. Jennifer Duggan, "China makes carbon pledge ahead of Paris climate change summit" *The Guardian*, June 30, 2015 at http://www.theguardian.com/environment/2015/jun/30/china-carbon-emissions-2030-premier-li-keqiang-un-paris-climate-change-summit
3. See note 1.

Interestingly, natural gas, which accounts for only 4 percent of the country's energy demand compared to more than 20 percent globally, was not specified in the document. But as China's economy continued on its upward trajectory, and reports that it had outpaced the US in energy consumption began coming in, there was a lot of optimism from gas producers that with the growth in environmental pollution and the government's policy to cut coal consumption, the demand for natural gas in China would grow, making a significant impact on the gas market. The rationale for this optimism was that since 2010, China's gas consumption has doubled, from 92.5 billion cubic metres (bcm) to 185.5 bcm in 2014.[4] Between 2000-2013, natural gas consumption in China rose nearly seven times between 2000 and 2013 – from 25 bcm per year to 168 bcm per year. Moreover, with China's gas import dependence reaching 32 percent in 2013, compared to just 2 percent in 2006, and China overtaking Iran to become the world's third-largest gas consumer after the US and Russia in 2012. Given that this accounted for only 5.5 percent of overall energy use – among the lowest shares in the world – it was expected that Chinese demand for gas would soon outpace that of most other gas-consuming and importing countries. These expectations were strengthened when in 2009, China surpassed Japan to become the world's third largest natural gas consumer, despite its miniscule share in the country's overall energy basket. Millions of dollars were invested in LNG infrastructure as well as in pipeline projects in gas-rich countries around the world, based on expectations of increased purchases by China.[5] In fact, China National Petroleum Corporation (CNPC) predicted that Chinese gas demand could possibly exceed 230 bcm per year by 2015, and could even reach a figure of 400 bcm per annum by 2020. Finally, with gas accounting for just 4-5 percent of the energy mix, the potential for growth of natural gas is enormous.[6]

4. China's natural gas demand sputters, *Petroleum Economist*, June 18, 2015 at http://www.petroleum-economist.com/Article/3463739/Natural-Gas-and-LNG/Chinas-natural-gas-demand-sputters.html
5. Ibid., *Petroleum Economist* (June 2015).
6. Michael Chen, "The Development of Chinese Gas Pricing: Drivers, Challenges and Implications for Demand", OIES Paper, NG 89, Oxford Institute for Energy Studies, July 2014.

However, over the last 18 months beginning end 2015, the slowdown in China's economy has caused the demand for gas to come down markedly, which casts doubts over the pace of future growth in the country's energy demand. Nonetheless, according to the International Energy Agency's (IEA) 2016 Medium Term Market Report, China will drive the increase in global gas demand till 2021. In a further attempt at encouraging the use of gas, the government has cut price of gas twice in September and November 2015 to stimulate demand and shift the consumption from coal. As a result, LNG imports in 2016 increased by 33 percent as compared to the year before, higher that the 30 percent forecast by some independent analysts and rose even higher in early 2017, partly in tandem with the policy increase gas usage to 10 percent of the energy mix by 2020, and partly as its domestic production stagnated. According to some analysts, by the end of the decade, China's gas imports, both by sea and through pipelines, may account for about 40 percent of the China's gas use, up from around a third in 2016.[7] However, with China delaying the fourth phase of its Central Asian Gas Pipeline, pipeline imports may be slowed down as domestic production showed an increase. According to forecasts from its National Energy Administration, China is aiming to increase production, including from shale, to 170 bcm, up from 137 bcm in 2016.[8]

China's Gas Procurement Strategy

Given its growing dependence on imports, China's gas procurement strategy is primarily based on three pillars, which are tuned to reduce its concerns and vulnerability on growing dependence on international markets and supply disruptions, including potential embargoes. Based essentially on the principle of diversification, these include the acquisition of overseas gas (and oil) blocks, including in countries that had inimical relations with Western countries; building strategic ties

7. China's Swapping Energy Independence for Cleaner Air", Bloomberg, January 11, 2017 at https://www.bloomberg.com/news/articles/2017-01-10/smog-choked-china-swapping-energy-independence-for-cleaner-air
8. China's 2017 natural gas output to jump to 170 bcm - energy agency, ET Energy World, February 17, 2017, http://energy.economictimes.indiatimes.com/news/oil-and-gas/chinas-2017-natural-gas-output-to-jump-to-170-bcm-energy-agency/57208375

with gas-rich countries and constructing pipelines from these sources, such as Myanmar, Central Asian Republics and Russia, which would not only lead to more integration with the Chinese market but would also ensure that China was not dependent on shipping energy through sea lanes that were dominated by rival powers. The energy component of China's 'The Belt and Road' (OBOR) initiative that was launched in 2013 by President Xi Jinping is also a recent initiative of this pillar, which aims to transform China's international energy policy by strengthening energy cooperation with energy supplying countries along the route in the long term; and developing its domestic gas reserves – including shale gas reserves – to reduce its dependence on imports.

Overseas Asset Acquisitions

China's distrust of world markets it perceives as being dominated, indeed controlled by Western powers through the international oil companies, and the resultant price distortions, has given rise to a policy wherein Beijing does not want to rely on the world energy market. At the same time, China is also against placing its energy imports in danger of being disrupted at sea through SLOCs that are controlled by the US Navy and allied countries. Given that 80 percent of its trade passes through the chokepoint of the Strait of Malacca, the concern, however tenuous, is that in the event of a conflict over Taiwan would render its energy imports vulnerable. As a result, China prefers to own or gain control over its energy resources as much as possible. As a result, China chose to acquire overseas oil and gas fields under what is known as its "Going-Out" strategy, which was the brainchild of former President Jiang Zemin, and at the time, ranked second among the 10 strategies of Beijing's "21st Century Oil Strategy". Moreover, apart from strategic issues, it also conformed with the commercial goals of Chinese national oil companies (NOCs), namely, China National Petroleum Corporation (CNPC), China National Offshore Oil Corporation (CNOOC) and China Petroleum & Chemical Corporation, more commonly known as Sinopec, as compared to domestic production costs, many of its overseas acquisitions were more cost-effective and allowed the companies to build up reserves at a cheaper price. With the government's active support, Chinese NOCs spread out all over the world, buying oil and gas assets in Africa, Central Asia, West Asia, Latin America and North America (Canada). Much of the Chinese NOCs' success was the result of the government's assistance and support which not only saw high level visits by Chinese political leaders, but also access to loans to target governments in the form of soft loans, as well as diplomatic support in the UN, military aid and infrastructure projects.[9]

As a result, since the mid-1990s, Chinese NOCs have successfully concluded a series of multi-billion dollar transactions which apart from buying oil and gas blocks, also included takeovers of publicly-listed companies, joint ventures with other IOCs for the development of deep water blocks and unconventional shale plays in North America and LNG liquefaction and export projects in Australia, North America and Africa. However, by the end of 2012, while it was expected that the acquisition policy will continue, there was a shift in strategy. Chinese NOCs were now focusing more on efficiency and return on investments as against the earlier strategy of acquiring volumes. Hence, the companies were expected to become more selective and strategic in the deals they chose to pursue in future.[10]

Pipeline Strategy

China's main gas demand is in the coastal areas. Owing to advantages in terms of transportation, pipeline gas is undoubtedly the first choice for gas imports. Central Asian countries are the largest source of pipeline gas imports for China. Turkmenistan alone supplied 46.48 percent of China's gas imports in 2013. With completion of other projects, Central Asian countries will supply even more gas to China.

Hence in 2002, the government began construction of the West-East Gas Pipeline in 2002 which has three phases. The first phase was to meet demand in the eastern and southern regions of the country with production from its western provinces of Tarim, Qaidam, and Ordos,

9. Margaret Ng Wing-Chu, "University China's overseas Oilfield Acquisition Strategy and its Implications", Reuters Fellowship Paper, Oxford, 2007 at https://reutersinstitute.politics.ox.ac.uk/sites/default/files/China's%20 Overseas%20Oilfield%20Aquisition%20Strategy%20-%20And%20its%20Implications.pdf
10. David Blumental, "The changing nature of China's global oil and gas deals", *China Economic Review*, August 8, 2014 at http://www.chinaeconomicreview.com/china-global-oil-gas-mergers-acquisitions-strategic-partners

as well as from imports from the Central Asian countries and was commissioned in 2004. The second tranche of the West-East trunk pipeline was to connect with the Central Asian Gas Pipeline carrying gas from Turkmenistan, Uzbekistan and Kazakhstan to the border in western China and supplemented with supplies of CNG from Xinjiang province. It was completed in 2011, connecting it to the key demand centres in the south-eastern provinces. The third phase, which was to supply gas to the western provinces, was launched in 2014 and was also fed by imports from Central Asia. Proposals for the fourth and fifth West-East Pipelines are still in the planning stages.

The majority of China's Central Asian gas imports come from Turkmenistan. According to Ashirguly Begliyev, Chairman of the state-owned company, Turkmengaz, by 2030 Turkmenistan plans to increase exports from 45 to 180 bcm per year, with China being the main market.[11]

In 2010, an agreement was signed with Uzbekistan to deliver 350 bcf per year, and it has also signed an agreement with Kazakhstan for the same. In fact, Kazakhstan plans to increase its supplies to China to 4.7 bcm per year once production of associated gas from its Kashagan oil field is increased.[12]

In fact, pipeline imports exceeded LNG imports from 2012, with Central Asian supplies forming a key factor in its larger regional strategy of greater integration with Chinese markets, which in turn is linked with Silk Road strategy of strengthening ties with Europe.

Recently, however, there are reports that China has delayed, or even suspended the fourth phase – Line D – of the Central Asian Gas Pipeline project, giving a blow to Uzbek and Kazakh export plans and transit fees for Tajikistan and Kyrgyzstan. It may also have contributed to Turkmenistan's new found interest in pursuing the South Asian and

---

11. Alexander Shustov, "Why China will remain Turkmenistan's main gas buyer", Russia Beyond the Headlines (RBTH), January 26, 2017, http://rbth.com/business/2017/01/26/why-china-will-remain-turkmenistans-main-gas-buyer_689386http://rbth.com/business/2017/01/26/why-china-will-remain-turkmenistans-main-gas-buyer_689386
12. Kazakhs boost flows for own gas to China Natural Gas World, November 30, 2016 http://www.naturalgasworld.com/kazakh-gas-to-flow-to-china-34676

European gas export projects, as prospects of increasing gas exports to China even further are now in doubt.

However, although China may increase its Central Asian gas imports in the future in line with its diversification of supplies strategy, it is also importing gas from Myanmar, and has signed an agreement with Russia. However, the China-Myanmar gas pipeline plays only a supplementary role in China's total natural gas import strategy. With the pipeline which was started in 2010 commencing operations in 2013, it was built with the purpose of serving mainly the south-western Chinese provinces, and at its full capacity could transport 12 bcm of gas from Myanmar's offshore gas fields every year, accounting for about 6 percent of China's annual gas consumption. However, China imported only 1.87 bcm through the pipeline in its first year of operation. The 793 km pipeline links the Myanmar port of Kyaukpyu with the Chinese city of Kunming in Yunan province. However, opposition in Myanmar centring around the fact that the local population will be deprived of these resources heading to China through their territory, thereby depriving Myanmar of any gains from this potentially valuable resources, has constricted the value and potential of the pipelines. Recently, there were reports that the flow of gas through one section of the pipeline in Yunan Province had to be turned off after it started leaking, although what caused the leakage is unclear.

At the end of June 2015, China began construction of the pipeline which is slated to import 38 bcm of natural gas from Siberia from 2018 every year over 30 years. Called the "Power of Siberia", the deal which was signed in May 2014 between Russia's state-owned energy giant Gazprom and its Chinese counterpart CNPC after months of negotiations, made headlines. Then, in November 2014, the two countries signed another agreement, known as the Altai agreement, which albeit non-binding, envisages supplying China with 30 bcm of gas for 30 years, which could commence from 2020.[13] (see Map 8.1)

13. Keun-Wook Paik, "Sino-Russian Gas and Oil Cooperation: Entering into a New Era of Strategic Partnership?", OIES Paper, WPM 59, Oxford Institute for Energy Studies, April 2015 at http://www.oxfordenergy.org/wpcms/wp-content/uploads/2015/04/WPM-59.pdf

Map 8.1

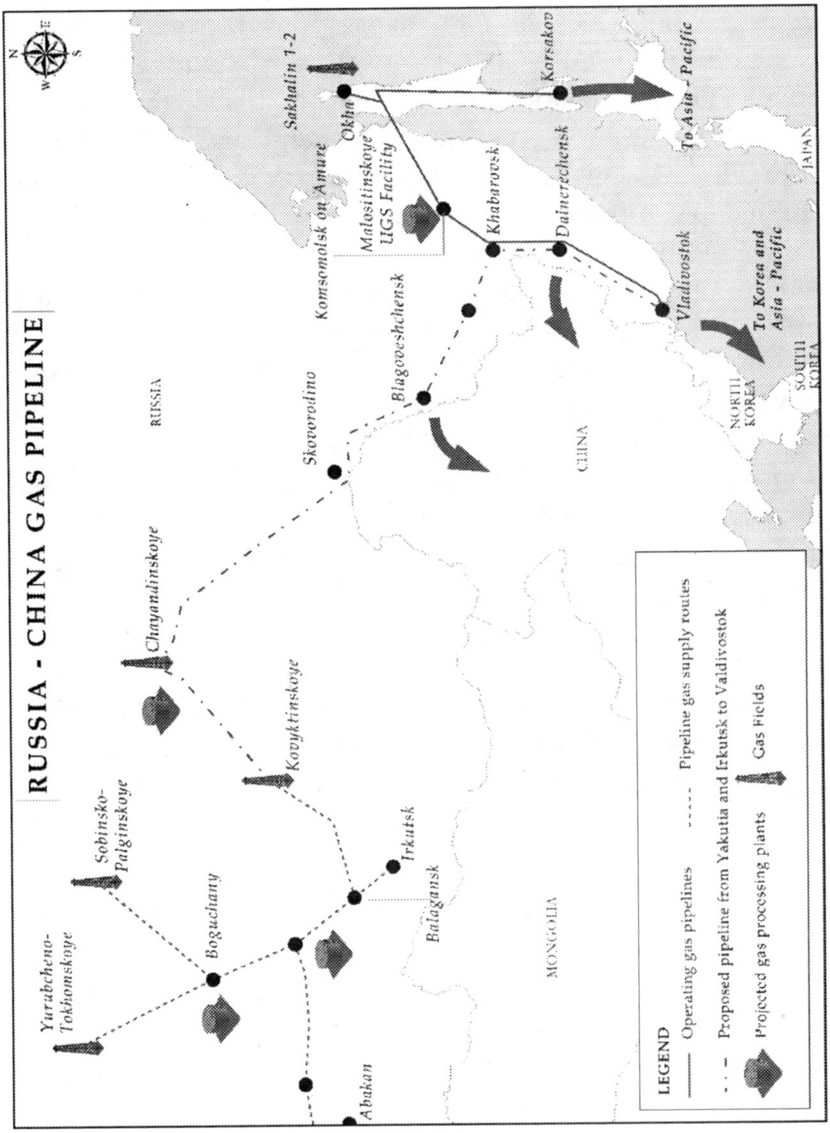
RUSSIA - CHINA GAS PIPELINE
Yurubcheno-Tokhomskoye
Sobinsko-Palginskoye
Boguchany
Kovyktinskoye
Chayandinskoye
Irkutsk
Balagansk
Abakan
Skovorodino
Blagoveshchensk
Komsomolsk on Amure
Malositinskoye UGS Facility
Sakhalin 1-2
Okha
Khabarovsk
Dalnerechensk
Korsakov
Vladivostok
To Asia - Pacific
To Korea and Asia - Pacific
RUSSIA
CHINA
MONGOLIA
NORTH KOREA
SOUTH KOREA
JAPAN
LEGEND
Operating gas pipelines
Proposed pipeline from Yakutia and Irkutsk to Valdivostok
Projected gas processing plants
Pipeline gas supply routes
Gas Fields

The two agreements were seen as path-breaking for a variety of reasons. First, the sheer cost of the $400 billion 400 km long project was seen as path-breaking, not only for the price but also as one of the biggest geo-strategic tools for both countries. The first deal, signed just two months after Russia's annexation of Crimea from Ukraine provoked a confrontation with Europe and the US that culminated in sanctions being imposed on Russia's energy and financial industries, it provided Moscow with the critical energy diversification strategy it required to compensate for the expected reduction in its European gas market and provided it with much needed finances. Secondly, if both deals go through, it could remove the possibility of any sizeable LNG supply to China and will establish Russia as a swing supplier between Asia and Europe, protecting Russia from competition from other LNG supplies to China. Third, it will to a large extent, put China's coal-reduction dilemma to rest by enhancing gas supplies; thereby ensuring its energy security, while at the same time allowing it to circumvent sea-based imports. At the same time, it also allowed Chinese companies to renegotiate the price of gas from Turkmenistan to its advantage by introducing another supply option.

LNG Imports

Since the first LNG terminal in Guangdong Province started operation in 2006, China's LNG imports have expanded to just under 20 million tonnes a year, about 15 percent of China's total annual gas consumption in 2014.

From the early 2000s, China launched into a LNG expansion drive, taking advantage of cheap supply deals of $3-4 per mm Btu with Australia and Indonesia. Since then, China has built 12 LNG import terminals, with 13 more terminals planned which, if successful, will take China's import capacity to 110 mt per year, with a total annual receiving capacity of around 38.4 million tonnes. As a result, there has been a steady expansion of LNG imports.

This is a far cry from China's gas scenario in 2015. Due to the slowdown in the economy, the expected switch to gas from coal had not been as quick as anticipated, mainly because of low demand, a result of lower industrial activity and power consumption. In fact, from September 2015, China had raised the price of natural gas for nonresidential users by 20.5 percent, in order to stimulate domestic exploration and production. Moreover, with coal prices at an all-time low, some power stations and petrochemical factories had begun reverting back to coal, despite the government's policy of encouraging cleaner fuels to cut pollution and emissions. As a result, although piped gas imports remained robust, LNG shipments had slowed down.

With respect to LNG, the biggest factor in China's loss of appetite was the price at the time. Although China bought LNG from other countries, Qatar was the largest source of LNG. As a result, in 2014, LNG imports from Qatar in 2014 were down by nearly 5 percent from a year ago, the first major contraction since 2006.[14]

LNG imports were also eroded by the pipeline deals signed with the Central Asian Republics (CARs), particularly Turkmenistan, and Russia. Moreover, with high domestic prices, China prefers to import gas through pipeline deals as against the more expensive LNG, which ranged between $3-4/mmBtu from low-end Pacific sources like Australia and Indonesia and the high-end West Asian sources like Qatar, priced between 9-12/mmBtu in 2014-15. Hence, Chinese pipeline imports saw a rise of 41.3 percent in March 2015 from a year ago.[15] Moreover, given that LNG contract pricing lags behind spot prices by around six months, the lower LNG prices only began making a difference from the second half of 2015. As a result, China's expected LNG expansion slowed down till early 2016, mainly due to the high import costs. Moreover, the economic slowdown also had an impact on demand as gas imports required a price that was acceptable to customers. According to some analysts, however, the landmark deal with Russia was expected to have a profound impact on the global gas market with the potential to create a new price benchmark that would put pricing pressures on other producers. The deal was reportedly priced at around $12/mmBtu as against a price of $14-15/mmBtu for Asia-Pacific imports LNG at the time the deal was signed

14. Colin Shek, "China's gas-import slowdown threatens LNG producers", *Al Jazeera*, June 2, 2015 at http://www.aljazeera.com/indepth/features/2015/06/china-gas-import-slowdown-threatens-lng-producers-150602104833809.html
15. "China's March natural gas pipeline imports rise 41.3% on year to 2.73 Bcm", Platts, April 23, 2015 at http://www.platts.com/latest-news/natural-gas/singapore/chinas-march-natural-gas-pipeline-imports-rise-26072059

in 2014, close to what most of Europe paid under discounted long-term contracts.[16] Nonetheless Chinese gas imports will, to a large extent, be contingent on domestic production, pricing as well as the direction of China's shale gas sector.

China's Shale Gas Policy

Much of China's recent scaling-down of natural gas imports has been due to the government's decision, in the face of the economic slowdown, to focus on developing domestic resources of gas, including its shale gas reserves. Following the success of the US shale resource sector, China had initially begun looking closely at developing its vast shale gas reserves. In 2012, the Ministry of Land and Resources said China has estimated shale gas reserves of 134 tcm, of which 25 tcm was recoverable. The US Energy Information Administration (EIA) 2013 on the other hand estimates however state that China's technically recoverable shale gas reserves total 1,211 tcf (34.3 tcm), double that of the US, and the largest in the world,[17] with the majority of the reserves being concentrated in three basins, viz., Sichuan, Tarim and Yangtze Platform, which together account for 89 percent of the estimated national reserves. (see Map 8.2)

In 2012, the government announced a plan to produce 60-100 bcm of shale gas by 2020 with the government taking on an active role in promoting shale gas development, by providing an attractive fiscal climate which included an upward revision of natural gas pricing and pipeline transportation and opening up of the sector. However, by the end of 2014, after two bidding rounds were held, the first in 2011, the 60-100 bcm target had been scaled down to half, that is, to 30 bcm. Meanwhile, progress was slower than expected as many of the winners of the bid lacked exploration experience. In fact, most of the shale gas R&D activities in the first two rounds were carried out by Chinese

16. Carolyn Davis, "Russia-China Natural Gas Pipeline to Create New Global Price Benchmark, Say Analysts", Natural Gas Intel, May 23, 2014 at http://www.naturalgasintel.com/articles/98478-russia-china-natural-gas-pipeline-to-create-new-global-price-benchmark-say-analysts
17. Technically Recoverable Shale Oil and Shale Gas Resources: China, Energy Information Administration, US Department of Energy, September 2015, https://www.eia.gov/analysis/studies/worldshalegas/pdf/China_2013.pdf

Map 8.2

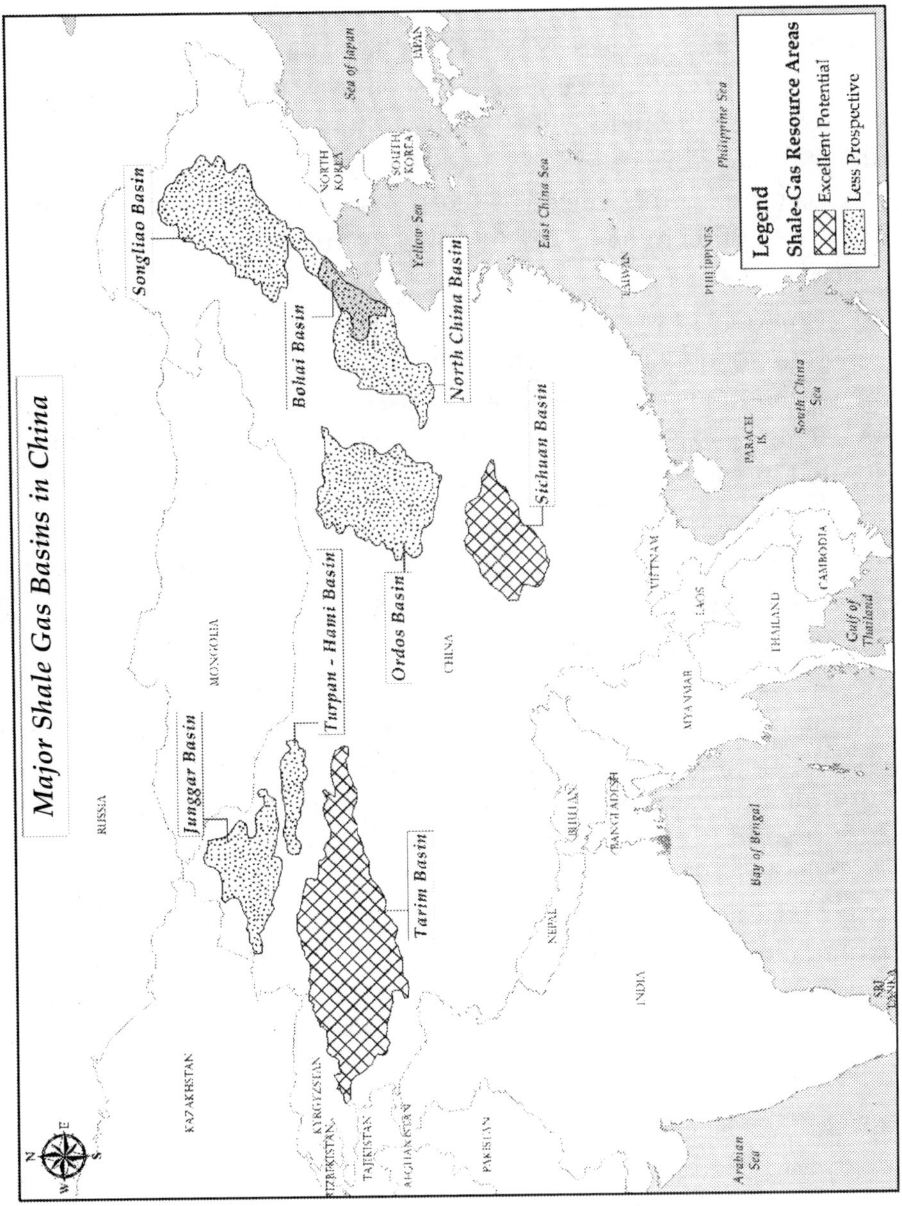
Major Shale Gas Basins in China
Songliao Basin
Bohai Basin
North China Basin
Sichuan Basin
Ordos Basin
Turpan - Hami Basin
Junggar Basin
Tarim Basin
Legend
Shale-Gas Resource Areas
Excellent Potential
Less Prospective
RUSSIA
MONGOLIA
CHINA
KAZAKHSTAN
KYRGYZSTAN
TAJIKISTAN
AFGHANISTAN
PAKISTAN
INDIA
NEPAL
BHUTAN
BANGLADESH
MYANMAR
LAOS
VIETNAM
THAILAND
CAMBODIA
NORTH KOREA
SOUTH KOREA
JAPAN
TAIWAN
PHILIPPINES
PARACEL IS.
Sea of Japan
Yellow Sea
East China Sea
Philippine Sea
South China Sea
Gulf of Thailand
Bay of Bengal
Arabian Sea
SRI LANKA

NOCs, like CNPC and Sinopec, as foreign companies were not allowed to bid in the first two rounds, although they were encouraged to enter into joint ventures with state-owned companies and share their technology and services. Most of the companies, however, did not have the requisite experience and knowledge with respect to shale E&P technology, although China claims to have the requisite technology for shale gas development. Several Chinese companies had even been exporting their machinery to the US shale industry, despite the fact that none of them have the full range of equipment required for such activities.

Moreover, the blocks that were offered were generally considered to be of poor quality and in difficult terrain, many of them being located in mountainous rocky desert and buried deep underground, resulting in extensive expenditure. Also, many of the country's shale fields are located in water-scarce areas, which makes the process more difficult.

Apart from upstream impediments to the development of shale gas in China, downstream hurdles such as the lack of adequate pipeline network impedes transportation and supply of resources.[18]

Despite these problems, China however came close to meeting the revised target for shale gas production in 2014, producing 1.3 bcm, compared with a goal of 1.5 bcm, although nearly 90 percent of it came from a single field, the Fuling block in south-western Chongqing municipality, being developed by Sinopec, with some 200 mcm being produced from 40 wells drilled by CNPC.[19] Recent reports have painted an even brighter picture. In September 2016, CNPC signed a second production sharing contract (PSC) with BP PLC for shale gas exploration, development and production in the Sichuan basin, the first having been signed in March 2016. BP's 2016 Energy Outlook in fact expects that by 2035, China will become the world's largest contributor to growth in shale gas production.[20]

18. Sophia Sun, "Shale Gas development in China", *Alberta*, at http://www.albertacanada.com/china/documents/ShaleGasDevelopmentInChina.pdf
19. Wang Zhongmin, "China's Elusive Shale Gas Boom", *Caixin Online*, July 4, 2015 at http://english.caixin.com/2015-04-06/100797698.html
20. "BP, CNPC sign second Chinese shale gas PSC", *Oil & Gas Journal*, September 1, 2016, http://www.ogj.com/articles/2016/09/bp-cnpc-sign-second-chinese-shale-gas-psc.html

Offshore Disputes

The South China Sea

Although a large part of its energy security policy is focused on acquiring offshore assets, enhancing domestic production and purchasing oil and gas, China is also seeking to expand its claim over territory in its near abroad that is expected to be rich in energy resources. This has, in turn seen it involved in numerous territorial disputes in its neighbourhood with rival claimants. At the top of the list is the South China Sea (SCS), which according to the US EIA, could be holding around 11 billion barrels of oil and 190 tcf of natural gas. On the other hand, China's state-owned company Chinese National Offshore Oil Company puts the number at 125 billion barrels of oil and 500 tcf in undiscovered resources.

At the same time, the SCS, being also bordered by Vietnam, Philippines, Taiwan, Brunei, Malaysia and Indonesia, is also significant to international shipping with a third of the global shipping passing through it each year, and more importantly, the Strait of Malacca and the Lombok Strait located in these waters, through which 80 percent of the total energy trade of the littoral states of China, Taiwan, Japan and South Korea traverses. Moreover, it possesses a large number of islands having strategic, legal, political and financial worth for the regional and international powers.

While the sea's strategic location makes it invaluable for China, the presence of the hydrocarbon and marine resources have intensified the competition towards claiming sovereignty over these resources, to a point where localised tensions have often evolved into larger conflicts between China on the one hand and one or more regional states, each claiming rights over the sea and islands therein. China claims its right on almost the entire SCS region where its claims rest on the historical nine-dash line, which include the Spratly Islands, Gulf of Tonkin, Hainan Islands and the Paracel Islands, and has established bases with a wide array of advanced equipment on some of these islands. In the recent past, the disputes have often been exacerbated by the presence of the US in the region to strengthen its alliance partners.[21]

21. Hafsa Khalid, "Pivot to Asia: US Strategy to Contain China or to Rebalance Asia?", *The Washington Review of Turkish and Eurasian Affairs*, February 2015 at http://www.thewashingtonreview.org/articles/pivot-to-asia-us-strategy-to-contain-china-or-to-rebalance-asia.html

East China Sea

Similarly, China has also accelerated its search for natural resources in the East China Sea in recent years, which, according to the EIA, holds between 1-2 tcf of natural gas reserves, with the Japanese government stating that it had installed 12 offshore platforms, mainly gas structures, in the area since 2012, and accusing Beijing of abrogating the June 2008 agreement wherein the two countries had stated that they would cooperate on the development of natural resources in the Sea. However, China resumed exploration in the East China Sea in 2013 after the Japanese government bought a disputed island chain from private owners, angering Beijing, although China's Foreign Ministry said its drilling activities were in waters which are were not disputed and were therefore legal.[22]

Strategising Supplies

While all the above strategies point to the intention of the government to ensure access to sufficient gas supplies to facilitate the transition from a coal-based economy to cleaner fuels, wherein gas plays an important role, the policy however failed in ensuring a synergy between the external strategies and domestic energy policy. As a result, today, China may be facing a glut in gas supply due to lower-than-expected demand. An important factor is China's economic slowdown. At the start of 2015, China's economic growth slowed to its lowest at 7 percent in the first quarter, down from 7.3 percent in the last quarter of 2014. More importantly, some key sectors displayed weakness, setting off concerns that the economy could be losing momentum. One indicator of this slowdown was that the output for electricity fell by 3.7 percent in March, the biggest since the 2008 financial crisis.[23]

But the main driver for the fall in gas demand is the National Development and Reform Commission's (NDRC) – the powerful

---

22. Philip Wen, "Japan finds China's expansion in East China Sea 'extremely regrettable'", *Sunday Morning Herald*, July 23, 2015 at http://www.smh.com.au/world/japan-finds-chinas-expansion-in-east-china-sea-extremely-regrettable-20150723-giiowk.html
23. Kevin Yao and KohGui Qing, "China growth slowest in six years, more stimulus expected soon", Reuters, April 15, 2015 at http://www.reuters.com/article/2015/04/15/us-china-economy-gdp-idUSKBN0N52E220150415

economic planning organisation – decision to increase gas prices to bring them in line with international gas prices, in order to attract investments in domestic gas development as well as to minimise losses on gas imports by the national oil companies, and encourage them to bring more gas into the country. However, the increased domestic price of gas proved to be a deterrent for industry as well as the power producers, who were already struggling due to a slowing economy and falling demand for power in general.[24]

Nevertheless, despite the slowdown and possible reduction in consumption of energy in some sectors, the outlook on gas is expected to remain positive, given the low penetration of natural gas in the economy, where even modest amounts of fuel switching to gas in the power sector and the transport sector would be sufficient for significant growth in consumption in the years ahead. Nonetheless, in order for China to attain its goal of lowering carbon emissions and pollution, which in turn would require access to more gas supplies, it would require to implement relevant policy reforms, particularly in the area of gas pricing. Currently, gas pricing in China is fragmented, with imported LNG being indexed to oil, while imported pipeline gas is subject to the government-prescribed price. This has led to distortions between domestically-produced gas price and imported gas price. The problem has been exacerbated as currently LNG imports far outweigh domestic demand.

At the same time, if the reforms being planned do succeed, and the demand for gas increases, supply may fall short of demand, despite the fact that China has substantial conventional and unconventional gas reserves. China will therefore have to fill the demand-supply gap through imports, which may have economic consequences, particularly at a time when the economy is showing signs of slowing. Hence, the stability and economic efficiency, of natural gas supply are very important in safeguarding China's energy security, particularly in an environment where the domestic price is lower than the purchase price. To ensure "stability" wherein supply can meet the demand and respond quickly to a sudden change in supply-demand balance, the

24. Justin Jacobs, "China's natural gas demand sputters", *Petroleum Economist*, July/ August 2015, p. 23.

setting up of a natural gas trading hub would allow the establishment of a gas price mechanism which would China's leverage in pricing power for natural gas imports in the gas market. While several Asian countries are looking at setting up an Asian gas trading hub, several Chinese analysts are advocating that it should be established in China.

How China deals with its energy issues will have an impact that will resonate far beyond its borders. While China's consumption of energy may set off a competitive race with other large consuming nations to secure supplies with, it is not only how much China consumes which will affect geopolitics, but also the strategies it employs to get its supplies. For example, China uses energy deals to establish or strengthen strategic partnerships for larger geopolitical goals, the recent deals with Russia and the Central Asian countries being a case in point. At the same time, these deals have the potential to have implications for the larger global gas market, and may change the current LNG pricing mechanism. Moreover, with the US switching its role from an energy importer to an exporter, it may have implications for its strategic and military ties with energy exporting countries, as they may now seek security in strengthening energy-based strategic ties with China, the largest energy market.

Hence, while China's rise is closely linked with its energy security, the rest of the world's energy security may well be determined by China's rise and the policies and strategies it employs to ensure its energy security.

9

INDIA – A LEGACY OF WASTED OPPORTUNITIES

With a huge and growing population, low per capita consumption but rapid industrialisation under the current government's 'Make in India' initiative, India is being seen as the energy market with the most promise. The International Energy Agency's (IEA) 2011 *World Energy Outlook Report* had in fact projected that India's demand for gas would increase incrementally by 6.5 percent per annum between 2008 and 2035.[1] More recently, BP's 2015 *Statistical Review of World Energy Markets* showed this figure to grow at a rate of 7.1 percent, which was higher than China's, whose demand had fallen to a 2.6 percent rate of growth in energy demand. At the same time, the government's Intended Nationally Determined Contribution Pledge of cutting carbon emissions by 33 to 35 percent by 2030 from 2005 levels, presents it with the dilemma to deliver sufficient clean energy at appropriate prices for different social segments, from the very rich to the very poor. Although Prime Minister Narendra Modi's penchant for renewable energy is well known – and considerable focus of the government's energy policy *is* on ramping up clean energy, notably solar, the latter cannot deliver the volumes required to meet the escalating demand.

Many saw natural gas as a means to enhance India's energy

1. "Are we entering a Golden Age of Gas", *World Energy Outlook*, Special Report, International Energy Agency 2011 at http://www.worldenergyoutlook.org/media/weowebsite/2011/WEO2011_GoldenAgeofGasReport.pdf

security, particularly following the post-2014 price drop and increased global supplies due to the US shale gas bonanza. In fact, the government even announced that henceforth, India's economy would be gas-based, with the share of gas in its energy basket rising from the current 6-7 percent to 15 percent by 2022, bringing hope and cheer to the beleaguered global gas industry.[2] The government also announced plans to double its LNG import terminal capacity over the next six years to 47.5 million tonnes from the current 21.3 m.t.

At the same time, the government is also a partner in the four-nation project known as the TAPI project, which envisages bringing gas from Turkmenistan; it is also in negotiations with several other countries, including Russia, Iran, Oman and Myanmar for more piped gas. Clearly therefore, natural gas is high on India's energy agenda on the grounds that it has the potential to replace coal and oil as a bridge or transition fuel to the government's goal of bringing about a renewable energy revolution by 2050.

However, several challenges will have to be addressed, most of which emanate from the ambiguities and lack of planning which continue to plague the domestic gas sector.

Challenges for India's Gas Sector

According to official estimates, India's proven natural gas reserves are around 1.4 trillion cubic metres (tcm), which comprises only 0.7 percent of global gas reserves. Hence, India cannot be described as a 'gas rich' country. Nevertheless, with 17 percent, that is around 1.4 billion of the world's population, its potential as an important and growing player on the international gas market has generated a lot of interest, given that demand in the traditional gas markets is slowing down. Together with China, demand for gas in these two countries is projected to grow from 11 percent in 2012 to 24 percent in 2035. However, according to estimates, India's share of the total world gas demand will grow to only 7 percent from the current 4 percent, as against China, which till the recent economic slowdown was expected to grow to 18 percent

2. Nidhi Varmaand Douglas Busvine, "India to gradually move to gas-based economy, Dharmendra Pradhan says", *Reuters*, May 6, 2016 at http://in.reuters.com/article/india-energy-economy-idINKCN0XX0PQ

from the current 8 percent as a percentage of world demand. The proportion of gas in India's domestic primary energy consumption was till recently expected to rise from 7 to 9 per cent, with coal and oil, at 44 percent and 25 percent respectively, remaining the preferred fuels, by 2035.[3]

Several factors will have to be taken into consideration for the modest projections for gas before gas can begin to compete with other fuels and in fact to ensure the growth of the gas sector. A look at the challenges that the gas sector is faced with is akin to a Catch-22 situation.

A Curious Pricing Regime

In the past, a major factor that has restricted the penetration of gas in the economy has been the high price of imported gas. Gas pricing in India follows a unique formula. Domestically produced gas price is based on the weighted average price of four global benchmarks, viz., the US-based Henry Hub, Canada-based Alberta Gas, the UK-based National Balancing Point or NBP, and Russian gas, and is based on the benchmark prices in the previous year and comes into force after a quarter's lag for a period of six months. For example, the price that would be applicable from April to September 2015, would be based on benchmark prices from January to December 2014.[4]

In 2002, following the discovery of large reserves of gas in the Krishna Godavari D-6 basin in India's eastern offshore basin by Reliance Industries Ltd (RIL), estimated at the time to hold around 10 tcf (0.283 tcm) of gas, raised expectations that it had the potential to change India's energy fortunes. Initially production, which commenced in 2009, was around 60 mmscmd, but soon after began falling and finally came down to less than 15 mmscmd. RIL attributed the fall on the geological complexity of the acreage; on the other hand, the government claimed that the company was not drilling enough wells,

3. Anupama Sen, "India's 'gas renaissance' – Rhetoric versus Reality", *Forum*, Issue 99, Oxford Institute for Energy Studies, February 2015, p.25.
4. Anand Kalyanaraman, "All you wanted to know about: Gas Pricing Formula", *The Hindu Business Line*, April 6, 2015 at http://www.thehindubusinessline.com/opinion/columns/all-you-wanted-to-know-about-gas-pricing-formula/article7074268.ece

and was waiting for the domestic price of gas to be increased, as RIL had taken the lead in demanding for market-linked pricing for gas.

Prior to the discovery, between 1997 and 2005, various committees had been appointed to work out an effective pricing mechanism for gas, which saw prices being increased a few times, although well below the cost of production. As a result. The state-owned companies and the government had been taking on the burden of the subsidies. It was only in May 2010 that the then UPA government decided to increase prices from $1.7/mmBtu to $4.2/mmBtu. However, the price increase was carried out only on the upstream side. Moreover, till 2013, gas produced by state-owned companies was priced between $2.52-4.2/ mmBtu, while the price charged by privately-owned firms was between $4.2-5.25/mmBtu.

This dual pricing mechanism also prevailed in the case of LNG imports, which commenced in 2004 to meet growing shortfall in domestic production. While LNG imports from Qatar were based on long-term contracts, prices of imports from other suppliers like Oman, Nigeria, Algeria, Australia, Trinidad and Tobago, Egypt, Malaysia, etc, were based on the prevailing spot prices. Cargoes from Qatar, which were linked to JCC crude oil prices under an agreed formula, were fixed at $2.53/mmBtu till 2008, which translated to a re-gasified price of $3.63/mmBtu ex-terminal, while those procured from the spot market were far higher, that is, between the range of $-29/mmBtu.[5]

In order to encourage domestic production, the Rangarajan Committee was set up to review gas pricing in the country. In its report which was submitted in December 2012, the Committee recommended that the price of domestically produced gas be raised to $8.4 mmBtu as the existing price was not sufficiently remunerative to encourage domestic production. Since India's dependence on gas was expected to rise over time, the rationale was that if prices were not competitive, it would not incentivise investment in domestic production; on the contrary it would lead to an increased dependence on imports.

5. Kamlesh Trivedi, "Indian Spot LNG Trade: How Indian Buyers Set New Ceiling for Spot LNG Price in 2008 and Emerging Trends for 2009, *The Energy Exchange*, 2008 at http://core.theenergyexchange.co.uk/agile_assets/725/TRIVEDI_GAS_MATTERS.pdf

However, imports continued to rise and in fact rose sharply to reach 15.2 bcm by 2011, as against 0.34 bcm in 2004. On the other hand, production, which was at 27.9 bcm in 2000, and had risen to 52.2 bcm in 2010-11, had fallen to 47.6 bcm in 2011-12. Hence, the revised price would benefit producers across the board.[6]

Nevertheless, the recommendation came in for a lot of opposition from the power and fertiliser sectors, which were the largest sectoral consumers, as every dollar increase in the price would increase their input costs by as much as Rs.3,000-4,000 crore a year for urea producers and as much as Rs.10,000 crore on gas-based electricity generation generating units, due to the highly subsidised rates at which they had to sell their resources.[7] It would also lead to an increase in the government's subsidy bill.

In June 2013, the government, accepting the Rangarajan Committee's recommendations, agreed to raise gas prices to $8.4/mmBtu, effective April 1, 2014. However, the new prices never did come into effect as the Election Commission deferred the notification till the completion of 2014 Lok Sabha Elections. Since the UPA had lost the elections, the new BJP-led NDA government decided that the whole issue of gas pricing needed to be re-examined and directed that the guidelines be kept in abeyance till 30 September, 2014, and that domestically produced gas should continue to be priced at the prevailing rate as on March 31, 2014,[8] that is, at $4.2 per mmBtu. Then, as global gas prices continued to fall, domestically produced gas prices were once again cut by a further 18 percent in September 2016, to $2.50 per mmBtu for the period October to March 2017. The low prices prevailing in the domestic market as well as subsidies in retail pricing of gas-based fertilisers, led to international oil and gas companies either exiting from the upstream or not bidding for exploration and production (E&P) contracts under the NELP scheme.

While domestic gas prices were being cut, the price of the

6. C.P. Chandrasekhar, "Cost of reliance on gas", *Frontline*, July 12, 2013 at http://www.frontline.in/columns/C_P_Chandrasekhar/cost-of-reliance-on-gas/article4840199.ece
7. Ibid.
8. *Report on Committee on Gas Pricing- 2014* at http://petroleum.nic.in/docs/committee_report_on_gas_pricing_2014.pdf

contracted deliveries of LNG into India continued to rule, drawing a much higher price than those in the spot market. But although weakening crude oil prices from the second half of 2014 was reflected in the crude-indexed term contracts by end-2014, the long-term contract with Qatar, which was linked to the JCC pricing mechanism over a 12-month period, continued to increase into December. As a result, with a dependency on LNG of 25 percent of demand – which has subsequently risen to 45 percent in 2016-17 – not only did India's LNG import bill balloon to $10 billion in 2014, buyers were faced with the challenge of passing on the costs to downstream buyers. This led to buyers either turning to the spot market, or opting for cheaper fuels like naphtha and coal over gas for power generation. Happily however, with the fall in prices from 2014, India began to acquire more LNG from the spot market. Also its successful price revision negotiations with Qatar saw its overall LNG import bill come down from $7.5 billion in 2012-13 to $6.7 billion in 2015-16.[9]

Low Production

One of the mantras of the political class in India is the need to strive for greater energy independence, based on the ballooning energy imports bill year-on-year. Ironically, while not ranked as an "energy-rich" nation, the Directorate General of Hydrocarbons (DGH), nevertheless states that much of India's demand for energy, particularly natural gas, can be met from domestic resources. According to the DGH, the country's conventional hydrocarbon resources are of the order of 28.1 billion tonnes of oil and oil equivalent (toe) gas, of which, as of March 2014 only 10,947 mtoegas could be established through exploration, of which only 4,098 million toe can be developed. Even then, over the past few years, production has grown marginally, if at all, and the DGH states that approximately 17 billion tonnes or 61 percent of the resources fall under the "yet to find category", and that out of the total sedimentary basins containing oil and gas, only 48 percent have been appraised. With 4 percent of the sedimentary basin

9. Sanjay Kumar Kar, "How bullish is the outlook for oil and gas industry in 2017?", *ET Energy World,* January 2, 2017 at http://energy.economictimes.indiatimes.com/news/oil-and-gas/how-bullish-is-the-outlook-for-oil-gas-industry-in-2017/56295012

declared a "no-go area", that is, areas where exploration activities cannot be carried out due to regulations/directives and restrictions, that leaves only 48 percent yet to be appraised or evaluated for hydrocarbon prospectivity through geological studies, geophysical surveys and exploratory drilling.[10] Much of this is in deep offshore and difficult geological formations, requiring sophisticated and expensive technology, which the domestic state-owned companies lack. With most of India's residual gas reserves available in deep offshore basins, the lack of access to sophisticated technology is one of the factors that has led to a fall in domestic output. Moreover, the prevailing low price for gas that is produced for domestic fields has prevented foreign oil companies with the requisite technology from entering the Indian E&P sector.

In order to resolve this problem, the government revised the New Exploration Licensing Policy (NELP) which had been launched in 1997, to attract the requisite investment and technology to increase domestic production of hydrocarbons. After nine rounds of NELP, the production of both oil and gas had continued to stagnate, leading to greater recourse to imports. A major failing of NELP was the unattractive terms offered, which deterred the international oil companies with the requisite experience and technology required for exploring difficult acreages. Another deterrent was the requirement for separate contracts for overlapping resources, which resulted in a long-winded exploration and development process. Moreover, interested investors were not allowed to select the hydrocarbon blocks and had to accept acreages the government offered. There were also complaints that accurate data over the capacity of the fields was not made available to the investors. As a result, after nine rounds spanning 15 years, although NELP succeeded in awarding 252 blocks for exploration of oil and gas and signed production sharing contracts (PSCs), only 100 have been surveyed while several of the blocks are under arbitration. Hence, while investments of around $22 billion have been made, production has not improved as expected.

10. "Hydrocarbon Exploration and Production Activities", Directorate General of Hydrocarbons, Ministry of Petroleum and Natural Gas, Government of India, 2013-14 at http://www.dghindia.org/pdf/2013-14.pdf

To resolve the problem, the government introduced major policy reforms in the upstream sector, and several more are reported to be under consideration. In October 2015, the Discovered Small Field (Marginal) Field Policy was introduced – which was subsequently rechristened as the Discovered Small Field Policy – to reduce the growing import dependency of oil and gas and to monetise several discoveries in the 'marginal' fields, which was assessed to be around 85 million tonnes of oil and oil equivalent gas reserves. The highlights of the policy included revenue-sharing contracts which required minimum regulatory burden for field monetisation; Single Licence for Conventional and Non-conventional hydrocarbons, including CBM, shale gas/oil, tight gas, gas hydrates and other resources to be identified in future; no restrictions on exploration activity during the contract period; up to 100 percent participation by foreign companies, along with joint ventures; crude oil and gas pricing and sale, where the contractor would be free to sell the crude and natural gas exclusively in the domestic market through a transparent bidding process; removal of cess on crude oil production, although the royalty rates would continue as under the NELP regime; customs duty exemptions for specified goods and services for contract areas.[11]

Moreover, the Hydrocarbon Exploration Licensing Policy or HELP was introduced on March 10, 2016, wherein an open acreage policy was introduced with the option to select the exploration blocks being provided without waiting for the formal bid round; revenue-sharing model with no cost recovery and operational freedom given to the operator; pricing and marketing freedom; single license for exploration and production of conventional as well as non-conventional hydrocarbon resources; an increase of one year in the exploration phase to eight years for onshore areas, and ten years from the earlier eight years for offshore areas, as well as reduced royalty rates for offshore blocks.

The Policy for Extension of Production-Sharing Contracts was introduced on March 10, 2016 as well, to enable oil companies to

11. "National Data Repository", Directorate General of Hydrocarbons, Ministry of Petroleum and Natural Gas, Government of India, February 10, 2017 at https://www.ndrdgh.gov.in/NDR/?page_id=2243

recover the balance reserves for a period of 10 years from 28 pre-NELP small and marginal fields after the expiry of the contract. However, the government would have to bear a higher amount than during the original contract period as well as a 10 percent higher percentage of the profit.

These reforms are expected to be ready by the end of the first quarter of 2017, after which companies will be allowed to bid under the new formulae. While the government is hopeful that this will enhance production in domestic acreages and attract more foreign and domestic companies which had hitherto shied away, there are several other challenges that need to be addressed before anomalies in the oil and gas sector can be removed. Once the bidding is opened, the success of the new policies will be tested.

Equity Assets

Apart from increasing output from domestic fields, India is also increasing its overseas equity acquisitions of oil and natural gas. While the initial focus was on oil assets, currently, India is also focusing on acquiring natural gas assets as well. However, in the past, India had more often than not lost out to Chinese companies, as Indian oil companies did not have the kind of financial heft or the government's backing as did their Chinese competitors. Therefore, in order to provide more leverage to Indian companies, the government has recently proposed to create a large oil company by integrating a number of public sector oil companies, including Indian Oil Corporation, Oil and Natural Gas Corporation, Hindustan Petroleum Corporation and others, that together would have not only the financial ability but also the economies of scale and higher risk-taking ability, to rival global oil majors as well as domestic private sector oil and gas companies when bidding for overseas energy assets. If successful, India may create more such integrated firms in other areas of the hydrocarbon sector.

The combined market cap of India's key oil and gas companies such as ONGC, IOC, OIL, HPCL and BPCL Ltd., is around $106 billion, which is less than the top oil companies such as Exxon Mobil Corporation, Royal Dutch Shell Plc or Chevron, but would give India an advantage over smaller companies including Russia's Rosneft, which has a market cap of around $70 billion or the UK's BP Plc., which has a market cap of $115.57 billion.

Although this has been welcomed by industry, there is some scepticism regarding the plan given that a similar move had been planned in 2005, but had failed to take off. Other challenges involved in such integration plans, including on the human resources side, have to be dealt with before such a venture can be successfully implemented.[12]

In the meantime, however, India has been on an asset acquisition spree. ONGC Videsh Ltd (OVL), the overseas arm of its state-owned parent company, Oil and Natural Gas Corporation), won the rights to bid for oil and gas development in its Farzad-B gas field, which OVL had discovered in 2008. Now it hopes to compete with several other IOCs and Asian firms for rights to develop the field. The field is believed to have in-place gas reserves of 21.7 trillion cubic feet in-place gas reserves of 21.7 tcf, of which 12.5 tcf are recoverable, in 2008.[13]

In July 2014, OVL also acquired a stake in Mozambique's offshore Rovuma Area 1, which holds as much as 75 tcf of gas reserves, and in September 2015, it acquired its third asset in Russia, when it took a 15 .percent stake in Vankor, Russia's second biggest oil field in East Siberia, from Rosneft. It is estimated that Vankor holds 173 bcm of gas apart from 476 million tonnes of oil and condensates.[14]

Poor Domestic Gas Infrastructure

Apart from the existing four terminals, located at Dahej and Hazira in Gujarat, Dabhol in Maharashtra and Kochi in Kerala, which were constructed to receive LNG mainly from Qatar, three new terminals

12. "Union Budget 2017: An integrated oil giant proposed to take on global rivals", *Firstpost*, February 10, 2017 at http://www.firstpost.com/business/union-budget-2017-an-integrated-oil-giant-proposed-to-take-on-global-rivals-3243252.html
13. "ONGC Videsh qualifies to bid for Iran oil, gas projects", *Business Standard*, January 2, 2017 at http://www.business-standard.com/article/companies/ongc-videsh-qualifies-to-bid-for-iran-oil-gas-projects-117010300607_1.html
14. "ONGC Videsh raises $1 bn in bonds to fund Vankor acquisition", *Business Standard*, December 18, 2016 at http://www.business-standard.com/article/companies/ongc-videsh-raises-1-bn-in-bonds-to-fund-vankor-acquisition-116121800311_1.html

with a capacity of 5 million tonnes capacity each are being planned or are under construction in Ennore in Tamil Nadu, Dhamra in Odisha and Kakinada in Andhra Pradesh, to rectify the earlier policy of constructing terminals in the west coast only.[15] (see Map 9.1)

The problem, however, is with the lack of connectivity between the terminals and consumer centres. A case in point is the recently constructed LNG import terminal in Kochi which is lying unutilised as the pipeline that was to connect the terminal to consumption centres has yet to be built. The current gas pipeline network at 16,250 km[16] is inadequate, with pipeline density in India being among the lowest in the world with the onshore natural gas pipeline density being only 3 km per 1,000 sq. km, as compared to 50 sq. km in the US, China and the UK. (see Map 9.2)

Realising the need to enhance the network, the state oil companies were awarded contracts to build and operate more infrastructure as natural gas transmission pipeline projects are very capital-intensive, and given the prevailing subsidies, there has been very limited private sector participation in the sector, which has also led to stunted growth.

In 2014, the government announced a plan to double the network to 30,000 km in the next few years with 11,000 km of new pipelines being authorised to be constructed over the next three to five years. However, according to the state oil companies contracted to build the additional network, the projects were unviable as the existing gas transmission network in the country was under-utilised due to paucity of gas. In 2014-15, against a demand of 405 mmscmd, availability was 123.25 mmscmd, which included production from domestic fields, as well as coal bed methane and imported, re-gasified LNG.[17] Part of this gap was due to the lack of re-gasification terminals or a limited surplus re-gasification capacity as key end-user industries, such as

15. Sanjeev Choudhary, "Government weighs doubling capacity of LNG terminal capacity", *The Economic Times*, June 7, 2016 at http://economictimes.indiatimes.com/industry/energy/oil-gas/government-weighs-doubling-capacity-of-lng-import-terminal/articleshow/52628254.cms

16. Gas Pipeline Network, Petroleum Planning & Analysis Cell, March 31, 2016 at http://ppac.org.in/content/154_1_PipelineandCGDStructure.aspx

17. *Annual Report 2015-16*, Ministry of Petroleum and Natural Gas, Government of India at http://www.petroleum.nic.in/docs/Annual_Report/AR15-16.pdf

Map 9.1

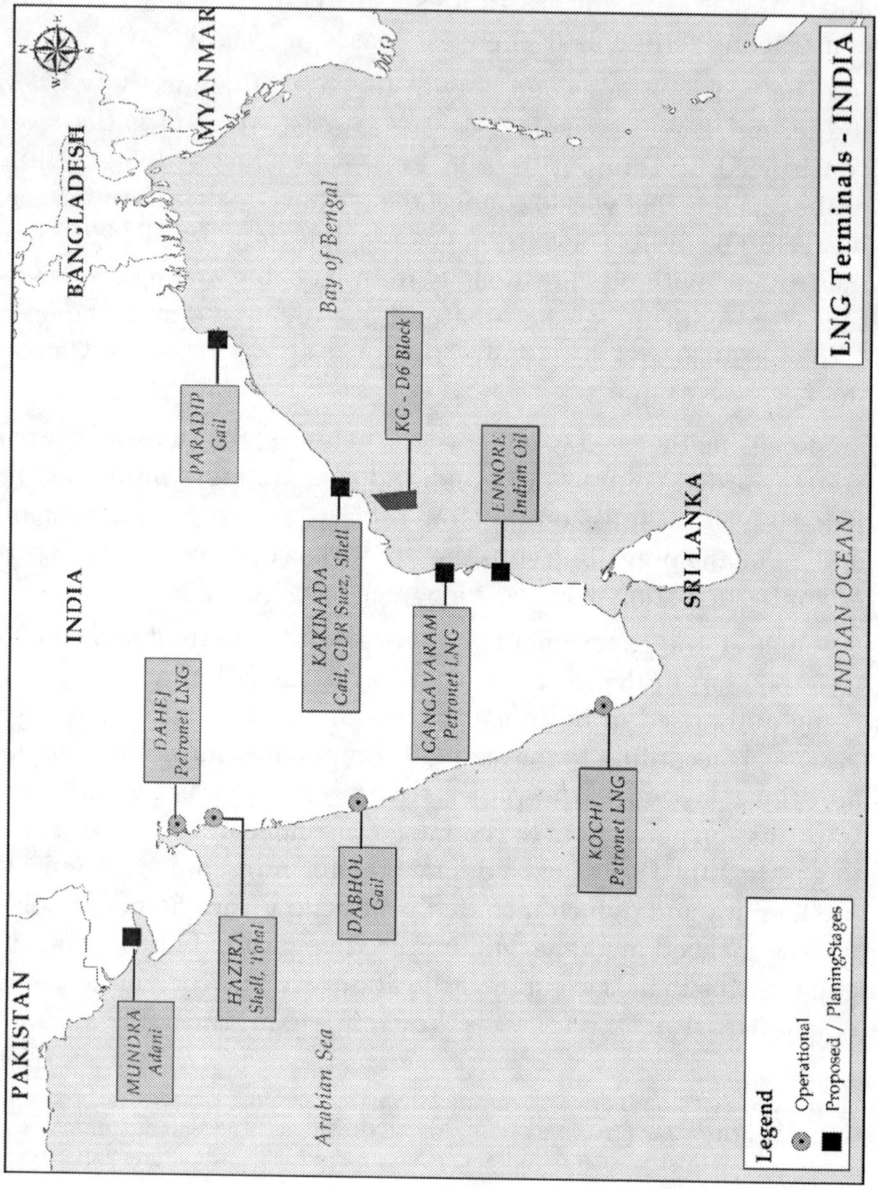
PAKISTAN
INDIA
BANGLADESH
MYANMAR
SRI LANKA
Arabian Sea
Bay of Bengal
INDIAN OCEAN
MUNDRA Adani
HAZIRA Shell, Total
DAHEJ Petronet LNG
DABHOL Gail
KOCHI Petronet LNG
KAKINADA Gail, CDR Suez, Shell
GANGAVARAM Petronet LNG
PARADIP Gail
KG - D6 Block
ENNORE Indian Oil
LNG Terminals - INDIA
Legend
Operational
Proposed / PlaningStages

Map 9.2

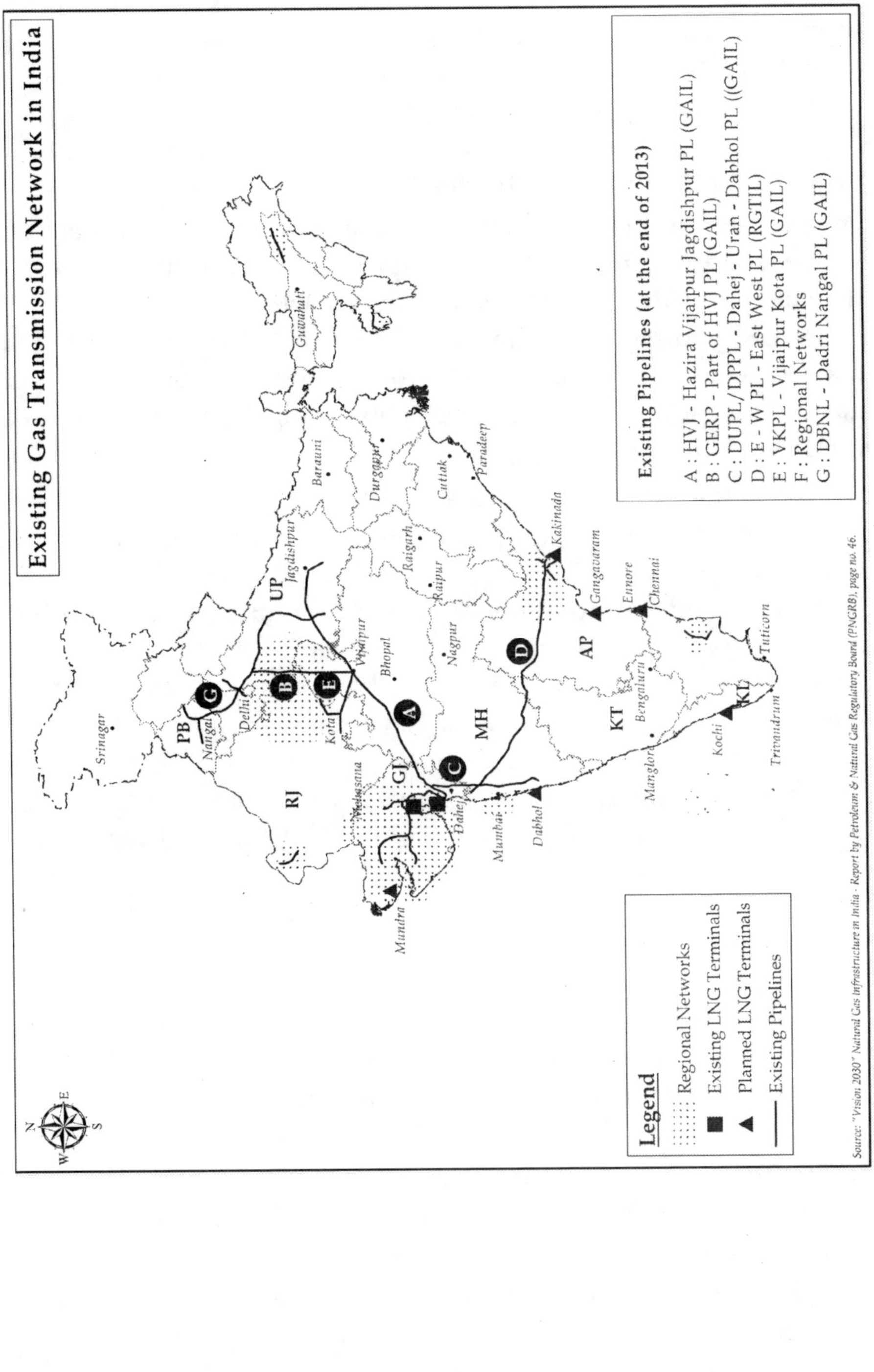
Existing Gas Transmission Network in India
Srinagar
PB
Nangal
Delhi
G
B
E
Kota
RJ
UP
Jagdishpur
Vijaipur
Bhopal
A
GJ
Mehsana
Mundra
Dahej
C
Mumbai
Dabhol
MH
Nagpur
Raipur
Raigarh
Barauni
Durgapur
Cuttak
Paradeep
Guwahati
D
Kakinada
Gangavaram
AP
Ennore
Chennai
KT
Bengaluru
Manglore
Kochi
KL
Trivandrum
Tuticorn
Legend
Regional Networks
Existing LNG Terminals
Planned LNG Terminals
Existing Pipelines
Existing Pipelines (at the end of 2013)
A : HVJ - Hazira Vijaipur Jagdishpur PL (GAIL)
B : GERP - Part of HVJ PL (GAIL)
C : DUPL/DPPL - Dahej - Uran - Dabhol PL ((GAIL)
D : E - W PL - East West PL (RGTIL)
E : VKPL - Vijaipur Kota PL (GAIL)
F : Regional Networks
G : DBNL - Dadri Nangal PL (GAIL)
Source: "Vision 2030" Natural Gas Infrastructure in India - Report by Petroleum & Natural Gas Regulatory Board (PNGRB), page no. 46.

manufacturers of urea for the fertiliser sector and power sector, found it hard to afford re-gasified LNG. Therefore, constructing more terminals will be contingent on the availability of additional gas supplies, the demand for imported gas (re-gasified LNG) versus alternate fuels, and time-bound clearances.

Transnational Pipeline(s) Woes

With all the problems facing the domestic upstream, as mentioned above, the government has to import large volumes to meet the demand-supply gap. Since LNG requires expensive infrastructure and is not competitive with domestically produced gas, a decision was taken that gas could be imported through pipelines from neighbouring gas-rich countries. However, as of now, not a single project has been implemented.

From the late 1980s, India began negotiations with Iran on importing gas through a pipeline project, better known as the Iran-Pakistan-India (IPI) pipeline project that was expected to bring 38 mmcmd of gas to India via Pakistan. Soon after, India also began negotiations with Myanmar and Bangladesh on another pipeline project that would entail bringing Myanmarese gas to India via Bangladesh. Again, in the mid-2000s, yet another project, which sought to bring gas from Turkmenistan to India, via Afghanistan and Pakistan, under the $10 billion TAPI project, was placed on the table. However, while the former two projects have all but been written off, the government seems more optimistic about the TAPI project, despite the fact that problems continue to plague the project. Although the question of assured supplies of gas have more or less been resolved with supplies to be sourced from the Galkynysh field– the second largest in the world after the South Pars field in the Persian Gulf, with reserves of 16 tcf of gas – and construction has commenced following the selection of Turkmengaz as consortium leader, albeit after considerable delay due to Ashgabat's refusal to grant equity to foreign companies.

Nevertheless, several challenges have to be overcome before the project sees the light of day, despite a timeline of 2018 being set for completion of the pipeline. First, the route through which the 1800 km long pipeline, carrying 3.2 bcf of natural gas per annum from Turkmenistan to India, will transit Herat and Kandahar in Afghanistan, before entering Pakistan, where it will reach Multan via Quetta before ending at Fazilka, is hardly deemed secure, making the project a security risk due to the ongoing conflict in these regions.

Moreover, the financing of the project – estimated at around $10 billion – has yet to be sorted out. Although the Turkmen President, Gurbanguly Berdimukhamedov, signed a decree in early June 2016 on the allocation of more than $45 million, i.e., 85 percent of the cost of construction, to finance the initial stage of the pipeline to the Afghan border, and the ADB has stated that it would consider providing financial support, there have been reports that the Islamic Development Bank (IDB), the Saudi Fund for Development, the Japanese government and the European Development Bank have also expressed interest in financing the project. However, given the complexity of the project and the security challenges involved, it is unlikely that financiers will take a risk without adequate insurance cover. Interestingly, one of the factors that contributed to the demise of the IPI project was the lack of insurance cover for the project.

The fall in gas prices from 2014 has been a setback. It may not only affect Turkmenistan's ability to pay its share of the construction at a time when the Turkmen economy is facing a major financial crunch due to the fall in gas prices, but also because the recipient countries may no longer be willing to pay the price demanded by Ashgabat. Earlier, India had agreed to pay a little over $9/mmBtu as well as $3/mmBtu for transportation charges.[18] However, with the current spot price for Asian LNG now expected to increase following the rise in oil prices, India may need to leverage its market power to negotiate lower prices.

Finally, with Iran now back in business following the lifting of the sanctions, the TAPI project may not get the same kind of backing from the US as it did previously. According to recent reports, China has expressed its opposition to the project as it conflicts with its plans for its CPEC (China-Pakistan Economic Corridor) project. That

18. "Japan May spot LNG prices fall to lowest in more than 2 years", Reuters, June 8, 2016 at http://in.reuters.com/article/lng-japan-spot-idINL4N1911PO

Turkmenistan is well aware of this fact is one of the reasons why it is pushing for the construction, as any delay may further delay the project or even put it on hold.

Ashgabat's concerns are not unfounded. For instance, India is negotiating with Iran for reviving either the sub-sea pipeline project supplied with gas from Iran's Farzad B gasfield, or alternatively, liquefying the gas and shipping it to India, either directly or through Oman. There have also been reports that Russia and India are exploring the possibility of constructing transnational pipelines which will bring oil and gas to India, through the restive Chinese province of Xinjiang,[19] as well as other options to bring Russian gas to India, via swap deals with China and Myanmar[20] or as LNG through the recently resurrected Chahbahar Port initiative.

Furthermore, there are also reports of a renewed interest to construct the 900-km pipeline from Myanmar, through Bangladesh to India (MBI) carrying 5 bcm per annum of gas from the Shwe gas field in southern Myanmar.[21] The pipeline was first proposed in the late 1990s, and following investments by Indian oil companies in Myanmar's offshore gas fields in the early 2000s, an agreement was arrived at between the respective countries in 2005 to construct the pipeline which at a cost of $ 1 billion, was to deliver 5 bcm per annum of gas to India. However, after Bangladesh made some preconditions on transit rights that India found unacceptable there was a breakdown in the negotiations, following which India proposed to go ahead with the negotiations on a bilateral basis with Myanmar, bypassing Dhaka. The new proposal envisaged bringing the pipeline through India's northeast region, but at an enhanced price. Protracted negotiations and a failure on the part of India to commit to the project saw Myanmar

19. Utpal Bhaskar, "India in talks with Russia, Iran on transnational pipelines", *Mint*, June 5, 2015 at http://www.livemint.com/Industry/lTBSa05Fk3Wlyrj9c6pthP/India-in-talks-with-Russia-Iran-on-transnational-pipelines.html
20. Raheja Vanya, "ONGC exploring swap deals to import gas from Myanmar", *Times of India*, December 7, 2016 at timesofindia.indiatimes.com/business/india-business/ONGC-exploring-swap-deals-to-import-gas-from-Myanmar/articleshow/55849335.cms
21. "Official talks on Myanmar-India-Bangla pipeline to start soon", *The Indian Express*, July 3, 2015 at http://indianexpress.com/article/business/business-others/official-talks-on-myanmar-india-bangla-pipeline-to-start-soon/

entering into negotiations with China regarding another bilateral pipeline project, which was successfully completed in 2013. As the gas that was proposed to be committed to India was ceded to China, the project was written off at the time. However, after the Awami League formed the government in 2009, relations with India improved substantially and the both sides have now agreed to revive negotiations for a trilateral pipeline.

While the several pipeline projects that have been on the table for decades are still ongoing, the crash in gas prices may, in fact, have put them on the backburner. With spot prices of LNG now becoming affordable, with further drops more than likely over the next few years, India seems to prefer pursuing the LNG option rather than opting for pipelines, given the geopolitical and strategic complications involved. What however, is evident is that the Indian gas scenario has now changed. The issue of Qatar's acceptance of a downward revision of prices for its long-term contract with India is a case in point. Moreover, with India emerging as a potentially major gas market, and given the supply glut in the LNG market, the advantage now appears to be in India's favour. However, whether India can gain from the current state of the gas market will depend on a number of factors.

Unconventional Gas

Apart from its policy on enhancing production from its conventional hydrocarbon reserves, India is also looking at exploring and developing its unconventional, including shale gas, gas hydrates and coal bed methane (CBM) resources.

With regard to shale gas, various agencies, including Schlumberger, US EIA, United States Geological Survey (USGS) and domestic companies, have estimated the shale gas and oil resource potential in selected sedimentary basins/sub-basins in India could range from 300 tcf (8.5 tcm) to 2,100 tcf (59.5 tcm). Recently, the government said that as per the notification of the former government's policy guidelines of October 14, 2013, for exploration and exploitation of shale gas, the national oil companies had been awarded blocks under the nomination regimes in three phases, for a three-year duration. Under Phase I, permission has been granted for 55 blocks to ONGC and OIL in Assam, Arunachal Pradesh, Gujarat, Rajasthan, Andhra Pradesh and Tamil

Nadu. Under Phase-II, the same two companies have to identify an additional 75 and 5 blocks, respectively. And in Phase III, they would have to identify 50 and 5 blocks to carry out shale gas exploration and exploitation.[22] However, despite the policy initiative, several challenges will have to be overcome before India can begin exploiting its shale in a comprehensive manner. The biggest challenge would be that of land acquisition and the relocation of displaced people. Moreover, production costs are higher in India as the rocks are found deeper in the ground, thereby necessitating additional technical development to bring down costs. Another area of concern is that of water, of which large amounts are needed and often in areas where it is scarce. Huge and perhaps often over-estimated figures are being cited; according to Chesapeake Energy, 65,000-600,000 gallons of water are required to drill one well. In India's water-scarce regions, this is a major disincentive.[23]

Moreover, India is also looking at developing its substantial CBM and gas hydrates potential. According to the DGH, the CBM resources in the country are to the tune of 92 tcf (2.6 tcm), while its gas hydrate resources are estimated at 1894 tcm in and around the western, eastern and Andaman offshore areas. The Petroleum and Natural Gas Ministry formulated the National Gas Hydrate Programme (NGHP) in 2000, and the first expedition was launched in 2006, which had established the presence of gas hydrates in the Krishna, Godavari and Mahanadi basins as well as in the deep waters off the Andamans. The next two phases of the NGHP are currently in an advanced stage of planning and are due in the period 2014-2017. [24] India is cooperating with other countries, including the US' Department of Energy and Japan, in exploration and development, besides data collection, analysis and identification of sites for pilot production testing.

---

22. "Identification of Extractable Reserves of Shale Gas", Press Information Bureau, Government of India Ministry of Petroleum & Natural Gas, May 13, 2015 at http://pib.nic.in/newsite/PrintRelease.aspx?relid=121651
23. Shailaja Nair, "Shale gas to rock the Indian energy scene? Some say yes, but...", *The Barrel*, November 10, 2010, at www.platts.com/weblog/oilblog/2010/11/10/shale_gas_to_ro.html, (accessed on July 17, 2011).
24. "India and US to join hands for gas hydrates", *Business Standard*, September 26, 2014 at http://www.business-standard.com/content/b2b-manufacturing-industry/india-and-us-to-join-hands-for-gas-hydrates-114092600811_1.html

However, while development of gas hydrates is still not commercially viable, the potential for CBM has been assured. Nevertheless, till date only 33 CBM blocks have been awarded with only one block being under commercial production, while 16 reserves have been relinquished by the owners, sources said. In order to give a fillip to the production of CBM, the current government is planning to amend the existing CBM Policy of 2009 to incentivise investment in the sector. Some of the issues that will be addressed are resolving the overlapping of CBM and coal blocks by putting in place a more workable mechanism to end the conflict of interest between the Petroleum and Coal Ministries, simplifying and liberalising the existing CBM contracts.[25]

India is also looking at accelerating its policy on acquisition of overseas oil and gas assets. With the recent fall in crude oil prices, the opportunity for acquiring such assets abroad has improved, and the government is planning to increase its forays in more countries with an increased energy diplomacy agenda and an enhanced kitty. Currently, India has 35 projects in 16 countries from Brazil to New Zealand which it has acquired through the overseas arm of its largest state-owned oil firm, ONGC.

Can the Inconsistencies be Overcome?

The Indian gas market is relatively young, with the first discovery in the country having been made only in the 1970s. Today, gas accounts for only 6 percent of the country's energy mix, compared with coal (40 percent) and oil (22 percent), hydro (2 percent), nuclear (1 percent), renewable energy (1 percent) and biomass (26 percent). However, according to the IEA New Policies Scenario 2014, the share of gas in India's energy mix is expected to grow over the next few decades, although projections of gas replacing coal in the power sector is unlikely to take place as gas-based generation is considered uncompetitive with respect to coal-based generation. On the other hand, with the government's stated goal of reducing oil consumption

25. Animesh Singh, "Amendments in Coal Bed Methane Policy in works to encourage output", *The Pioneer*, March 4, 2015 at http://www.dailypioneer.com/business/amendments-in-coal-bed-methane-policy-in-works-to-encourage-output.html

incrementally over the next few years, the expectation is that natural gas, being a more environmentally acceptable fuel than oil in the transport sector, as well as in the residential sector, may be used as a substitute.

With the International Monetary Fund (IMF) projecting India's growth to grow from 7.2 percent in 2014[26] to 7.5 percent in 2015 – which has subsequently been downgraded to around 6.7 percent due to the recent demonetisation drive – India certainly has the potential to leverage its growing demand for energy market in the larger global geopolitical and strategic arena, akin to China. Although a latecomer in the game of energy politics, India is finally leveraging its strengths as a growing energy market, indeed, one of the few consumers whose appetite for energy has not diminished despite the dismal global economic scenario.

In the LNG world, India is being watched with interest due to its potential as a LNG market, despite its current comparatively low consumption for gas. In 2015-16, India imported 16 million tonnes of LNG, but some forecasters predict it will import nearly 50 million tonnes by 2030. In a further attempt at increasing gas use in the fertiliser and power sectors and to encourage mid-stream infrastructure creation, from LNG terminals to pipelines and city gas distribution networks, the government has halved the basic customs duty on LNG imports from 5 percent to 2.5 percent.[27]

At a time when the gas market is over-supplied and several new LNG projects are expected to come on line, including in Australia, new US export terminals, and Africa, India is seen as a bright spot in an otherwise dark scenario, at least for the next couple of years. However, with the rise in crude prices, and demand expected to increase from other Asian and European markets as countries are attempting to make

26. "Country and Regional Perspectives, World Economic Outlook: Uneven Growth—short- and long-term Factors, Chapter 2, International Monetary Fund, (IMF), April 2015 at http://www.imf.org/external/pubs/ft/weo/2015/01/pdf/c2.pdf
27. "Arun Jaitley halves import duty on LNG to 2.5 per cent", *The Economic Times*, February 2, 2017 at http://energy.economictimes.indiatimes.com/news/oil-and-gas/budget-2017-arun-jaitley-halves-import-duty-on-lng-to-2-5-per-cent/56926865

the transition from oil and coal to cleaner fuels, including natural gas, the window of opportunity for India may not remain open for very long. While India's potential as a huge gas market is not in question, the inconsistencies in its policies, and the lack of related infrastructure raise doubts whether India will be able to get its act together in time to benefit from the prevailing low gas price regime or whether it will have lost a golden opportunity to position itself as a country that has what it takes to call the shots in the global energy market.

10

What Lies Ahead for Gas in the Future?

From a fuel that was used in regionally disconnected markets, natural gas was projected to take over as the fuel of choice for many consuming nations across the world. Its versatility and the fact that its carbon emissions are lower than either coal or oil, makes it well placed to be the 'bridge' or transition fuel between fossil fuels and renewables. Between 1990 and 2010, the share of gas witnessed a rise in demand, particularly in the emerging markets of the Asia-Pacific region, including China, and the West Asian countries, partly due to increasing environmental concerns as well as abundant supplies. In fact, natural gas succeeded in increasing its market share by 60 percent during this period. But although the International Energy Agency (IEA) remains optimistic over the future of gas, the dilemma for gas producers and exporters is two-fold: how to make gas more competitive and thereby increase its share in national energy baskets as against coal; and second, to increase its share in the transport sector vis-à-vis the current leader oil and future electric vehicles (EVs).

The IEA, in its 2016 Medium-Term Gas Market Report, paints a more sombre canvas for the gas market, stating that while oil markets will start rebalancing from 2017, an oversupply in natural gas will continue until the end of the decade, causing prices to remain depressed. Multiple factors have been cited for the forecast, including cheap coal, plummeting renewable energy costs in key gas markets like Japan and South Korea on the one hand, and lower economic growth and environmental concerns in China, besides the price factor.

So, does this mean that the prospects for the gas market are set to be gloomy for the foreseeable future? According to the *BP Energy Outlook 2035*, published in 2015, despite the current gloomy outlook for gas, demand for gas worldwide is projected to increase by 1.9 percent annually till 2035.[1] But perhaps the most important factor that will determine the future of gas is whether in the face of the growing concerns regarding climate change, gas will be able to compete with 'greener' energy resources. However, the transportation cost of gas is higher than the other fossil fuels, be they over land or sea. While the cost of laying pipelines over long distances, along with transit fees and construction of compressors adds to the expend, in the case of LNG, the liquefaction, regasification and compression costs and transportation in special vessels makes the delivered cost of gas much higher than either coal or oil, thereby acting as a deterrent, particularly for the cost-sensitive developing countries. In Asia, which is projected to generate the majority of the growth in demand for energy resources in general, and where the fall in gas prices had, in fact, been the most dramatic, natural gas remains less competitive compared to cheap coal and policy support for renewables.[2] But even in Europe, gas consumption was the lowest in 2014 since 1995, partly because of the slow pace of recovery following the 2008 financial crisis, and partly due to energy efficiency and the move towards renewables. As a result, according to the IEA's 2016 medium-term gas market report, since 2012 the demand for gas globally has increased by just 1 percent per annum, as compared to the 10-year average of 2.2 percent, and from 2015 to 2021, demand will pick up marginally, increasing at an average annual rate of 1.5 percent.

No doubt, the fall in prices from 2014 did revive interest in gas in

1. *BP World Energy Outlook 2035*, February 2015 at http://www.bp.com/content/dam/bp/pdf/Energy-economics/energy-outlook-2015/Energy_Outlook_2035_booklet.pdf
2. Medium-Term Gas Market Report 2016, International Energy Agency at https://www.iea.org/Textbase/npsum/MTGMR2016SUM.pdf

some countries. A case in point is India, where the government announced that India would be moving to a gas-based economy; several other countries in South and West Asia too are looking at an incremental increase in their gas consumption. At the same time, the abundance of supplies in the US from shale reserves has seen gas replace both coal and nuclear plants. And as US imports of gas came down, it freed up cargoes originally meant for the US, for other markets. Around the same time, a number of new producers also began entering the market, including Australia and Papua New Guinea from the Asia-Pacific region, and Trinidad and Tobago and Nigeria in Africa, while traditional producers and exporters like Qatar, Norway, Brunei, Russia, Indonesia, Equatorial Guinea and Malaysia increased their output. The combination of these two factors therefore rendered the market to be over-supplied, causing prices to drop further.

Furthermore, an economic slow-down in China saw the demand for energy consumption falling, albeit marginally, but nonetheless dealing a blow to producers who were looking to the growing Chinese market to absorb much more of the new supplies. According to the energy regulator, the National Development and Reform Commission, (NDRC), China's total natural gas consumption rose by around 1 percent to 6.6 percent in 2016 up from 5.7 percent in 2015.[3]

But it was in Europe, the largest market for gas, that demand did not pick up as expected. The 2008 financial-led economic crisis, from which the developed world has still to emerge, caused demand to fall considerably, began raising the share of renewable energy in their energy basket in order to meet their carbon emissions cut commitments.

Geopolitics Versus Price

A large part of the reason for the lack of growth in gas in Europe is due to its policy to reduce its dependence on Russia, its main supplier. Russia's proclivity to undermine rival supplies to its most important market by disrupting gas supplies transiting recalcitrant states in the

3. Jennifer Li, "China Gas to benefit as coal to gas switch brings on millions of new users in northern areas", *South China Morning Post*, February 14, 2017 at http://www.scmp.com/business/companies/article/2070796/china-gas-benefit-coal-gas-switch-brings-millions-new-users

past (Ukraine, Belarus) or fomenting conflicts in states (Georgia) to prevent alternative lines bypassing Russia from being constructed, has been a growing area of concern. The recent conflict between Russia and Ukraine has in fact brought a renewed urgency for many of the EU states to wean themselves from their dependence on Russia for energy, particularly gas, supplies. Furthermore, with Russia's recent announcement that it would stop using pipelines transiting Ukraine after 2019, the European states are now faced with seeking alternative transport networks to bring gas from Russia or construct the missing links connecting newly proposed pipelines – the Turkish Stream and the recently announced expansion of the Nord Stream link. In the likely event that these alternative pipelines are not constructed, due to a number of factors including regional tensions and huge capital costs in a low price environment, Europe may find itself being left with few alternatives to Russian gas.

The US too is encouraging the EU states to look at alternative sources for its gas, both for weaning Europe away from dependence on Russia as well as a future market for its own exports, which it plans to commence soon. According to reports, the US company Cheniere Energy, plans to supply eastern European countries with LNG in a few years, including a floating regasification terminal off the coast of Croatia, which would allow American companies to enter the central and eastern European market,[4] thereby further loosening Russia's hold over Europe's gas market. Meanwhile, following the launch of its energy security strategy in 2014, the European Commission has been trying to ensure energy security for its member-states by exploring carious sourcing options including from the Caspian Sea states, West Asia – including post-sanctions Iran – and North Africa.

Aware of the need to broaden its market beyond Europe, particularly after the Ukraine crisis,[5] Moscow, since 2014, has been looking eastward, towards Asia and particularly China. Both countries

4. Charles Kennedy, "North-American LNG Could Weaken Russia's Grip On Europe", Oilprice.com, July 29, 2015 at http://oilprice.com/Energy/Natural-Gas/North-American-LNG-Could-Weaken-Russias-Grip-On-Europe.html
5. "Energy Perspectives: Long-term macro and market outlook", Statoil, June 2015, p. 34 at http://www.statoil.com/en/NewsAndMedia/News/Energy Perspectives/Downloads/Energy%20Perspectives%202015.pdf

have signed mega deals for gas in 2014 and 2015. At the same time, wary of too much reliance on the Chinese market, and cognizant that Beijing is also contracting large volumes of gas from the Central Asian states, Moscow is also negotiating with India, as well as other South Asian countries like Pakistan, for supplying gas, both via pipelines as well as LNG.[6] While negotiations are on with Pakistan to construct a $2 billion pipeline called the North-South pipeline – the first major Russian investment in Pakistan after decades – which on completion is expected to pump imported LNG from Karachi, and possibly Gwadar, to Lahore,[7] it is also exploring various pipeline route options for bringing gas to India, including through the Central Asian states or Iran and even China, as well LNG through swap deals with Myanmar.[8]

One of the emerging rivals of Russia for its eastern as well as potentially European markets is Turkmenistan. Currently, however, Ashgabat, which was completely dependent on Russia for export routes, and turned to China as a diversification strategy, finds itself becoming increasingly dependent on the Chinese market. As a result, Ashgabat too is looking further a field, but its options are limited due to the lack of export outlets. Despite the interest shown by the EU states in Turkmen gas, the Southern Gas Corridor project has been held up due to differences amongst the potential partners over pipeline capacity and the legal disputes over sovereignty between the Caspian Basin states.

Apart from Europe, which remains an attractive market due to the price factor, the future growth of the gas market is expected to be in Asia. While Japan and South Korea have been the main LNG consumers, the outlook for further growth in Japan is not bright. With

---

6. "India eyeing LNG imports from Russia", *LNG World*, June 8, 2015 at https://www.lngworldnews.com/india-eyeing-lng-imports-from-russia/
7. Zafar Bhutta, "$2b North-South pipeline: Pakistan asks Russia to further cut LNG supply fee", *The Express Tribune*, February 11, 2017 at https://tribune.com.pk/story/1322815/2b-north-south-pipeline-pakistan-asks-russia-cut-lng-supply-fee/
8. "India, Russia to study building $25 billion pipeline", *The Economic Times*, October 16, 2016 at http://economictimes.indiatimes.com/industry/energy/oil-gas/india-russia-to-study-building-25-billion-pipeline/articleshow/54878729.cms

nuclear energy poised to make a comeback, Japan may see its LNG import decline continuing in 2017. According to the Institute of Energy Economics (IEEJ) if around 14 nuclear plants restart by the end of 2017, Japan's LNG imports in 2017 could drop by more than 5 percent from 2016 levels.[9]

In 2014, the Asia-Pacific region consumed around 650 bcm of gas, a fifth of the world total, and by 2014, demand in the non-OECD Asia-Pacific region is expected to grow at a rate of 3.5 percent, that is around 1,300 bcm or around 28 percent of the world total.[10] In South Asia too, the sensitivity of the countries to energy prices is a key factor in demand as displayed by the differences between the partners over gas pricing – as well as security issues – which has seen the TAPI gas pipeline project languishing for decades. Currently, with the price of gas ruling at historically low levels, an over-supplied LNG market, and post-sanctions Iran back in the game providing more supply options, some of the signatories of the project, viz., Pakistan and India, are looking at re-negotiating the pricing terms for Turkmen gas, as well as long-term contractual obligations. At the same time, the longer the negotiations drag on, the potential for cost-escalation of the project increases, making it unviable.

In fact, the issue of LNG pricing will play a major role in the future of the gas market, in general, and in the Asia-Pacific region, in particular. Asian countries, especially the Asian OECD nations, have been paying a premium for gas supplies due to oil-linked pricing, which is much higher than hub-indexed prices, and long-term take-or-pay contracts with no flexibility to resell the gas, due to the destination clause, low demand flexibility and the lack of a regional spot pricing mechanism. Much of the current new supply coming into the market was due to the expectation of high and growing Asian demand, particularly from China.

---

9. Aoshima Momoko et.al., "Economic and Energy Outlook of Japan through FY2017", Institute of Energy Economics, Japan, December 22, 2016 at https://eneken.ieej.or.jp/en/press/press161226.pdf
10. "Energy Perspectives: Long-term macro and market outlook", Statoil, June 2015, p.34 at http://www.statoil.com/en/NewsAndMedia/News/EnergyPerspectives/Downloads/Energy%20Perspectives%202015.pdf

However, the recent successful re-negotiation by India's largest LNG importer Petronet of its long-term contract with Qatar's RasGas, whereby it not only paid less than half the contracted price but also got a waiver for the penalty for importing less gas than was agreed in the contract, may have changed the market irrevocably, as other Asian countries, including China and Japan, too began negotiating for better terms with suppliers.[11] Japanese utilities, in fact, are not only renegotiating contracts, but also questioning issues such as oil-indexed pricing mechanisms and the destination clause that prevent the reselling of surplus cargoes. Tokyo has also indicated its interest in establishing Japan as an LNG trading hub in order to gain more influence over the LNG market.[12]

Changing Market Dynamics

The influx of extra supplies triggered by the earlier phase of high prices and the shale revolution had made the outlook for gas prices even more bearish than for oil. As a result, Asian consumers who were paying the highest prices for LNG are now not only planning to re-negotiate their long-term contracts, but are also looking at setting up a spot-price benchmark for Asian LNG.

With regard to long-term LNG contracts as well as those in the planning stage, there are several options for both producers and consumers, including retaining oil-indexed mechanisms with price ceilings, hub-indexed pricing, and the inclusion of a future Asian spot price in the contract, if and when it is introduced. Although oil-indexed gas prices do not reflect developments in gas markets as there is decreasing competition between oil and gas at the end-user level – notably in the power sector – many producers are more comfortable

---

11. Siddhartha P. Saikia, "Post-crash in gas prices, India's Petronet to rework pricing for LNG from Exxon's Gorgon project in Australia", *Financial Express*, May 31, 2016 at http://www.financialexpress.com/economy/petronet-starts-talks-to-redo-pricing-for-gorgon-lng-deal/269570/;James Paton and Anna Shiryaevskaya, "China Joins India Seeking Better LNG Contracts for Buyers", Bloomberg, March 11, 2016 at http://www.bloomberg.com/news/articles/2016-03-11/china-joins-india-seeking-better-lng-terms-as-contracts-weaken
12. Mayumi Negishi, "Japan steps on gas in bid to reshape LNG market", *The Wall Street Journal*, June 19, 2016 at http://www.wsj.com/articles/japan-steps-on-gas-in-bid-to-reshape-lng-market-1466325065

with oil-indexed prices as several development costs of gas are linked to oil prices. Moreover, they cite the lack of liquidity, limited curve, fears of manipulation and concerns about volatility, for continuing with oil-indexation. Finally, oil-indexation allows flexibility in pricing. For example, when spot gas is cheaper than oil-indexed contract prices, the buyer can reduce the offtake on volumes and go for cheaper hub or spot supplies (or vice-versa), as was seen recently in India's case.[13] But at the end of the day, a major reason for producers' preference for the long-term oil-indexed pricing mechanism is that they provide them with the security required for the huge investment needed in upstream production infrastructure and associated transport networks.[14]

Nevertheless, at a time when spot gas prices are ruling, and expected to remain low for some time, large consumers of gas are unwilling to pay higher oil-indexed prices. In fact, the outlook for gas prices has become even more pessimistic than that for oil, with some analysts predicting that with global LNG supply poised to increase by about a third over the next three years, it will push over-capacity to around 10 percent, causing prices in Asia to plunge further. As a result, the countries which had signed long-term oil-indexed contracts when crude prices were higher and had suffered the most, are now negotiating for revised terms.

But in all this turbulence, the outline of a truly global gas market is emerging, led by the expansion of the LNG trade. Following the fall in US gas prices due to the shale revolution, and the move towards a more flexible form of pricing in Europe incorporating both hub and oil-indexed mechanisms, Asian LNG, which was almost entirely oil-indexed and priced much higher than in the other two markets, became an attractive market. For example, following the increase in shale gas production, US gas was prices below $2/mmBtu, while the price of

---

13. Anne-Sophie Corbeau, Anne Braaksma, Farid Hussin, Yayoi Yagoto and Takuro Yamamoto, "The Asian Quest for LNG in a Globalising Market", *International Energy Agency*, 2014 at https://www.iea.org/publications/freepublications/publication/PartnerCountrySeriesTheAsianQuestforLNGinaGlobalisingMarket.pdf
14. Gazprom, "oil-link vs spot gas prices, and storage, the Barrel", April 23, 2015 at http://blogs.platts.com/2015/04/23/gazprom-gas-oil-link-spot-prices-storage/

delivered gas in Asia was going for $15/mmBtu or more. Moreover, Japan, the world's largest LNG importer, accounts for approximately 34 percent of the LNG market. Combined with South Korea which accounts for a little over 13 percent, it accounts for a little under 50 percent of the market, while Asia as a whole accounts for around 75 percent.[15]

However, with the drop in the price of oil, the delivered price of spot LNG to Asia has come down from $18.3/mmBtu in April 2014 to less than $7/mmBtu in March 2016, thereby narrowing the window of profitable opportunity. Currently, US exports to Asia (Japan) can be delivered between a low of $5.60/mmBtu to $5.89/mmBtuand a high of $6.97 and $8.24, including transportation costs, depending on whether it is shipped via Panama or around South Africa, respectively.[16] The opportunity for US LNG exports to Asia are bright, provided more production does not enter the market and drag prices down further. However, if a global market dominated by spot prices does take shape, the US can position itself as a swing producer, akin to Saudia Arabia's position in the oil market, and will allow it the space to assert itself.

Moving Towards a More Integrated Gas Market

Although demand for gas has come down in some East Asian countries like Japan, and South Korea, overall, the Asian countries are expected to be the drivers for the growth in demand for gas, including LNG. As mentioned earlier, while India has announced that it will increase the use of gas in its overall energy consumption, China's demand for gas too will continue to grow, albeit at a slower pace. Some of the traditional gas exporting countries like Malaysia and Indonesia are expected to become net LNG importers, while the use of gas in several West Asian countries is poiseu to multiply. Moreover, the number of importers grew in 2015 including Jordan, Pakistan, Poland and Egypt.[17]

15. International Gas Union, *2016 World LNG Report*, at http://www.igu.org/publications/2016-world-lng-report
16. Ronald D. Ripple, "U.S. Natural Gas (LNG) Exports: Opportunities and Challenges", IAEE Energy Forum, Third Quarter, 2016 at https://www.iaee.org/en/Publications/newsletterdl.aspx?id=341
17. International Gas Union, World Gas LNG Report 2016 Edition, see note 15.

However, neither the older or more recent consumers are ready, nor willing, to pay the high premiums paid by Asian consumers, as compared with their European and North American counterparts, and are seeking cheaper supplies and exploring alternatives to their traditional contracts and price structures. Some companies are pushing for, and succeeding in getting more flexibility in their contracts, particularly with regard to destination clauses, with some major Asian consumer governments negotiating with producer governments to explore alternatives to oil-linked pricing and destination clauses. The case of India's Petronet's deal with RasGas and re-selling gas acquired from the US are some concrete examples.

Although long-term contracts indexed to crude oil prices are still the main pricing mechanism adopted by Asian consumers, more and more gas (LNG) is being bought on the spot market as well as one-term transactions under short-term contracts.

Several Asian countries like Japan, China, and Singapore, are also trying to develop regional trading hubs with the goal of increasing price formation transparency. With an end goal to creating a global LNG market, Japan is planning a strategy for setting up a new procurement model whereby diverse players will make short-term, spot purchases or more resilient contracts for LNG supplies, although the conventional procurement model of long-term contracts will continue for the time being. The EU too published a strategy for LNG and gas storage in February 2016, and is trying to get international cooperation toward further utilisation of LNG and establish an integrated LNG market.[18]

In the meantime, various countries have accelerated initiatives to create LNG trading hubs. In 2014, Japan opened an over-the-counter (OTC) trading system for LNG, with the aim of developing an LNG trading hub, while Singapore's Stock Exchange launched the Singapore SGX LNG Index Group or SLInG in June 2015, which will provide free-on-board (FOB) prices for cargoes from Singapore to different destinations, reflecting regional spot prices. So far, thirteen market

18. "Strategy for LNG Market Development: Creating flexible LNG Market and Developing an LNG Trading Hub in Japan", Ministry of Economy, Trade and Industry, Government of Japan, May 2, 2016 at http://www.meti.go.jp/english/press/2016/pdf/0502_01b.pdf

players have signed up to participate in the Index Group, and ten more were expected to join. China too launched the Shanghai Oil and Gas Exchange, which will trade in both pipeline gas and LNG, in July 2015.

However, all three exchanges have to overcome challenges before they can emerge as certified trading hubs. While Japan lacks pipeline connectivity with other Asian markets, and low liquidity and price transparency, high levels of government regulation deter China as an attractive option as a regional benchmark. In the case of Singapore, trading volumes have been too moderate to establish a hub on the lines of its North American or European counterparts.[19]

Although a beginning has been made and may see the establishment of an Asian gas trading hub, a fully globalised gas market is still elusive in the absence of a global gas price. According to the IEA, certain factors are crucial for the development of trading hubs – gas price liberalization, particularly the inability to pass through gas purchase costs to customers, non-interference of governments, and third-party access to gas infrastructure. Most Asian markets still lack these factors barring Singapore. Moreover, the Asian gas markets are not as mature as their counterparts in North America and Europe were when these hubs were created. Most Asian countries depend mostly on LNG imports, barring China, which imports both piped gas as well as LNG, while Europe and North America rely mainly on domestic production and pipeline imports. Some of the countries – Japan and China – have initiated some changes, such as liberalisation of Japan's wholesale gas market which is expected to be completed by April 2017 and unbundling of pipeline transportation and storage infrastructure in China of the three major national companies, as well as price reforms. However, India and South Korea are yet to initiate the requisite reforms on pricing or liberalisation of their gas markets. In the case of Singapore, while it appears to be the strongest candidate for a regional gas hub, it is a relatively small market and may become a pricing hub for small-scale LNG trade in Southeast Asia at best. Therefore, in the near future, instead of an Asian gas hub emerging, more flexible pricing mechanisms may be expected to emerge in Asia,

---

19. "Natural Gas Prices in Asia, Natural Gas", *International Energy Outlook 2016*, Chapter 3, Energy Information Administration, US Department of Energy, May 11, 2016, at http://www.eia.gov/forecasts/ieo/nat_gas.cfm

with a mix of oil indexation, hub prices, and spot indices being used by various countries,[20] along with cancellation of destination clauses.

Already, spot and short-term LNG contracts of less than four years have increased from 5.4 percent in 2000 to 29 percent in 2014. Also, over the next decade, large amounts of LNG contracts will expire, allowing buyers to negotiate better terms in forthcoming deals, including short-term contracts and/or reduced volumes, or simply pick up supplies from the spot market. With over 120 million tonnes a year of new supplies being contracted from 2015, the advantage is now with the buyers.[21] But for how long?

Under the current and near-term low price scenario, LNG producers and exporters have not much option but to offer better terms – and prices – to buyers in order to retain their market share. With huge investments involved, they have little option. However, in the case of planned, but yet to be implemented projects, it is likely that many will be deferred. According to some analysts, the number of delayed projects has increased from 40 to 63 from 2014. While initially the more complex and costlier projects like oil sands, LNG and deep-water projects were the main casualties, as the oil price continued to slide through 2015, the oil companies began deferring the smaller, simpler projects, while smaller producers too began deferring projects from 2015.[22] Some of these included Petronas' Kasawari offshore gas development project in Malaysia's Sarawak province, Woodside's Cossack North offshore project in Australia, Royal Dutch Shell's proposed LNG project in Kitimat, Canada and Chevron-PTTEP's Ubon offshore project in Thailand, while GAIL India sought to defer a 20-year contract to buy LNG from Gazprom, as the latter has deferred its Arctic Shtokman project.[23]

20. Anne-Sophie Corbeau & David Ledesma, "LNG Markets in Transition: The Great Reconfiguration", King Abdullah Petroleum Studies and Research Center, April 2016, pp. 8-9 at https://www.kapsarc.org/wp-content/uploads/2016/05/LNG-Markets-in-Transition_A-Corbeau-and-D-Ledesma.pdf
21. Ibid., pp. 6 and 11.
22. "Report finds nearly $230 billion in oil and gas projects deferred", *Offshore Magazine*, January 29, 2016 at http://www.offshore-mag.com/articles/2016/01/report-finds-nearly-230-billion-in-oil-and-gas-projects-deferred.html
23. Debjit Chakraborty and Rajesh Kumar Singh, "India's Top Gas utility Seeks to Defer Gazprom's LNG Contract", Bloomberg, July 25, 2016 at http://www.bloomberg.com/news/articles/2016-07-25/india-s-top-gas-utility-seeks-to-defer-gazprom-lng-contract

Some producers are nevertheless ready to ride out the (price) storm. Qatar, the largest LNG exporter, while not planning any major investments, has been diversifying its market worldwide, covering both the European and Asian markets and offering revised terms to its long-term clients. Unlike its competitors, Doha has a major advantage, as not only is its production cost one of the lowest in the world, it has also acquired its own fleet of LNG vessels, including the huge Q-Flex and Q-Max ships that can cover the world giving it a wider sweep.

Moreover, despite the current bleak outlook for the gas market, there is a fair amount of optimism that despite the possibility that Australia and the US were preparing to ship out over 100 mtpa of LNG by 2020, the market will be able to absorb the extra supplies, as demand for gas picks up over the next two years due to growing concerns over climate change. Many are hopeful that despite projections that growth in the renewable energy market will impact demand for fossil fuels in the global energy mix, the latter will remain the dominant players on the global energy market and can be expected to remain so for decades to come. In fact, Maria van der Hoeven, the IEA's executive director, recently stated that there was no future emission reduction scenario under which oil and gas do not play "a significant role", and said that fossil fuels will still account for 60 percent of primary energy demand in 2040 even if the world proves successful at getting on a pathway to limiting temperature increases to 2 degrees celsius. Moreover, gas producers and exporters are upbeat that although demand for coal and oil may see a fall, demand for gas will grow due to its lower carbon emissions as well as greater availability.

Another sector which has the potential to see the demand for gas increase substantially is transport. According to some sector experts, natural gas use in the transport sector has the potential to displace around 1.5 mbd of oil by 2030, while a 10 percent diversion of LNG in the heavy transport market would generate 70 million tonnes a year of extra demand, which is equivalent to a year's supply to Japan. However, the lack of refuelling infrastructure is an obstacle in many countries, although some countries, including India have been early proponents of replacing oil with gas, both to reduce its growing oil import dependence as well as to tackle growing air pollution on its city roads. Another area where gas as an alternative fuel can make a mark is in shipping. Tougher emission regulations in the US and the EU have prompted the increased use of LNG as a transport fuel. HIS Markit, an energy consultancy firm, forecasts that around 17 bcm of LNG demand would come from the shipping sector over the next decade, provided systems can be developed to address the issue of storing LNG, given that gas has a larger volume than bunker oil, requiring a larger amount of storage space, a major setback for ship operators in terms of freight earned by cargo.[24]

If and when demand does pick up however – expectedly from 2020 onwards – will there be sufficient supplies, given the huge capital investments and long gestation period, particularly from difficult geological plays? Hence, at a time when gas demand begins picking up, there is every likelihood that gas prices may ascend to the highs of the pre-2014 period.

It is exactly this factor that has seen some countries forming strategies to counter such an eventuality for their energy security. In an attempt to revisit an idea in 2012, executives from the energy industry of five Asian countries, viz., India, Japan, China, South Korea and Taiwan, met in New Delhi in December 2014 to discuss ways to form a group of buyers that would help them strike better deals for their LNG imports. More recently in June 2016, India's petroleum minister Dharmendra Pradhan said that India would be taking the lead in creating an alliance of gas importers across the world for "reasonable and affordable" pricing of the fuel.[25]

All in all, despite the gloomy outlook for the gas market in the short term, is likely to look up over the medium and long term. However, creating demand to absorb the new supply will be a key challenge, and much will depend on the national energy policies of key Asian countries. With several new producers slated to come into the market, low prices will in all likelihood continue for a while. While this will

24. Ian Lewis, "Oil's sibling rival", *Petroleum Economist*, Vol. 83, No. 8, October 2016, pp. 24-25.
25. "India taking lead to create alliance of gas importers: Pradhan", *One India*, June 14, 2016 at http://www.oneindia.com/india/india-taking-lead-create-alliance-gas-importers-pradhan-2127534.html

benefit importing countries, it has affected the profit margins of the producers, with economically viable proven reserves being revised downwards by at least 63 percent in the US alone, while in other regions, such as Australia's Gorgon plant, as well as Russia and Canada, producers are facing a disadvantage vis-a-vis their competitors in West Asia, whose cost of production is much lower.

As a result, it is necessary that a price that will not only be beneficial for producers and consumers alike, but will also be competitive relative to other competing fuels will be required to be worked out. While pricing, contract durations and flexibility of destination are areas of interest for consumers, return on investment and market share is of the highest importance for the producers.

The gas, and indeed the energy world order, is in flux. While the contours of a global gas market, as opposed to the current fragmented and regionalised one, is taking shape, it is difficult to predict with accuracy how it will develop in the medium to long term. The globalisation of gas trade does indeed offer opportunities for new actors – both producers and consumers – to enter the scene. However, it will place some producers under pressure to adjust their business models, and the future of the market will depend to a large extent on how and if the traditional producers are ready and willing to adjust to the changes in market fundamentals, which will also have implications for other policy areas, including security, domestic and foreign policies.

INDEX